THE HIGHER SELF VOICE ON . . .

SOUL PSYCHOLOGY

Our Journey
Through
the Human
Kingdom
Universe

By Janet Richmond

Cover Art by Janet Richmond

Using unique unconscious techniques given me by the Higher Selves, I incorporate the Divine energies into my art. Called Catalytic Empowered Art, it helps manifest a desired change within one's life pattern. Each piece is infused with a specific concept of desired outcome whether for healing, resolution, empowerment, or manifestation of specific situations or conditions. The energy is slow moving but constant and continues working for one's lifetime always bringing change to a higher level.

The artwork on the front cover was created to bring about *Expanded Creativity* for the viewer in the Highest Ideal. You do not need to meditate on it. Just focus your attention on it from time to time allowing the desired change to manifest more quickly.

Table of Contents

PART IV: The Astral

PART V: Connecting the Dots

PART VI: The Neutralizing Process
and Its Practical Applications

EXPANDED PERCEPTIONS:

APPENDICES

Author's Preface

SOUL PSYCHOLOGY opens the world to new philosophical, spiritual, and psychological concepts regarding the soul, the mind, the Heavens, and the evolutionary process of the humanities. There are other books that discuss the existence of the soul, the phenomena of past lives, and even what happens in the afterlife, but this is the first book that offers a gestalt viewpoint as it clarifies and expands on what a soul is, how it relates to the mind of our current life, its role while we are in body and in between lives, and its evolutionary journey over eons of time as it moves through its infinite human experiences.

The book delves deeply into how our prior lifetimes have led to the creation of our belief systems, our unconscious conditioning and our self-identities all of which permeate and define each successive life as we journey through the *Human Kingdom Universe.* The complex misunderstandings, false beliefs, and deep wounds taken on and held at the soul level can blow our lives out of control. Understanding these thus provides answers as to why our lives are what they are and why we face the difficulties/ problems/painful situations/conditions that we do.

SOUL PSYCHOLOGY also teaches us how to *neutralize* the causal energies that will free us from those unwanted patterns. Neutralizing is the elixir for the soul and enables us to heal within one life what our soul has been attempting to do over eons of time. Readers will discover and become intimate with their silent partner—their soul—and its messages.

This book is relevant to anyone looking for clarity, balance, and resolution. It unfolds in six parts, allowing the reader to learn through the eyes and experiences of others, including myself. This makes it easy to connect with the new ideas so that by the end, the reader is at home with the material. *SOUL PSYCHOLOGY* opens the metaphorical Pandora's Box, but instead of the world's ills, out comes clarity, fascination, solutions, and most of all hope. This is information and *not* a religion. Belief and worship are not a part of it. The non-judgmental, expanded viewpoint is provided by the Higher Selves. In the same way that Freud pioneered psychology, the study of the human mind, the Higher Selves' multi-layered information offers soul psychology, the study of the human soul.

The following ideas and concepts not only changed the way I saw the world and myself but also gave me answers to bigger questions that dogged me. The Higher Self viewpoints from the 5th Dimension - the next level of evolutionary existence—opened my heart and eyes and brought me the opportunity to heal myself at deep levels.

Now, with deep gratitude for having had access to Higher Self perspectives, I have written this book to pay forward all that I have gained. From my heart to yours, I invite you to read on.

Janet
janetrichmond.com

Before You Pass Go

My first book—*CHOICES: Neutralizing Your Negative Thoughts and Emotional Blueprints*—and this book, share one basic concept: our "beingness" doesn't end at the skin. Although there is much more to the energy field around each person than I will present here, there are four parts of our etheric world that the Higher Selves emphasize (and which was fully explained in *CHOICES*). In short, etheric energy envelopes surround our physical body similar to an auric field. The four envelopes of energy are:

1.   Thought Form Body

2.   Habit Body

3.   Emotional Response Body

4.   Creative Body

The first three envelopes house the energies we have created for ourselves over the eons of lifetimes lived in the Human Kingdom. They also are the fuel for the manufacturing plant we carry—the Creative Body—that creates the situations and conditions in our lives.

Once we understand our energetic side, we also have the power and ability to change the patterns that we are unhappy with. We can neutralize them. We don't have to wait around for someone else to fix our lives for us. We become the directing identities. This viewpoint then helps us to move away from the idea of blaming others, Mother Nature, our parents, bosses, mates, the government, the economy, etc., and to realize that we are not victims. If we are unhappy with our outer reality, we can neutralize the energetic patterns that fuel it, enabling joy to manifest in our lives.

1. Thought Form Body

   Every time we think a thought, it creates an energy form/identity. Once created, the energy exists forever. What happens to it then? Where does it go? It goes into an etheric body we carry around us called the Thought Form Body, where all our thoughts of all time (all of our lifetimes) are stored. Each thought carries a magnetic type of energy, and every kind of thought has its own unique magnetic signature. When a thought moves into the Thought Form Body, it is magnetically attracted to other *like* thoughts with the same signature. Over time, the like thoughts become a larger and larger conglomerate of the same like thoughts resulting in what is called a *thought form.* This process is true for all thoughts—good, bad, or indifferent. And because we have had thoughts from the first moment we arrived in the Human Kingdom, we carry with us an infinite number of thought forms. Some are huge. Some are minute. And most others greatly vary in size somewhere in between.

2. Habit Body

   The Habit Body is not in magnetic nature. Instead of thought forms, the Habit Body contains habit imprints. Imprints are created every time we think a thought and every time we perform an action. With every thought or action, an impression—the imprint—is made in the Habit Body energy field. Think of the energy of the Habit Body being like the smooth sand on a beach after the tide has gone out and where no one has yet stepped foot. The imprint could be likened to a fresh footprint in that wet, smooth sand. With every step in the same footprint, it becomes deeper and deeper. In the same way, every like thought and action deepens a habit imprint as well. What we have then in our Habit Body are deep, deep imprints in the symbolic sand.

Why are these imprints significant? They are important because unlike the magnetic energy of thought, the Habit Body carries an energy that propels us to action. Although there are imprints of various depths, all imprints propel us to repeat the actions and thoughts that created them. And the deepest ones contain the most powerful propellant energy. This energy fuels our most ingrained habits and pushes us to repeat the actions over and over again.

3. Emotional Response Body

In each lifetime, we go through a series of experiences as we make our way from childhood to adulthood and through the death and dying process. When a significant event happens, we often have some emotional reaction, and when we do, we find ourselves targeting our emotional response upon the event. Every event is neutral, but depending on the circumstances around the event for each of us, we will have our own individual reaction to that event. When we "attach" that emotional response by believing the event is inherently the reason for what we are feeling about it, we have established an energetic connection between the event and the response, creating what the Higher Selves call an *emotional blueprint*. Thus, the event is no longer neutral for us.

Once the event has the emotional reaction attached (the blueprint), the subsequent events of that same type (whether in the same or later lifetimes) will trip the replay sequence of the emotional reaction, as if we hit the replay button on a recorder. In this way, not only does the event take on a definitive color of positive or negative with each reoccurrence, but the emotional reaction also grows in power and becomes more intense and entrenched. This is because the blueprint carries with it the power of *all the prior reactions* from this and other lifetimes.

For example, when an event makes us angry, we would feel the anger we had previously placed around the event from all our lifetimes. Since we all create our own unique blueprints, sometimes we may react to an event with rage while other people (who don't have the same blueprint) may barely have a reaction at all. What is interesting is when we are angry, we usually feel we choose our reaction (our feelings about the event) because it seems normal and justified. But we are actually triggering the reactions we have processed over and over again with the same event. There is little choice in the matter.

4. Creative Body

Think of the energetic field of the Creative Body as our own private manufacturing plant. It carries within it the *Creative Life Force Energy*, an energy that manufactures the situations and conditions of our outer reality 24/7 by weaving together the energies with which it is supplied. Like any manufacturing plant, this etheric body needs fuel and supplies to function. Its fuel consists of all of the thought, habit, and emotional blueprint energies that we have created. So the Creative Life Force could be viewed symbolically as a great sculptor who has set up his art production in a field containing debris and materials strewn everywhere. He runs around with the deep need to create and obsessively makes his artwork from all of the available supplies, using the most plentiful materials.

It is the same with the Creative Body. It does not base its creations on what we want or whether we are good people.

Instead, as it is an impersonal energy, it uses the supplies provided with no preference except that the energies most commonly used are the most abundant ones. We all have fuel that is powerful and unlimited in nature, and yet, so much of the time, the energy supplied is negative. Thus, much of what is manifested in our lives includes difficulties, problems, upheavals, struggles, doubts, and fears. Of course, we have positive experiences occurring as well, and don't we want more of those? We want to reduce the negative fuel and empower the positive fuel.

It is the energies of thought (thought forms), habit (habit imprints), and emotion (emotional blueprints) that make up all we believe in, all of our self-identities, and all the ways we have defined ourselves and the world. These are the foundation of our complex nature. *What the Creative Body weaves into existence for each of us reflects perfectly on the outside what we carry energetically within our etheric bodies.*

Neutralizing

These bodies work together in a conglomerate state. The first three bodies are carried within our Creative Body, operating simultaneously in a complex process of energetic "magic" that powers us without our knowing much of the time. Fortunately, the Higher Selves gave us the technique of neutralizing, which allows us to move into the driver's seat. With it, we can change our outer reality by altering the type of supplies we give the Creative Body.

Neutralizing, when it pertains to thought forms, is the process or act of rendering the magnetic energy of thought harmless by bringing the magnetic signature of that thought into a non-magnetic state. This process is done with the *Divine Light*—the Divine Energy of the

Originating Source—that each soul carries. When referring to this Light within, we term it the *Pure Soul Essence.* This Divine Light provides the exact perfect opposite match for the thought energy, merges with it, and brings the thought energy into a neutral state. The habit imprints are neutralized differently. For them, the Pure Soul Essence Light moves in and fills the deep crevasses to disarm the propelling force behind them. For the emotional blueprints, the Light dissolves the energetic bond that holds emotions firmly attached to any event. The emotions themselves are not dissolved; they are set free from the attachment. The process neutralizes all the energies simultaneously as they all interact and are interconnected with one another.

Energy Identities

Energy identities signify all the thought forms, habit imprints, and emotional blueprints that each soul creates and accumulates over the span of its entire journey through the Human Kingdom Universe. These are all soulless and mindless energy forms, energy without Soul/Mind reasoning and consciousness.

A few examples of energy identities are the following:

- Thought forms could be of the "I am sick" or "I need a job" or "I am lonely" type.

- Habit imprints could be associated with eating dessert after every meal, reaching for your child's hand every time you go somewhere on foot, or at the extreme end, addiction patterns.

- Emotional blueprint examples could include a fear reaction to loud noises, embarrassment when put in the spotlight, or shyness when meeting someone new.

There are an infinite number of energy identities, and they have accumulated over the entire span of our journey though the Human Kingdom Universe. However, even as powerful as they are, they are easily addressed with the Divine Light of the Pure Soul Essence we all carry.

Because some of the terms used in this book are either unique or have precise meanings from the Higher Self perspective, a glossary is provided. (See Appendix I.) In addition, I have provided an expanded discussion on the Higher Selves—who they are and our connection to them (see Appendix II)—as was explained to all of us many years ago.

You are now ready to pass go. I invite you to enter the world of *Soul Psychology.*

PART I

The Soul/Mind, Soul Psychology, and Soul Scrambles

CHAPTER 1
What Is the Soul?

HIGHER SELF QUOTE

The inner essence of every soul at any level carries within it a connection to the Totality of Originating Source (the Higher Self term for God/Allah/Jehovah/etc.,). And because Originating Source is ever-experiencing and ever-expanding, the Totality that you carry is also constantly expanding and experiencing, for it is locked into all that goes into Originating Source.

Soul Consciousness

It might surprise you to know there is no such thing as a young soul. Not only did we all begin our evolutionary journey in the Mineral Kingdom and continue through the Plant Kingdom and Animal Kingdom, but also we are now moving through the Human Kingdom. In the Human Kingdom alone, we have already spent eons of lifetimes on our evolutionary journey.

As humans today on this planet, we have experienced virtually millions and even billions of events, situations, and conditions as a result of our tens of thousands of lifetimes. And we come into every new life carrying at the energetic level all the experiences from our previous lives. We are truly more complex than we have ever thought ourselves to be.

When and How Did Evolution Start?

In the beginning, billions and billions of eons *before* the existence of the Milky Way, there was only the *Originating Source of All There Is,* and it was unevolved and inexperienced. And yet, contained within the Totality of this unevolved energy were masculine and feminine components. During the course of what we refer to as an eternity, this energy grew and built until these male/female elements connected and gave birth to the first universe (and there have been several previous universes before the one we inhabit). Much like when two parents join and give birth to a child who carries the essence of who the parents are, the Originating Source joined its male and female energies, giving birth to itself by manifesting the *expressions* of its Totality. In that first birthing pattern, Originating Source experienced its first vibration based on the experience of giving birth to that universe.

These expressions were deintensified to lower and lower frequency levels, to the point where the solar systems and galaxies were born and became the material world of the 1st Dimension or the Mineral Kingdom. This material world then became the foundation of a dense reality (running at an extremely low frequency rate) that was the starting point of the evolutionary process. Once born, the expressions within the Mineral Kingdom began the journey back to the Originating Source (through plant, animal, human, and beyond), carrying within them the same innate drive of the "parent"—the drive to discover, experience, create, and expand. This journey entailed moving up the ladder of evolutionary frequency one step at a time, one experience at a time, just as a newborn baby would learn about its world by one touch, one smell, one taste, one sound, and one look at a time. This process continues, unending.

The Pure Soul Essence

These material world expressions (in the Mineral Kingdom) of Originating Source were its newborns—inexperienced, but each particle contained the Pure Soul Essence, that symbolic spark of Light that carries the Totality of Originating Source Energy. Each spark of Light remains connected with the parent by a symbolic but real thread of Light. This thread is forever there, forever connecting each expression—each soul—to the vast Totality of the Originating Source, providing a conduit and a channel between parent and child.

The Originating Source, on a moment-to-moment basis, is fed all of the experiences from each soul in every dimension through this thread, which is the mechanism whereby the Originating Source learns and expands. From the time of the first universe onward, each and every event that has ever been experienced by any part of the universe, even the densest mineral, has fed into and increased the vibratory frequency of the Originating Source for infinite eons of time. And in return, all of the knowledge gained by the Originating Source is fed back to each expression (each soul) along the same thread. The Pure Soul Essence within each soul carries *everything that Originating Source was, is, and is becoming.*

This Pure Soul Essence could be likened to the DNA we receive from our parents. Just as every cell in our body has the full DNA double helix (even though a cell may be manifesting one small element of the DNA such as a skin cell or brain cell), so does each expression (each of Originating Source's newborns) carry the Totality of the Originating Source within the Pure Soul Essence—all the purity, perfection, knowledge, love, and so much more.

Every expression of the Originating Source is an actual being. They all are souls. And the Pure Soul Essence is carried within each soul, from the lowliest grain of sand to the highest, most evolved being. From that perspective, every soul is equal. Every soul is as pure, perfect, and important as every other soul.

The Human Kingdom Universe

The Human Kingdom Universe includes Earth and all planets (whether or not they house the humanities), as well as the Human Kingdom Heavens where the humanities go when they are out of body between lives. It also includes the *Astral*, which could be viewed as the force fields of energy around the planet. This universe is an enormous amount of *space* where the humanities reside, existing side by side with the Mineral, Plant, and Animal Kingdoms. It is the part of *All There Is* and is held at the frequency level of the physical world *ruled by the five senses.*

The Human Kingdom is comprised of both the incarnate *and* the disincarnate state. Most of us tend to think of the disincarnate state as something that belongs in Heaven and as such, is separate and apart from the Human Kingdom. This is not the case. A human is human—in body or out—no matter which side of the veil they are on.

Human Evolutionary Focus

Life as a human is not a crapshoot. A soul does not take on a body and incarnate on this planet or any other planet as a victim of circumstance. Souls reincarnate on any given planet having made the individual choice to play out their current life for an infinite number of possible reasons. The soul may want to grow, learn, and resolve pain, fear, doubt, rage, etc. The mind of the current life, once in body, has no conscious recollection of its soul's decision as to why it has taken on the life it has. This makes understanding the journey more difficult for us to grasp while living that life. Yet, we are the directing identity of our lives. We are not victims nor have we become puppets to something external to us.

We play out patterns based on our soul's belief that these experiences—negative or positive—would be helpful to us. Often the purposes for the experiences are misread, misunderstood, or seem insignificant altogether once we take on the body. The soul cannot pick up the phone and call or text us to remind us what we need to heal or balance or learn. This can be frustrating, especially when experiences are negative in nature, since at first we don't understand that we have set up the circumstances of these experiences. However, nothing happens to any individual in a body that has not been agreed upon at the soul level. It is at the soul level where true Free Will resides. And although the soul has laid out situations and conditions for itself before birth, we still have choices once in body. A soul has the option at any point in time to alter its journey by changing its Soul/Mind in regard to its prior decisions.

Once we are humans, there are untold, infinite numbers of combinations and permutations of situations and conditions that any one soul can experience in its enormous journey in this kingdom. This is why each soul is a snowflake; no two are alike. This book will assist you in understanding yourself at the soul level and help you to change your life experiences to those that are more joyful, harmonious, peaceful, and successful in every way.

The Mind and the Soul

The soul is the collective minds of the past and contains at that level a Thought Form Body. In the Thought Form Body of the soul are the collected thoughts connected to that soul from all of the past nows. These, then feed and reinforce the current mind pattern, reinforcing the Thought Form Body of the current mind in the current lifetime.

To set the scene for our journey through the Human Kingdom, we see that the evolutionary processing within the Human Kingdom marks a distinct shift from the three lower kingdoms (Mineral, Plant, and Animal). We have a reasoned thought process and ability to communicate that does not fully exist in the lower kingdoms. Humans move up in evolutionary frequency by expanding our levels of awareness instead of by changing our physical bodies to become more complex. We are aware that we have a soul and a mind. We may not be clear as to what they are or how they are defined, but we know they exist.

What, then, is the *soul* and what is the *mind?* These terms are common and their definitions are dependent upon the philosophy, religion, or science from which they are derived. In this book, these words are defined by the Higher Selves. Though possibly different from what you may already understand, if the information is allowed to flow and the words are clear, judgment can be avoided. Judgment in any arena caps the frequency level of thought and understanding that one can reach.

The soul carries the energy of awareness. This idea can be hard to grasp, as our concept of awareness is that it is (we are aware) or it is not (we are clueless). Instead of looking at it from the either/or viewpoint, envision the energy of awareness as levels beginning with no awareness, which then increase in awareness the higher a soul goes in frequency. At the mineral level, there is very little awareness. The soul has just begun its journey back up the frequency levels. At the plant level, too, there is also little awareness. By the time we get to the higher levels of the Animal Kingdom, we see that awareness has expanded. There are some animals, for example, that can even identify themselves in a mirror, having therefore a sense of self.

Once we move into the Human Kingdom, the awareness levels continue to expand exponentially as the soul moves through its journey in this Free Will world. Awareness can be viewed as the *energy of consciousness*. Consciousness at the soul level is different from and more expanded than consciousness at the mind level. Where do we get this awareness? We get it from the experiences of each life. The more lives we live, the more our awareness grows.

What is the mind, then? It is the mental and emotional process in this current life. It is how we think, feel, react, and process our experiences. It is an aspect of (a part of) the soul—a newborn *Soul Aspect* in a newborn's body. A Soul Aspect is part of a soul that has broken off or aspected out to experience, learn, and express as the *mind* of each new life. Each aspect is separate but equal in the same way an amoeba that divides creates two amoebae that are fully functioning.

We then go through each life, learning and growing with all the situations and conditions we experience. The mind is the

7

mechanism that allows the soul to experience while in body. Just as the Originating Source had to create expressions of itself in order to experience, so does the soul. The mind is the way our souls learn more and more about how to swim (or anything else) by going out and actually swimming. We can learn a lot by listening to a lecture, reading a book, and seeing a video about how to swim, but until we actually try it, we do not know if we can do it.

At death, the current mind from this lifetime joins the conglomerate awareness of all the previous minds from all the previous lifetimes. The Higher Selves describe the soul as *the conglomerate of the minds of the past.* Each mind becomes a part of the totality of the soul consciousness. The soul carries the totality of all the experiences, knowledge, belief systems, self-identities, etc., that have come from the eons of lifetimes we have lived. It evolves by adding more and more minds to its beingness, which brings additional experiences and knowledge along with many misunderstandings, false beliefs, confusions, and conflicts.

As the soul incorporates and processes each lifetime in turn, it then often takes an active role to plan each of the next lifetimes. In the very early stages of human evolvement, the soul has little awareness to even understand that planning a next lifetime would be beneficial and might reincarnate simply for very basic emotional reasons—anger, love, revenge, grief. In time, a soul eventually takes on enough awareness to plan lifetimes in order to fill in the gaps of learning or to repair its false beliefs.

When we are born into each life, we come in deaf, dumb, and blind. (No rudeness or insult is intended here.) We are ignorant as to what our soul is all about or even that there is more to us than meets the eye. This means that there is a huge realm of soul awareness that is hidden from the mind of each life. This can be misleading, as the soul is a huge force behind all that we are. It is at the soul level that we define ourselves and hold onto our limited truths that rule our current life patterns. The soul operates behind the scenes to determine the characteristics of our lives.

Think of the Soul/Mind as if together they form an ocean. The ocean (like the Soul/Mind) is deep, highly complex, rich with resources, often rife with pollution and multi-layered, with the deepest part of it completely hidden from the waters at its surface. The mind level could be likened to the upper levels of the ocean, where we normally interact and experience it. We swim, surf, fish, sail, explore, snorkel, play, create, and work in these upper layers. Most of us never delve far below the surface of the ocean (into our soul). It is those deeper levels of the ocean, symbolically our soul, that provide the foundation of what happens at the upper reaches, symbolically our mind. It only seems like the weather and other external elements affect the surface of the water (our lives). Yet if the lower ocean levels are calm, unpolluted, and full of life, the upper levels are provided with great riches, resources, and opportunities for enjoyment, productivity, and meaning. But if the lower levels are disturbed with geothermal events, the surface of the ocean may experience traumas such as volcanic eruptions, tsunamis, or life-threatening high tides. And if the lower levels are polluted with garbage, the upper layers will house fewer resources, more junk, and will make life on the top more difficult.

What happens within each of us at the soul level is as important as what happens at the mind level. Our souls are our identity in our conglomerate being. The mind is our identity in this current life.

However, both the soul and the mind (the Soul/Mind) are indelibly intertwined, and we can help ourselves best by understanding both. Studying the vast ocean at all its levels enables scientists to understand how the lifeblood of the planet works and how it impacts global life. In the same way, we can greatly benefit from understanding more about the human ocean that is our Soul/Mind.

Soul Set

Sometimes, when a being gives up its body (dies), that soul is overwrought with distress, jealousy, rage, vengeance, obsessive love, or other emotional blueprints. These powerful emotions are usually directed at other people (or situations and conditions) from the experiences, events, or people of that life. Thus these souls may take on what is called a Soul Set: the body is laid aside and the soul continues to live through and play out of the mind level of the prior life. The individuals who play out of a Soul Set can become stuck in their own evolutionary process. Because they maintain their emotional focus on various situations, places, or people from their prior lives, they aren't continuing to learn and expand their own awareness. These souls may or may not already be in the Human Kingdom Heavens. However, either way, they are intently focused on what they have left behind. Under more common circumstances, when a body is laid aside, the soul moves into the Human Kingdom Heavens to begin its schooling pattern and therefore is not still *set* in the pattern of the prior lifetime.

Every soul carries with it both the *male nature* and the *female nature*. However, as a soul collects experiences lifetime after lifetime, it can take on the flavor of either frequency. Thus, based on the predominate experiences a soul plays out, it may maintain a sense of identity based on the dominant sexual nature. It could be viewed as a masculine soul if it often plays out of the masculine experiences or a feminine soul if it more often plays out of the feminine experiences.

Soul Scrambles™

Each soul, in its defining of terms, many times becomes confused as to what the real issues are, and therefore negative experiences, in many instances, are repeated over and over again because the soul has not fully understood the inner workings that contributed to these various negative experiences.

Just as psychologists study behavior, emotions, and patterns from one's current life experiences, , the psychology of the soul focuses on the experiences the soul goes through during its human evolution from lifetime to lifetime.

To best understand soul psychology, I begin by describing *Soul Scrambles™*. A Soul Scramble indicates a dysfunctional, limiting, and often painful pattern in our lives that keeps us firmly stuck in a rat wheel of repetition. It is often born from personal events and/or cultural conditions when a mind makes (and locks into) one or more erroneous conclusions and misinterpretations during its life experiences and/or during the death experience. The scramble further develops during the long and problematic path of many lifetimes as the soul continues to accumulate more misconceptions (as it adds experiences from each new life) and becomes more firmly imprisoned in its false beliefs. Scrambles grow more complex, convoluted, and difficult to understand and move beyond. These Soul Scrambles - and *no human soul is free of them* - are the foundation of what an individual attempts to undo while in body. They have a powerful effect upon a soul's choice regarding its subsequent reincarnations.

All souls in the Human Kingdom Universe are on complex journeys, with the goal being to move into higher frequency levels of awareness and consciousness. Many of us are here on this planet, at this point in time, to unscramble the false beliefs we have taken on over the eons of lifetimes. As we free ourselves from the fetters and blinders of these false beliefs, we undo our scrambles. In this way, we increase the frequency of our conscious awareness. Because our journeys involve eons of lifetimes and carry many Soul Scrambles (that operate solely and/or work with one another), we are mostly blind as to who we truly are. But we do not have to be stuck; we are not powerless. There is a way to heal all the wounds and misunderstandings we carry. The fascinating explanation of Soul Psychology is more than a fleeting or superficial concept. Once understood, you will have the advantage of a huge jumpstart to infinite self-healing and self-balancing of any and all life patterns that may have been dogging you.

CHAPTER 2
Charlie

There are countless ways that a soul can develop and play out its Soul Scrambles. The Higher Selves first introduced the concept with Charlie's personal story. His scramble began with a difficult life as a woman and clearly illustrates the emotional, mental, and psychological impact from the beliefs that we take away from our lives.

The Higher Selves Introduce Us to Charlie in 1990

You might be interested in the history of a soul we'll call Charlie. Charlie has problems in his soul space for there were many different conditions that contributed to the end result of this lifetime (on this planet). Charlie was the first person to be infected by the AIDS virus. Knowing his story and understanding how Charlie reached that point through his own soul pattern will perhaps help each of you to understand your own patterns and the patterns of others.

Charlie was out of body when he told us the story of his Soul Scramble. He was *reflected* and recorded by Joan Culpepper during a group session in 1990. (Reflection is a process of mirroring or acting out in words and/or body language what a disincarnate human wishes to convey. It differs from the normal idea of channeling in that at no time does the reflector go into trance, and there is never any mixing of the soul energies between the disincarnate and the reflector.) The Higher Selves encouraged Charlie to explain his Soul Scramble both to start the process of forgiving himself and as a learning experience for all of us present in Joan's group. Charlie's story had the great benefit of showing us how a soul's evolution occurs over many lifetimes. It also showed us how easily a soul can unknowingly start down a difficult and complicated path, thereby creating a Soul Scramble that can then take an extremely long time to understand and to unravel.

Because Charlie was gay during his last incarnation on Earth and because he was the first to contract the AIDS virus, it is important to give his story the proper context. Whether a soul comes in as hetero- or homosexual, it is the choice of the soul, and there is no right or wrong. Part of the human soul's journey includes the desire to understand and to balance its male and female nature. This is done in many ways as the choices are unique to every soul.

Today we know that anyone can contract the AIDS virus, but during the 1980s, the information and understanding about HIV was just beginning as scientists moved slowly from ignorance to understanding. The AIDS virus, HIV, was not a term used by scientists until 1986 and by 1990 was still only beginning to make its way into minds of the general public. We now know that one can have the virus without yet manifesting the disease AIDS, but at that time, many were still unaware. Therefore, the Higher Selves used the term "AIDS virus" instead of HIV to be clear. Also, in the early days, AIDS was at first seen by many as a homosexual disease. The Higher Selves explained it like this:

There have been many questions raised on this planet in areas that deal with the AIDS virus. The major issue has been the idea that AIDS was specifically a homosexual disease. Had a heterosexual person been the first to receive the virus, there would have been no major issue made about the sexuality or anything else. It would have been considered as a very bad disease. Therefore, we would like you to understand that the AIDS virus is the end result of a major thrust in evolution of the virus itself unrelated to the sexual orientation of the infected.

Charlie's Story in His Own Words (briefly edited)
In sharing with the group, Charlie described specific lifetimes he had from the hindsight and Higher Self help. He did not possess a deep wisdom superior to those of us in body because he had crossed over. He was a confused human who misinterpreted many of his experiences and drew erroneous conclusions.

As far as I have been able to determine, my evolution of my soul has been rather ragged. This does not mean that I am not evolving. It means that, in many instances, when I was in my body, whatever that body may have been (male or female) and wherever that body was placed (whatever planet I was on), it was as if I misunderstood completely what I was to do.

First of all, I was a female in the lifetime that started this scrambled soul psychology. It was not on planet Earth but on another planet. I was a free spirit and a rebel. But in that system and at that time, the female was not appreciated and was governed by any male who happened to be in her pattern.

My father had died when I was very young. My older brother became the controlling male in an otherwise female family. Being the free spirit that I was, I was in trouble most of the time. And the more trouble I got into, the more rebellious I became about my situation. Jane has helped in this respect, for Jane tells me that she had a problem with male domination at one time, and it took her off of her soul evolutionary understanding for a while. {The Jane that Charlie mentions is a disincarnate that Joan and the Higher Selves had helped years earlier. Jane has been educated by the Higher Selves and now helps other souls in the Human Kingdom Heavens who have had difficulties with their evolutionary movement forward. {See Appendix III.} *I have gained hope from Jane because I now understand more clearly how these attitudes can become ingrained and can create future situations and lifetimes that have nothing to do with the lifetime where the problem started.*

As I continued in that first lifetime where the end result of this AIDS virus came into play, I consciously, actively, resented that I was a free spirit housed in a female body. I knew (in my consciousness in that lifetime) I did not belong in a female body. My spirit was too free and I was too rebellious to be held down by another, and therefore I must have been intended to be a male. Additionally in that lifetime, I became embittered about my situation because no matter what I tried to do or where I tried to go, I was always held back, always taken control of by males.

I died in that lifetime in a state of utter frustration and bitterness, and I carried with me the lack of being able to identify my free spirit with the female body. I incarnated in the next life as a male. Because I carried that energy forward (the idea of males being superior to females), I developed, through several different lifetimes, a superior, arrogant attitude, not only toward females but also toward most people.

The scientific side of my soul was far more developed than the emotional side. In those male lifetimes, I strove to reach the top. And I always did because at an unconscious level, I attempted to make up for all that I had lost in that female incarnation. In scientific exploration, I became very proficient in areas that dealt with laboratory experiments with weapons of war and destruction. This occurred, of course, on different planetary systems other than Earth and out of different vibratory frequencies. But each of these planets served a purpose by allowing me, in that male pattern, to develop and find a place I could put my frustration and anger.

During those early male incarnations, I moved into a destructive mode, insofar as the types of experimentations and systems that I worked toward were concerned. You must understand, however, I did not intend in any conscious way to be involved in destruction. It was my mindset (as was true of the mindsets of those with whom I worked and those on this planet) that weapons were needed in order to protect and to keep others from invading our space. In several incarnations, I developed very potent weapons from nature. I assisted many germs in their evolutionary vibration for I was able to make them extremely potent. And when unleashed . . . I do feel bad about this now. I can't really conceive of having been so unconscious . . . {Charlie chokes up here} *but those potent germs killed on contact. And I was proud of my contribution.*

When I reached a point in my evolutionary awakening where I understood I needed to help that part of my soul to advance into a higher vibration, I experimented once more with taking on a female incarnation. And I was never, ever, comfortable with it. Because of that prior incarnation of the female, there was the association of being powerless as a female. Added to that were those lifetimes where great power was reached through my scientific advancement (as well as other positions of power and authority I moved through.). This meant I carried a lot of scrambling within the soul. When I reached a point of soul desperation regarding the inability to adjust to any female incarnation I found myself in, I sought counsel out of body. I spent the equivalent of several lifetimes out of body working with educators in the Human Kingdom Heavens. It was an attempt to understand the pattern along which I was advancing and to discover the options that I had in order to attempt to save myself from further soul scrambling.

When I was ready, I took on a female body again. I felt fairly comfortable in that lifetime and was able to enjoy a beautiful love relationship with a man who did not attempt to control or coerce me. The experience gave me the additional soul programming of being equal while in a female body. Additionally, it greatly assisted the emotional nourishing of my soul, for the emotional side of my nature had not been fully activated and was at war within the soul space to advance on its own. I was unaware until it was pointed out to me by several of the educators that a soul can war within itself and can create tremendous schisming and take value systems that have been shaped and can overpower them and reshape them. When people speak about the battle between the white and dark forces, I know what the battle is. I have fought the battle within my own soul—the scientific powerful male aspect part of me wanting to dominate and destroy the emotional more feminine side of my nature. But, in the play out of those two aspects of the soul while in body, I was confused as to what I had come in to do.

While taking on female incarnations, I continued to attempt to reach the highest level of emotional development of that feminine side of the nature, not necessarily while in a feminine body but the feminine side of the self. As I plodded along, I continued to make mistake after mistake. I became a soul frustrated in rage because I could not get it together. The educators {the Higher Selves, Master Teachers, and guides that play the role of counselors in the Human Kingdom Heavens} *informed me that these were misconceptions. But the arrogant part of the nature in the soul was still present. It was unable, many times, to understand, because in its arrogance it would not listen!*

I reached the point finally through a long, slow process (both in and out of body) of understanding that I, as a soul, was lost. As I viewed all of the crimes I had participated in, all of the destructive acts that came about based on work that I had done, my inability to fully cope, and my inability to understand that emotional feminine aspect of my nature, I came to believe I was a lost soul. I knew that I would never be able to repent for those evil deeds and for my own inability to be a whole and complete person.

I was desperate. I went into intensive therapy (if you could view an out-of-body experience as being involved in intensive therapy) and in desperation, allowed the educators to give to me as much as they could in order to assist me in reaching a point of laying claim to my own soul in a state of wholeness. And I understood that to atone for what I had done I would have to duplicate in my life what I had done to others. I knew that I had to die most horribly over and over again so I could repent and save myself. {Charlie begins crying.} *I knew that I had to develop the other facets of my soul or that the scientific powerful aspect would destroy me.* {More crying} *And the very thing that I came to do for repentance in this last life started the whole process all over again.* {Referring to the AIDS virus}. *And I'm so sorry.* {Crying continued} *I'm so sorry. When I chose . . .* {At this point Charlie becomes so overwrought that Joan has to pause the reflecting in order to calm him down.}

When I chose to be born in this lifetime on planet Earth, I chose to be born in a male body. And while I did not define the terms (as far as "I will go there and I will die of the

AIDS virus"), I defined the terms such that I would do my repentance by dying from a horrible disease caused by a germ. Putting on a body is like going to sleep. You're deaf, dumb, and blind as to what the soul is all about. You fumble, and you don't know why you do things. And in the need on my part to develop the other facets of my soul, in taking on the male body, I attempted to work out the identifying of the male body with power and destruction. I wanted to be an emotionally loving individual, thus choosing to be gay. {There is no implication here that the only way to be emotionally loving is by being gay. This was Charlie's belief system related to his individual scramble.} *But when I got into the body, I forgot everything, even who I was. The emotional and arrogant sides of my nature did battle. I misidentified in my mind what I was here to do. I was homosexual, identifying in my unconscious soul space with those female incarnations where I had had pleasant equal relationships. The arrogant, rebellious side of my nature asserted itself and the need on my part to be the free spirit took sway. I learned that I could be whoever I wanted to be for it didn't matter what the world thought. And then . . . my soul prophecy came true . . .* {Charlie continues to be overwrought.}

CHAPTER 3
Exploring Charlie's Story

HIGHER SELF QUOTE ON CHARLIE

In the fabric of despair that Charlie has woven himself into through these various lifetimes, he still doesn't clearly understand the overall process. But he is reaching a point of being able to come into a higher understanding of all that has been processed and which ended in this lifetime.

Charlie clearly explained how his Soul Scramble was born, developed, and became such a painful, devastating, and dominating force in his soul for hundreds of lifetimes. It came to a head in his latest life here. His story illustrated how we can take on misunderstandings that bring blame, shame, guilt, and despair into one's life. It further showed how harmful it is when we lock into false beliefs as if they are made of concrete. But because we are born into each life deaf, dumb, and blind as to the reasons we chose to be there, instead of expanding our awareness, we tend to intensify and entrench those beliefs. As they become stronger and more convoluted, the harder it is to detach ourselves from their foundational structure. Often our scrambles define who we are, like Charlie identifying himself as rebellious and arrogant. These self-identities can be so powerful that we often cease to question (while in body) why we behave the way we do.

> *First of all, I was a female in the lifetime that started this scrambled soul psychology . . . I was a free spirit and a rebel. But in that system and at that time, the female was not appreciated and was governed by any male who happened to be in her pattern.*

Here, Charlie sets the scene by describing the cultural belief system which created rigid boundaries. It was a culture that didn't allow movement out of the structure. The males were dominant and had all the authority and responsibility. The females were completely subservient and unable to act in an independent manner. It was the viewpoint of the culture that supported the behavior by Charlie's brother that then in turn led Charlie to misunderstand the feminine nature. If he had had a life in another type of culture, this exact Soul Scramble may not have occurred.

> *. . . I consciously, actively resented that I was a free spirit housed in a female body. I knew . . . that I did not belong in that female body . . . because no matter what I tried to do or where I tried to go, I was always held back, always taken control of by the males.*

This is the onset of Charlie's deep misunderstanding that females are powerless and unable to be free spirits. He based this decision on that life and said, "*I died in that lifetime in a state of utter frustration and bitterness, and I carried. . . . that energy forward . . .(in the next life).*" It is implied that other females in his family did not have issues with the male domination. There is also an element of this Soul Scramble that came from Charlie's own individual rebellious nature. Therefore, not every female from that society would have come away with the exact same misunderstandings. The next phase for Charlie was to incarnate as a male over a series of lifetimes since his idea of being female was now so negative.

The scientific side of my soul is far more developed than the emotional side... because at an unconscious level, I attempted to make up for all that I had lost in that female incarnation. In scientific exploration, I became very proficient in areas that dealt with... weapons of war and destruction. This... served a purpose by allowing me, in that male pattern, to develop and find a place that I could put my frustration and anger.

Charlie's belief that the female was powerless also therefore affected his decisions as to the type of male lives he chose. His rage, born from that place of powerlessness and his conviction that he had led a wasted life, fueled his actions in future lifetimes. His choices moved him into an arena where he could play out his frustrations by developing weapons of war. Charlie said, "*I attempted to make up for all that I had lost in that female incarnation.*" Ironically, he became proficient in an area that allowed him to be dominant, thereby playing out a similar male role he was disgusted with when he had been dominated as a woman.

In several incarnations I developed very potent weapons from nature. . . . And when unleashed . . . I do feel badly about this now. I can't really conceive of having been so unconscious . . . but those potent germs would kill on contact. And I was proud of my contribution.

Charlie showed us how in any one lifetime we can misunderstand and misinterpret what we do. All souls take on cultural beliefs, such as the use of germ warfare to protect family and country, and these were the cultural perspectives Charlie chose to be born into. And in those places, he was a hero, of sorts. In time, with the help of hindsight, he wondered how he could have been so unconscious about what he had done. This was the beginning of the deep guilt and shame that became firmly implanted in his Soul Scramble. Charlie felt like the men in that restrictive culture had victimized him. Later in his journey, he took on the belief that he victimized others by developing germ warfare.

When I reached a point of soul desperation . . . I sought counsel out of body. I spent the equivalent of several lifetimes out of body working with educators in the Human Kingdom Heavens . . . in an attempt to save myself from further soul scrambling.

Charlie was clear that it was his decision to seek counseling. Heaven is part of the Human Kingdom and as such, operates under Free Will. As a result, one has to decide to get help while in the disincarnate state just as one does while in body. When we experience trouble while living in body, we can stick our heads in the sand, try to solve the problem by ourselves, or we can reach out. The same goes when out of body. Heaven has resources for those who do want help. And out of desperation, Charlie reached out. We may feel a few years in therapy is sufficient . In Charlie's case, he spent over a century in the process.

When I was ready, I took on a female body again. I felt fairly comfortable in that lifetime in a female body and was able to enjoy a beautiful love relationship with a man who did not attempt to control or coerce me. The experience gave me the additional soul programming of being equal while in a female body.

The idea of being equal as a female was a step forward for Charlie although it had a downside because of the scramble he was in. His female side, now feeling more like an equal, would fight the masculine nature to get what it wanted/needed, adding to the battleground scenario as his lives unfolded. It further empowered the female rebellious nature, which also added to the intensity of the conflict. This shows how a positive element in a soul's growth can actually add to further scrambling. There is so much emphasis to always think positive, but here is an example where a positive feeling/concept was a double-edged sword.

Additionally, it greatly assisted the emotional nourishing of my soul, for the emotional side of my nature had not been fully activated and was at war within the soul space to advance on its own. I was unaware . . . a soul can war within itself and can create tremendous schisming . . . the scientific powerful male aspect part . . . wanted to dominate and destroy the emotional more feminine side of my nature. But, in the play out of those two aspects of the soul while in body, I was confused as to what I had come in to do.

Charlie was confused when in body, not only because he did not remember what the purpose of that life was, but he was also unaware that parts of his soul were "at war" within. This is key. All of us have internal battles that we are unaware of. It makes it more difficult to move forward in this Free Will Kingdom and can increase the time frame for us to find resolution. Once we become aware, our blinders fall away much more quickly. It may still take time to resolve the issues, as it had for Charlie. However, Charlie didn't have the benefit of knowing the neutralizing techniques. Our road can be much easier because we do.

> *While taking on female incarnations . . . to reach the highest level of emotional development of that feminine side . . . I continued to make mistake after mistake. I became a soul frustrated in rage because I could not get it together. The educators . . . informed me that these were misconceptions. But the arrogant part of the nature in the soul was still present . . . and was unable, many times, to understand, because in its arrogance, it would not listen.*

There are two parts of this that are important. The first is that on this long journey, we can make mistakes over and over again. This is part of the human experience, and this is why our journey through the Free Will Kingdom takes so long. And second, even though Charlie has gone for help with his confusion, like many of us in body he did not want to hear. Charlie's inability to hear the educators due to his arrogance was a significant reason why it took so long to resolve his scramble. He was resistant, and as such, repeated his patterns over and over, unable to move away from his hardened belief system or *solidified truth*—a belief that is so ingrained in the Soul/Mind that it is unquestioned and unexplored. Even though we may not have his exact Soul Scramble and the resistance for the same reasons as Charlie, this resistance at the soul level is an important element of most Soul Scrambles. Resistance is something we have to become aware of and neutralize in any of its forms.

As I viewed all of the crimes that I had participated in, all of the destructive acts that came about based on work that I had done, my inability to fully cope, and my inability to understand that emotional feminine aspect of my nature, I came to believe that I was a lost soul. I knew that I would never be able to repent for those evil deeds and for my own inability to be a whole and complete person.

Charlie fixated on another major misunderstanding, which only added a great weight of despair and shame onto his plate. He believed he was a lost soul.

First, no soul is ever lost. However, in the Human Kingdom there are times when souls get sidetracked or so entrenched in a pattern that millennia go by. There is no time pressure to finish the human journey. There is no reward or prize if one soul does it quicker than another. No soul is more special, and no soul is more elite. Heaven is still in the Human Kingdom, and the line between incarnate and disincarnate is very thin. It is normal and understandable that some souls will figure things out more quickly or sometimes more slowly than other souls whether in body or in Heaven.

Second, this belief that he was a soul lost became a huge barrier for Charlie. It was the foundation for the subsequent belief that he could never repent for all he considered to be his evil deeds. Charlie could find no worth in himself, not even the slightest hint of self-value.

This pattern of worthlessness is carried by virtually all of us in different degrees. We have all had lives and situations in our journeys where we have felt/believed that we had failed and made unforgivable mistakes. In Charlie's case, his sense of failure, worthlessness, and regret was so deep that he could not find a way to forgive himself.

> *I was desperate. I went into intensive therapy . . . in an attempt to reach a point of laying claim to my own soul in a state of wholeness. And I understood that to atone for what I had done I would have to duplicate in my life what I had done to others. I knew that I had to die most horribly {of a disease from a germ} over and over again so I could repent and save myself . . .*

It was not the educators who told Charlie that he had to die a horrible death to save himself. It was Charlie's decision based on his false belief that atonement and suffering was the only way to save his soul. Not only did the situations and conditions for the life he had here lead to a painful and agonizing death, but in the end, instead of leading him to a state of atonement and self-forgiveness, they added yet another layer to his Soul Scramble, making it even more difficult to forgive himself.

> *Putting on a body is like going to sleep . . . you fumble, and you don't know why you do things. . . In taking on the male body, I attempted to work out the identifying of the male body with power and destruction. I wanted to be an emotionally loving individual, thus choosing to be gay.*

Charlie brought balance within his soul by having his female nature present within a male body. He hoped this would affect more cooperation and connection between the male and female parts. This is *not* the only reason an individual would choose to be homosexual in a life. Whatever the reason, it is a soul's choice. The reasons would be unlimited and would generate from an individual soul's belief patterns. Also, his description "that putting on a body [was] like going to sleep" implies that he was awake while out of body. However, we can see that this was also not the case. He was just as confused when out of body as when he was in body, though perhaps from different directions.

When Charlie finished his story, this is what the Higher Selves explained:

> *Each soul must learn to forgive the self. In learning to forgive the self for any negative situation in your life—forgiving the self for being poor or out of work, for example—it is removed. Forgiveness is important in every area of every life, either in body or out of body. Charlie is as pure and perfect as any other soul, and yet Charlie (as is true of any other soul) has not fully recognized his own perfection. In addressing the perfected-ness of the self (through forgiving the self of all perceived imperfections), each soul can stand in a much freer state.*

With Charlie as with all of us, forgiveness of the self is not an easy task. Fortunately, as we learn more and more about how the soul's journey works and as we find ourselves moving up the ladder of increased understanding, we will find self-forgiveness to be a possibility and much easier to accomplish than we had thought. Suffering is not the way to dissolve a Soul Scramble. We can neutralize the false beliefs, known and unknown, that hold us in a place of suffering and scrambling. This enables us to find the self-forgiveness that will end the scramble.

The Impact of Charlie's Story

Charlie's story became the foundation of the growing understanding about the psychology of the soul. The learning we do in between lives in the disincarnate state will be tested when we are playing out of the mind level while in body. We learn on the proving grounds of experience. We have to practice what we have learned to feel confident that we can do it. For example, isn't one's honesty only truly tested when confronted with a choice where being dishonest is the easier path? We may have many insights and realizations while in the disincarnate state, but the *verification* of new awareness and clarity is achieved while in body. And it can be difficult because we carry all our thoughts, beliefs, judgments, habits, and emotional responses with us into every lifetime, and for the most part, we are completely unaware.

Charlie thought he made choices while in body, but real choice is not at the conscious mind level. It is at the soul level. And because he had not yet resolved his myriad of false beliefs, his worst nightmare came true. His self-identities and belief that he was lost led him to recreate the same acts for which he had sought repentance. While in body, Charlie spread the AIDS virus to others, and thus, unwittingly, played a role yet again with germ warfare (though by a different process) by unleashing the disease upon the planet. We often become so entrenched in the patterns of our past lives that we unwittingly play out those patterns while in the deaf, dumb, and blind human form. Charlie's soul consciously chose for him to suffer in order to atone, which reinforced the negative, shameful feelings that he already carried about himself. His beliefs were misconceptions and were *not* a reflection of his pure and perfect soul essence.

Being present when Joan reflected Charlie was a life-altering moment for all of us. We cried along with him. We felt his pain so deeply and could not find it in our hearts to judge him as evil or bad in any way. It was not clear if Charlie knew in his conscious mind during this life that he spread the disease or whether that knowledge came to him when he died. We were given no information as to the year of his death or how far along the scientific understanding about AIDS had been at that point. But what we did have was the benefit of the insights Charlie had gained from the Higher Selves. He opened his heart to us that day, and we gave him our heartfelt support. Most of all, Charlie showed all of us that the more we understand, the more difficult it is to judge, criticize, and blame.

To Recap

Breaking down by category what we've learned from Charlie's story will help orient you as you read the rest of the book. The three general areas of information are as follows:

Misunderstandings: Charlie takes on some serious misunderstandings that both fed his Soul Scramble and intensified it.

- There was no freedom when in female body.

- He was powerless as a female.

- He was a soul lost.

- He could never repent for his evil deeds.

- He had to atone in order to forgive himself for what he had done.

- Atonement meant he had to suffer for the acts he had committed.

Information about the Disincarnate State, Heaven, and the Human Kingdom Universe:

- If you want help with your problems, even in Heaven, you have to ask. Heaven is still part of the Human Kingdom and operates under Free Will.

- There are educators available, but they can't force you to listen or to understand.

- There are more planets that house life than just Earth.

- Souls can be just as confused in Heaven as we are here.

- Wisdom is not automatically bestowed upon us when we cross over.

- We choose our next life from the soul level.

What We Have Learned about the Soul:

- We reincarnate as both sexes.

- The female and male sides of the soul can evolve at different rates.

- We can be in conflict/at war with ourselves.

- We don't remember what goals we planned for ourselves when operating out of the mind level while in body.

- The culture/society we are born into can have a great effect on our belief systems.

- Souls can develop Soul Scrambles that drive the choices in how we reincarnate.

- Working through Soul Scrambles can take hundreds of lifetimes/years.

- Souls can take on the attribute of either the male nature or the female nature for some or much of the journey through the Human Kingdom.

The knowledge you have gained from learning Charlie's Soul Scramble provides the perfect starting point for understanding the power of one's perspective. It is our belief systems that are the foundation for our viewpoints about life and all it entails.

CHAPTER 4
Viewpoint: Is Charlie a Victim or Victimizer?

Each soul is a celebration of life in its highest, most beautiful perfection. It is only through the externalized viewpoint (brought to life by the individual and by others around the individual) that the celebration of life becomes distorted and defused. The judgments begin and the individual then begins to adopt an attitude that is not geared toward properly loving the self.

Viewpoint is a powerful persuader. It is the fuel that justifies our actions and our words. It is what gives us our opinions, weak or strong. It is the foundation for how we see the world, others, our lives, and our purpose. Charlie's story is only the first step to help you understand the tremendous impact our beliefs, viewpoints, and judgments have on our lives.

How can viewpoint affect our decisions and actions? Charlie's story helps us explore the answer since he had created for himself, through his belief systems, a rat wheel that kept him on a repetitious and entrenched pattern.

What Is Charlie?

a. Victim

b. Victimizer

c. Both

d. Neither

e. All of the Above

f. None of the Above

Okay, so what is Charlie? Don't worry. All of the answers are correct! Your answer comes from the viewpoint you have about the scenario. That is why you cannot fail this quiz. Everyone's viewpoint is valid for him/her.

a. Victim

If we met Charlie toward the end of his life when he was alive here, our hearts would have broken for him. We would have seen the ravages of AIDS on his body and mind, the fear of the unknown nature of the disease, the isolation he felt as all those around him were afraid to be near him and in some instances, even talk to him. We would have seen him as having this disease by happenstance or fate, and we would have believed no one deserves the horror he experienced. We might have also seen him as a victim of the male dominant culture he was born into in that first Soul Scramble life and perhaps a victim of his own confusion and lack of self-awareness as well.

Our viewpoint would be clear. Charlie was a victim.

b. Victimizer

If we knew Charlie at the time when he first became ill but functioned and lived life as a rebellious type, we may have seen him as uncaring and arrogant, exposing others to a contagious disease that he had contracted. Charlie believed that he had been a victimizer because of the lethal germs he had developed and also by how he handled himself in the last life with HIV. From this viewpoint, it would be easy to see Charlie as a victimizer, perhaps even as heartless.

c. Both

How could he be both a victim and a victimizer? Because his soul pattern contained elements of both polarities. People are complex and often not one-dimensional. Charlie was no exception. He felt like a victim in life as a woman—a victim of the male-dominated society. He also felt like a victimizer as the architect of germ warfare.

d. Neither

Now that we have read Charlie's story, we understand why Charlie chose the route he had taken. We understand that he was not a victim, for it was he that decided to take on the horrible death by disease as a way to atone. He did not remember what he was to learn from this death, but because he chose this death, he was not a victim of nature.

He was also not a victimizer. He was caught up in his complex and entrenched Soul Scramble, playing out from that long-ago female lifetime the rebellious nature developed out of the great frustration of being so controlled. His actions could be perceived as thoughtless and uncaring, but he was reacting against the shoulds and shouldn'ts as if he was justified to do what he wanted. He was much more like a rebellious child, not fully understanding his purpose. More importantly, in the same way that we understand that Charlie chose this AIDS outcome for himself, those who he had infected also made that choice. Each person would have had his own reasons at the soul level (though unremembered) for making the choice to be infected. This is a Free Will Kingdom, and we cannot do something to another that the other doesn't agree to (at the soul level). So, if there are no true victims, there are no true victimizers.

e. All of the Above

How could the answer be all of the above? Each viewpoint is valid for the person making the choice. Every viewpoint has an element of validity. Viewpoint is subjective and dependent on where you stand in any one moment. Change your position and suddenly your viewpoint changes. So no matter what answer you gave, you have answered correctly.

f. None of the Above

By now you know this isn't about whether Charlie is a victim or a victimizer. In a way, it was a trick question as I was the one who posed it. The question itself encouraged the various answers. In reality, being a victim or victimizer is not what defines Charlie or anyone. Charlie's soul is as whole and perfect as any soul. It is his and our perspectives that create the judgments and labels. At the higher levels, there is no such viewpoint. The soul's perfection is clear. Charlie is soul struggling to see his own perfection. And this is the journey we are all on.

We have seen for perhaps the first time how a soul's journey greatly affects one's life pattern in the life we live now. It is evident that what we feel, see, and experience in our own current life is but a small part of a much larger picture. We also see how our viewpoint affects our judgments. The wider the perspective, the less room there is for judgment. There is only room for understanding—understanding that we all are on a journey and everyone has their own unique history, their own unique reasons for being who they are and for doing what they do.

CHAPTER 5

The Truth, the Whole Truth, and Nothing but the Truth

HIGHER SELF QUOTE

In the highest level, truth does not exist. For moment-to-moment what is seen as truth evolves and grows and becomes an ever-evolving truth. It is in this sense that we have requested each of you to remain as unlimited as possible in what you would lock down and call "the truth."

So what is truth? Truth is relative to each individual and is related to the viewpoint one is coming from. Truth expands as the viewpoint expands. The more we understand, the more we see that any judgment we may have at any moment is on shaky ground. For everything about a person is relative to their soul's journey—where they have been, what they have experienced, why they chose the path they are on in this life, and what misunderstandings and misconceptions are motivating their journey. What are their Soul Scrambles? We are all in the same boat. Whether judging others or judging ourselves, at the mind level we are coming from the place of limited understanding. We don't know our own journey, our own misunderstandings, let alone someone else's. Here is an example of the Higher Self viewpoint about truth. The story is based on common elements that are familiar to all of us.

HIGHER SELF QUOTE

A truth can become a shadow on your path of exploration. For once one has locked into any truth, any philosophy, one has given over the power of expansion to a limited vibration, to the boundary where this belief happens to be at any given time.

Ann and Tom

Ann and Tom married young. They lived in the States. They both worked and didn't have any children. As the marriage moved into its sixth year, Tom cheated on his wife. Ann found out and decided to end the marriage, no questions asked. She thought with great relief, "Thank goodness I found out what a jerk he was before we had kids. Now I know the truth about him." And she blamed Tom fully for ruining their marriage. She left him and filed for a divorce. It was black and white for her. She was bitter and angry and felt blindsided by his betrayal.

A few months later, she walked to her car on the way to work and thought, "I'm so lucky that Tom screwed up so that I had an excuse to get out of that empty marriage." This thought amazed her! She realized for the first time that it was an empty marriage long before Tom had ever cheated on her, but she had avoided thinking about it for years. Once this thought came to her, she could no longer squash it. It was out of the box and shocking. Why, she wondered, hadn't she paid attention sooner, and why had she needed an excuse to leave an empty marriage? How could she have rationalized so well and believed all of her own excuses for so long? Not wanting to go into another relationship and have problems again, she decided that she needed help to understand the whys. With a recommendation from a friend, Ann went into therapy.

Therapy was a new experience for her, but she was motivated to understand herself more and to become more discerning in life. Over the months, she realized she had something to do with the empty marriage. She had never fully committed to the relationship as there was always a part of her that she withheld. She understood she never was fully open and vulnerable with Tom. She also realized she was the same way with her work. She knew she worked hard at her job, but she was always out by six and rarely worked overtime. She found herself looking at the want ads online almost every weekend. There was nothing wrong with her job. She was happy there and well paid. But somehow there was the sense that something better was out there, and she didn't want to miss any opportunity.

As therapy continued, she looked for the causes of her resistance to commit. And in this search, she saw her father in a different light. Her dad had died when she was eight years old, but her memories were clear, though formed from a child's perspective. During his life, her dad had moved jobs and cities often and took the family with him. Once or twice a year, the family moved when Dad said it was time. On each occasion, he talked about the move as something exciting, something that would lead to a better life. Ann was too young at the time to understand more than that.

Now that she was in therapy, Ann pieced together that her father ran from his own limitations, his inability to hold down a job, and his constant self-sabotage due to his drinking. She understood that because of the limited perspective of a child, she had taken on the idea "the grass is always greener on the other side of the fence." She felt her inability to commit was anchored in the misunderstandings she held from her upbringing.

The concept Ann had previously held about her father shifted, and she now saw him as a flawed human being. She no longer held the simple picture of him as the hero. With that vision came some resentment and anger. She blamed her father for her problems. She knew this meant she, too, had to accept some responsibility for the failure of her marriage. Her inability to commit resulted in her not being the wife to Tom she would have been otherwise. At this point, Tom became only half-bad in her mind. He was still a jerk, but this idea was tempered by her taking on 50% of the blame of her failed marriage. But her 50% she firmly placed on her father's shoulders.

Armed now with greater understanding, Ann moved back into single life with the determination to live past the surface, to live out of a deeper place, and to commit more fully to her job and to a mate when the time came. She wasn't sure how to make those shifts but believed consciousness would make the process both possible and easier.

A few months later, Ann met Kirk. During the early stages of the relationship, Ann shared her insights and understanding with Kirk, feeling that, by sharing, she was being more open and vulnerable in this relationship. She thought she was doing what she needed to do to make sure this relationship lasted and that should something happen to break them up, it would not be because of her.

They fell in love and moved in together. A couple of years passed, and they fell into more superficial communication patterns. They both had their own work, their own friends, and though they socialized together with other couples, they did less and less of that as the months went by. Both were friendly to each other and let each other know where they were and when they would return, but in time they grew apart. Ann realized this and was content, at first. She was confident in Kirk's loyalty to her, and she stayed in her comfort zone of not really being fully connected. She saw that it was not the ideal relationship—therapy had taught her something—and even as she recognized her patterns, she rationalized that no relationship was perfect and felt she couldn't have everything. For Ann, though not fully conscious on her part, true connection and commitment still carried a discomfort that she didn't like to experience.

Ann became restless. She wanted children but knew her relationship with Kirk wouldn't work with children. She felt she would be alone in the parenting. She realized that not only was she in danger of being cheated on again, but she also found herself again looking at the want ads. This shock came when she fully acknowledged to herself that she was thinking at some unconscious level that a new job—perhaps out of town—would give her an excuse to leave Kirk. She knew for certain that here again was her old pattern. No matter how much she thought she understood, she had fallen back into her old ways.

Determined to change but not wanting another relationship that would repeat a similar ending, she broke it off with Kirk and searched for other answers.

This was when Ann discovered my web-radio show called the Higher Self Voice. She listened to the archived shows she'd missed and then listened live. She not only appreciated the Higher Self information but also loved the conscious healing meditations provided on each show, as they were powerful for her. At first, though she didn't understand it fully, she felt the energies at a deep level. At times, the topics spoke to her personally. She realized how essential the neutralizing process was if she really wanted her old patterns to change, so she earnestly used neutralizing on a regular basis.

Things did change. Shifts in her thinking appeared. She felt more empowered, more serene, less restless, more willing to work extra hours, more open to things she hadn't been before. She even felt the connections to her friends shift. There were a couple friends she no longer hung out with, and yet she became closer to others. Some shifts she noticed were profound and others more subtle, but she had no doubt the work helped her to release and dissolve her habits, her unconscious beliefs, and overall patterns. The voices in her head and her feelings of bitterness, betrayal, and hurt lessened and many even disappeared. She became more understanding of herself and others with her blame and judgment patterns significantly reduced. She slept better and experienced less anxiety. Overall, Ann resonated with the information and knew that she was preparing for the right relationship at the right time. She knew that neutralizing the negative and empowering the positive meant that more enriching and joyful possibilities would manifest for her.

After working on her own for several months, Ann decided to schedule a private session with me and discovered from the Higher

Selves that Tom and she had co-created being together in this life at the soul level (before either of them had been born). She learned that both of them had patterns that they had repeated in many lifetimes, and they were both determined to heal themselves in this life. Because their patterns worked well together, they had set up the general circumstances for their lives with the hope that the pain and suffering from the loss of their marriage would propel both into the search to heal.

Now armed with this new information from the healing session, Ann realized she was *completely* responsible for her patterns. She saw that it wasn't her dad's fault, Tom's fault, or even about fault. Instead, she understood she came into this life with the scramble centered around difficulties with commitment and was grateful that all the circumstances she and Tom had hoped would play out did so. She had been motivated to search for answers. She understood that Tom, rather than being a jerk was a wonderful soul who had honored his agreement to be part of her life pattern, which resulted in her finding the way to balance and happiness. Finally, the self-blame she had taken on herself became self-acceptance, fully knowing she had taken responsibility for her patterns.

Ann felt comfortable reconnecting with Tom to share with him her new understanding and appreciation for his part in motivating her to heal. Tom was mostly confused as some of what Ann talked about was foreign to him. Over time, with further discussions, the seeds of these new ideas grew. He thought about himself and his life's patterns in new ways, and his journey to self-awareness took hold. He, too, started the search for answers, though he found his place of solace with yoga and meditation practices.

Ann, after taking on the lifestyle of neutralizing, dissolved her old belief system. About a year later, she met Jim, a loving man who connected with her in ways she hadn't experienced before. They married and had children. Ann found the grass is greenest where she was and no longer looked for something else, or someone else. There was no longer a need to avoid the discomfort she used to feel upon connecting because there was no discomfort anymore.

The Truth Will Set You Free?

HIGHER SELF QUOTE

By reaching a point of being able to stand within the center, accepting neither the truth nor the untruth, you will greatly accelerate and expand your ability to live an unlimited, non-judgmental state of beingness.

There is one adage about truth we often take for granted. "The truth will set you free." The Higher Selves don't use many sound bites and instead explain this concept of truth in more depth. So, let's look at this adage using Ann and Tom's story as context.

Which truth set Ann free? There are many moments of truth in this story. First, there is the truth when Ann discovers that Tom has cheated on her. This truth frees her from the marriage but also brings in feelings of hopelessness, anger, and blame. And what about the truth that her dad was not the hero she had thought but a flawed father that caused her problems? Did this free Ann? Or did this move Ann further into a place of blame and resentment and powerlessness?

It is when Ann discovers that she and Tom made a co-created pact to help each other heal, she understood in her heart that she was not a victim as she had planned the situation before her birth, and she had successfully brought it into her life. The circumstances she had set up with Tom had successfully motivated her to find answers and to heal herself! This truth was of the freeing sort as she had moved into another level of awareness. She understood her journey with expanded perception without the judgments and faultfinding.

There are usually only momentary truths as truth is ever-evolving. Truth is an organic, dynamic force in life. It is a vertical concept, carried at every level, and as it moves into higher and higher frequencies, each truth or every concept expands. At each new level we discover there is more to a concept than we first believed. Truth expands as we remove our blinders one by one or twenty by twenty allowing us to see things/people/ourselves from a wider perspective than before.

Ann moved through her own series of truths. There is always more expansion even beyond what she knows now, but she had reached the truth she had wanted to reach when she planned this life. Truth unfolds like stepping-stones up the path of a hillside. In this analogy, at each level, the stepping-stone that you are on is the one you are ready to be at. But, we are not meant to lock into one of the momentary truths—one of the stepping-stones—and build a house there. For example, if Ann had never progressed passed the first truth in her story—that Tom was the jerk and her anger toward him was justified—and built her house there (symbolically), she would have locked into a life of bitterness and powerlessness, feeling like a victim. This house would have become her prison.

Ultimately, truth is ever-evolving. You are where you are, experiencing what you are in the moment, and learning, growing from that. As we progress up the ladder of our truths, we begin to see we haven't failed and it is not about blame. Instead, life offers us stepping-stones where the events and people that we manifest are opportunities to become aware, to heal, and to move to the next stone. As we go to the more expanded frequencies of truth, the sting goes out of what we think of as failure, whether our own or what we believe to be someone else's. We realize we did not screw up but we manifested a situation that forced us to become conscious, aware, and discerning. This stepping-stone process is how we learn and evolve and how the evolutionary process works. And we set up some of it in general for each life before we are born.

The journey chosen by one may not follow the same path as the journey chosen by another. One party may use the situation co-created in one way and the other person in a different way. I recommend that we do not judge what the other person is doing as wrong. We don't know enough about ourselves so how can we judge others? And when we do, we most often *misjudge* them.

Truth at the Soul Level

Truth does not have to be something that you *consciously* believe in at the mind level. It can also be what you hold onto at that unconscious soul level. It is these soul level truths (whether we are aware of them or not) that direct our lives. These truths are so snarled and misunderstood because they have been created over eons of lifetimes. Charlie is a perfect example of this. Like Charlie, we all have truths we have brought into this life, which have given birth to the difficult/painful/unjust situations and conditions that lead us to search for answers. Most of us, unfortunately, carry our truths at such a deep level that they have become *solidified*. We view them as self-evident and unquestionable. They are entrenched, and most often, negative. Some common examples: I am too emotional; I will never have financial security; I can't do this because . . .; I'm not good enough; I don't deserve . . .; or I'm a loser/failure/worthless. It is these kinds of embedded negative truths that hold us prisoner.

At this point in time in the Human Kingdom Universe, we are going through an unbelievably fast acceleration and unveiling. (See Expanded Perceptions—The Divine Paradox) So it's an opportune time to be aware of what we are holding onto. We all feel secure with the truths we have lived with for a long time, lifetimes long. They are familiar and comfortable in that we know them well and have developed work-arounds, defense mechanisms, and various ways to cope. Yet, if we hold onto these old truths, we are more or less frozen in our belief systems that hold us to lives we aren't happy with. But by allowing the old truths to dissolve and the new to be expanded and unfolded, we will manifest so much more of what we want and who we truly are just as Ann did in her story.

Ironically, once we understand that truth can be limiting, it is an incredibly freeing concept. It may seem overly complex and difficult. Yet it gives us permission to question; something we are all really good at doing. And now we will do it from the viewpoint that something, some idea, or some concept may no longer work for us and may not be in our highest ideal.

But where do all these truths come from? How do we get the beliefs that we carry around with us? They come from every life we have ever had, from the cultural, ethnical, spiritual, and psychological truths we have taken in, most of which we are not aware of in this current life. Symbolically, the truths we have taken in over the eons could be seen as a massive entangled root system at the foundation of who we think we are. It is snarled and knotted and is part of virtually all of our patterns. It looks like the huge bramble bush or thicket that surrounded Sleeping Beauty's castle, protecting her for 100 years until her Prince Charming found her. Ours may seem impenetrable and beyond our ability to do anything about it (especially because being in the Human Free Will Kingdom we do not have a Prince or Princess Charming to save us), but we *are* able to move into that deep root system ourselves and neutralize it. But let's understand more about this bramble bush, this dense undergrowth and overgrowth that prevents those in the castle from seeing clearly what is in the world around them. It also prevents anyone looking in from the outside from seeing the glory and beauty of the castle and all who live there.

This dense undergrowth is something we all carry. What are its origins? How does it become part and parcel of our Soul Scrambles?

PART II

Soul Scramble Development While Incarnate (In Body)

CHAPTER 6
Soul Scramble Origins

HIGHER SELF QUOTE

Making judgments by stating emphatically a belief or a disbelief in any given situation (whether it be information or conditions that exist in the life patterns of others) creates a limitation. A belief or a disbelief greatly limits the person placing that judgment and the person or the condition that judgment is placed against.

Beliefs

At the beginning of my first book, *CHOICES,* I describe a one-panel drawing of a man who holds onto the bars of a jail cell window, looking out onto the beautiful countryside beyond. He despairs that he is in prison and not free to enjoy the beauty of the countryside. He feels alone and without options. But as we look at the picture, we see what he doesn't—there are no other walls in the jail cell; he is free to leave at any time. All he has to do is turn around, shift his focus away from the bars in the window, and he would see that he was free. His *viewpoint* kept him prisoner.

We create so many of our own jail cells and prison walls by the beliefs we carry. In this book, I take the belief concept to a deeper level, to the level of how the journey of the soul affects and creates its beliefs and how the beliefs become Soul Scrambles.

Where do our beliefs come from? They come from the experiences we have had and the conclusions we've drawn from them in each and every lifetime. And most of the conclusions we have drawn are based on misunderstandings, misconceptions, and misinterpretations. These misunderstandings are the basis for our limiting belief systems, the truths that we use to explain ourselves and our world. As the mind of each current life joins with the minds of our past lives (our soul), we add to and empower these truths, intensifying and increasing the density of the carpet (or bramble bush) of our energetic foundation—our thought forms, habit imprints, and emotional blueprints. And what else do we do? We lock into our limited truths, false beliefs, and rampant misunderstandings. Our scrambles become complex and entrenched. Over time, these scrambles are why it is so hard to *turn around* to see that our prison walls are not real but *a closed viewpoint* that we hold onto. Also, these beliefs become our self-identities. They determine how we live our lives, how we define ourselves, and how we manifest our reality every day.

Most of us experience tough times, difficult problems, and many patterns we can't seem to resolve, dissolve, or even work around. We may not understand this *but what we manifest in our lives—the events, experiences, and people—reflect perfectly on the outside all that we believe on the inside.* Often, we also haven't fully understood that it's our *own thoughts and emotional responses* over eons of time that have created what we carry inside and have kept us on the spinning wheel in a rat cage. It may be difficult for some to come to terms with how we are responsible for our own patterns, but we are the true creators of our pathways. In each current life, we respond and play out our lives based on what we have experienced and accumulated over time. Remember, the soul is the most significant part of the symbolic Soul/Mind ocean, and it determines most of the conditions of the lives we now live.

The Power of Perspective

How we see, judge, and interpret our world is all processed through the veil of the belief systems we carry and the perspectives we hold. The following old Chinese proverb illustrates the freedom from worry, fear, doubt, anxiety, and stress when one stands in the middle of neutrality without an entrenched perspective.

The Story of the Taoist Farmer: A story taken from an ancient Chinese text written/compiled by the Huainanzi (the philosophers of Huainan) under the patronage of Liu An, King of Huainan, in the Han Dynasty during the second century BC. Lightly edited for clarity.

"Once upon a time, there was a man living on the northern border of China who was very good at raising horses. Everyone called him Sai Wong (meaning 'an old man on the border'). One day, one of Sai Wong's horses escaped from the stable and ran across the border straight into the territory of the Hu people. Upon hearing this news, all his neighbors came to comfort Sai Wong and hoped he wouldn't be too upset about it. To everyone's surprise, Sai Wong was not affected by the news and said with a smile, 'A horse running off might turn out to be a good blessing in disguise.'

Several months later, not only did this runaway horse return, but it also brought with it another fine horse from the Hu's territory. When his neighbors heard the news, one after another came by to congratulate Sai Wong. This time, Sai Wong frowned and said to everyone, 'Getting a fine horse for nothing could be a bad omen in disguise.'

Sai Wong had a son who enjoyed horseback riding. One day, his son went riding on this fine horse from the Hu's territory for an excursion and accidentally fell off the horse and broke a leg. So Sai Wong's neighbors came to comfort him. They asked him not to take it too hard. Surprisingly, Sai Wong said to everyone peacefully, 'My son breaking a leg might be a blessing in disguise.' His neighbors were all puzzled by his response and decided Sai Wong must have lost his senses due to grief.

However, shortly thereafter, the Hu people began a large-scale invasion against China. All the young men in Sai Wong's area had been summoned to join the army and defend the country. Because the Hu people were very swift, daring, and skillful at fighting, most of these newly recruited young men were killed on the battlefield. Yet, Sai Wong's son survived the war because his severely broken leg prevented him from joining the army. It was then that Sai Wong's neighbors discovered the wisdom hidden in his words."

What can we learn from this? First, unlike his neighbors, Sai Wong did not judge each event like others did. It turned out that his more neutral viewpoint, the wait-and-see attitude, was the more accurate approach. More importantly, the assumptions that the neighbors made were based on their perspectives. The neighbors' subjective perspectives were that events are bad or good or lucky or unlucky. Sai Wong, however, had the ability to stand in the center of neutrality. He did not get caught up with or get limited by a perspective. Instead, he was open to see what unfolded and saved himself much time of worry, regret, anger, and frustration. By standing in that neutral place, he did not lose himself to *emotionalizing* (getting carried away with the emotional side of) the events. He allowed each event to be what it was without judgment.

Of course, this is a simple story and life is rarely that simple. But a strong perspective can be a powerful prison and can color how you (and others) feel, how you view your life, and how you experience events.

What is the Goal?

The ultimate goal is to free ourselves of the beliefs and judgments that stem from the long-term accumulation of misunderstandings. When we reach that goal, we will see all perspectives or at least a much wider viewpoint. We will see an event in the purity of its neutrality. For example, picture yourself driving on a freeway. You can see about half a mile ahead. You are moving fast, and according to your perspective, you will reach your destination 10 miles away quickly. What you don't see is the accident that has just happened four miles ahead. The pilot in the traffic helicopter above sees the accident because he looks at the freeway from a wider perspective. He knows the pileup ahead will slow traffic to a halt and could even mean injuries for those bearing down on the problem. Plus, he knows the closest exits for the cars coming from behind to use to avoid the pileup and to prevent an even more problematic scenario. The pilot sees that bigger picture. For us, as the drivers, reaching the traffic jam means frustration and distress because our belief was that our trip would be fast. This belief was based on limited information. Had we had the benefit of the higher perspective, we would have exited early and gotten to our destination without anger or worry.

We can bring this type of higher viewpoint into our world. We can get up in that helicopter when we neutralize the energy identities that are the foundation of our viewpoints. (Remember, neutralizing is the act of rendering harmless the energy identities that create our viewpoints, thereby taking away the fuel that supports our belief systems. This allows in the larger perspectives and brings us to a state of balance. Neutralizing opens us up to new ways of seeing that facilitates more understanding, options, and opportunities.) Symbolically, it also means that we don't need to wait for the random possibility that we tune into traffic updates on the radio at the perfect time to learn of the accident. We can instead drive through this life as if in a helicopter able to see there are really no prisons and we are not locked into the limited lives we have been living. We don't have to be anchored by our ruts, patterns, or routines that have little meaning and/or that are the source of our misery.

Are there even higher viewpoints (truths) than a helicopter? Yes. In this analogy, there could also be the viewpoint from the moon, the sun, or even from the outer edges of the Milky Way Galaxy. There is no limit on the expansion of truth. There are always higher and more expanded viewpoints.

We don't need to know all that has happened to us that has created our belief systems. We don't need the expanded understanding of our soul history like Charlie did. We can, however, understand more about the process in general—the whys, the wherefores, and the hows related to our beliefs. Behind them all are the misunderstandings and misconceptions that we have accepted as truth. Where do our beliefs come from? How do they become so deep, tenacious, and entrenched and often create our knee-jerk reactions?

Personal Experiences versus Cultural Norms

HIGHER SELF QUOTE

Each time you move out into the everyday world, you are constantly assaulted by situations that you accept as a belief or disbelief. You allow limiting thought judgments to become an ever-expanding part of your everyday world.

Basically, there are two general arenas where we take on and then continue to empower limited and limiting beliefs. The first arena relates to the events *we personally experience* as individuals. The second arena relates to the *general cultural/societal norms* and viewpoints we are exposed to in each life. There are in both cases significant events/situations and insignificant ones. The insignificant ones have little impact on our soul's evolutionary journey. It is the more significant events—especially the ones we have judged as negative—that have the greatest effect.

Here are some examples of beliefs coming from *individual* significant experiences:

- We lose both parents at a young age and are put into the foster care system. The pain and ugliness we experience leads us to believe that we will never be happy or successful in life with such a terrible childhood.

- We lose our job and became homeless and we come to believe that the government caused all our problems.

- Our house was hit by lightning, burned down and a family member was lost/severely injured. We emerge from the situation believing that life is a crapshoot, and we are doomed to be its victims.

Of course, there are an infinite amount of situations and conditions that could happen to individuals. When they are significant or important to us, we come away with strong feelings and powerful conclusions about them. And usually, the conclusions are laced with confusion and misinterpretation that stem from our limited perspectives at the time.

In the cultural and societal arena, the significant influences are from the daily, weekly, monthly, and yearly conditions we live within that create an ongoing conditioning we all experience in every life. The values and beliefs present in these societies are taken in almost by osmosis as we learn from our parents, peers, teachers, spiritual advisors, the governmental authorities, etc. This is the conditioning that everyone within a particular society is exposed to, not just you as an individual.

Here are some examples of beliefs coming from culturally based conditioning:

- From Charlie, we know that the male dominant culture he incarnated in was part of the reason his developed his belief that women were powerless, and he wasn't meant to be a woman.

- For someone who lived in a society dominated by a tyrannical religion or where religion justified cruelty to others, a belief could develop that God is unjust, controlling, and punishing.

- If born into a society that operates a caste system, beliefs at every level of the caste would reflect the level an individual would develop. Those in the lowest caste would think they are worthless and those in the highest would think they were better than others.

Societal norms of many types have been incorporated into our souls, layer by layer, lifetime after lifetime. It's no wonder that all of us have more beliefs than we can imagine which then play out within our life's patterns. We are influenced throughout every life by both personal and cultural experiences. Both affect who we are at the soul level. And it is the soul that carries great influence in the current life.

No two souls have identical experiences, so no two souls will come away from an event, a lifetime, or a society with the same misunderstandings and beliefs. However, there are commonalities. Even though the details vary, the belief system born from our many personal and/or cultural experiences have significant similarities. Over time, we all have taken on what could be viewed as generic beliefs. If we neutralized these belief systems we would change our life for the better. Fortunately, we can do just that!

CHAPTER 7

Creation of a Compounded Soul Scramble

If you can step back from all of your beliefs and unbeliefs and objectively live within the center of the two, you will find tremendous clarity of vision and higher frequency of understanding as well as an unlimited level of ever-expanding awareness, knowledge, and wisdom.

How Events Evolve into Beliefs

Every *event* is a neutral occurrence. It is our viewpoint about the event that makes it negative or positive. This may seem like an outrageous statement. A simple example is a snake event, which is contact of any sort with a snake. If you are terrified of snakes, you would have a difficult time seeing a snake as a neutral commodity. But no matter how we feel about snakes (or anything else), there are others who feel differently. There are people who study snakes and find them fascinating, those who find snakes curious or interesting, and those who break out in hives looking at a snake in a book. If any event such as the snake event were inherently negative or inherently positive, everyone every time would react the exact same way. But this doesn't happen with snakes or any other event. Each individual *attaches* his/her own mix of emotional reactions to every event, creating an emotional blueprint.

Once an emotional blueprint is created, it determines over and over again how we will react to the event each time it recurs. Just as an architectural blueprint determines how a building will be built, an emotional blueprint determines how we are going to feel about an event.

To further complicate things, each time we experience a similar event, we may also add other layers of emotional attachments because an event may not happen in the exact same conditions each time. For example, let's use a child who is in one of his early lives as a human. When he is small, he walks through the woods with his father and they see a snake. The father, who is cautious around snakes, takes a path of avoidance. He impresses upon the child that snakes can be dangerous and to make sure to steer clear but he also gives him simple information about the lives of this reptile with no legs. The beginning of uncertainty, caution, and even curiosity takes hold within the child related to the snake event.

The next type of snake event happens when the child is about four or five. The child sees a snake while he is with his mother in a marketplace at a booth where poison snake venom is sold. The child is curious so stops and looks closer. Perhaps to entertain the child, the vendor thrusts a snake toward his face as a joke. His mother screams, and the boy's shock attaches fear to the snake event. Now for him, the snake event triggers caution, curiosity, and fear.

The third time the child sees a snake, he is alone outdoors and accidentally steps on one that bites him. This adds terror and fear of death to the blueprint of the snake event, as he wonders if he will die from the poisonous venom.

Each snake event had different circumstances. Each time the boy added complexity to his response pattern, and this was from just one life. In general, emotional blueprints start out simple and then can grow bigger and more complex as time (lifetimes) goes by. With all the emotions flowing, the thoughts and actions happen simultaneously, creating an Altered Reality (a complex energy identity) within our etheric bodies related to this one event.

This is how belief systems take root, expand, and become intricate and complex as they weave in and out of all of life patterns. In our example, the child, in just one life, has already built a blueprint about snakes that will likely continue to be empowered over his journey. From now on, he would experience the fear emotion any time he heard talk about a snake or saw one. The event will never be neutral again in any life (unless the blueprint is neutralized). In addition, these events rarely happen alone in one's life pattern. The complexity can be huge and pervasive. Our experiences around the everyday and the extraordinary events evoke thought, action, and emotional responses to those events that then become the foundation of our beliefs—in this case, that the snake is something to be feared.

How Beliefs Evolve into Soul Scrambles: The Jake/Janice Story

HIGHER SELF QUOTE

The majority of beliefs that are carried have their originating base in the area of unremembered experiences that have no basis of fact in this reality. And yet this projection from these unremembered experiences brings into this lifetime a discoloration insofar as how the belief system will be built.

The Soul Scramble of Janice/Jake is an example of a conglomerate system of beliefs and their origins that I combined based on information from friends, clients, and myself. It is woven together by using specific events in a soul's life over its journey through the Human Kingdom Universe. It reflects the impact of individual experiences (rather than the cultural and societal beliefs), and it illustrates in a more multidimensional way how our scrambles become so complex.

This Soul Scramble shows the development of an extreme phobia of the healing arts. In the first life beginning this Soul Scramble, Jack (the male nature of this soul), lived many millennia ago in a traditional tribal situation. At a young age, he assisted a shaman as his apprentice for many years. He discovered (unknown to the general tribal population) that the shaman was power hungry and used his position as a healer to gain information to manipulate others in order to self-aggrandize. Over time, Jack found the healing arts to be distasteful. Because it was his first and only direct experience with a healer, he incorrectly connected the entire profession with the character of this shaman. He came away from that life distrustful of healers based on his individual experience.

In the next few lives, the distrust continued in similar fashion until the time Jack lived in a rural setting 1,000 plus years ago. He and his wife lived in a sparsely populated region. At one point, his wife got very ill and despite his distrust, he took her to the local healer in the region, as there was no other option. This healer was mostly incompetent, with little knowledge and more interest in his next drink. The healer performed a harmful procedure resulting in the death of Jack's wife. Jack left that life with more than distrust as now he had added the emotional attachments of hatred and rage. The failings of this healer were now personal for Jack.

Over many other lifetimes, Jack continued to build his negative beliefs and feelings to the point where he had chosen many times to die early rather than to get help from a healer/shaman. He also refused to get help for his family members. While in body, he thought he was doing the right thing but at the soul level between lives, he came to realize he had made decisions that meant both he and others died younger and suffered much more than necessary. As a result, another powerful feeling was added to the mix of this Soul Scramble—self-blame. Consumed with guilt, he was determined to change this pattern.

Jack received the help offered in the Heavens (just as Charlie did) and grasped that his hatred and rage toward the healing arts were blinders which led him to make poor decisions. He knew he needed balance and discernment rather than a knee-jerk reaction that dismissed all healing avenues. After going through an intense learning process with the counselors in Heaven, he developed a plan. Jack returned to the next life as a woman—Janice. He chose to reincarnate as the female child of a midwife during the time of the Inquisition. The soul felt this situation would give her (and

Jack) the opportunity to see the healing arts from the perspective of a close, personal, and loving relationship between a mother and daughter.

Unfortunately, the scramble became even more complex. While growing up with her mom, Janice did see the positive role her mother played in the birthing process. And Janice found value in the healing arts and became a midwife herself. But she ran into problems with the church. She had based her practice on what she had learned from her mother. She gained great wisdom, experience, and a deep commitment to put caring and expertise into her own midwifery practice. But unlike her mother, who always worked within the church's beliefs and gave credit to church authorities, Janice focused on her practice rather than the church or its edicts. Janice was not as prudent as her mother had been. She turned a blind eye to areas where she could have been more discerning. She ignored the church's dictums if they meant endangering her patients. This led to feelings of ill will between her and those spiritual authorities in charge. She irritated the religious officials and according to them, undermined the church's authority. Janice put her skill and knowledge before religion because of her genuine determination to be an ethical and professional healer.

The church tolerated this attitude as long as she was successful at birthing the infants. But the church pounced on her the minute she assisted a very difficult birth of an important person where the child died. The church authorities put Janice in prison for not calling in the priests for their prayers, as they were convinced that with God's help, the child would have lived. Now considered a heretic, she lived in prison until her death. Upon dying, she carried from that life a deep sense of powerlessness (the church would always have the power), self-blame (she had come to believe she made the unforgivable mistake of pride to stand up to the religion instead of embracing humility) and confusion (how could spirituality and the healing arts ever work together). Rather than resolving this Soul Scramble, Janice/Jack's soul was now more determined than ever to avoid all things medical. And their belief system around the healing arts became more complex, convoluted, and dark.

Now we come to the current lifetime where yet again Jack/Janice's hope was to resolve their now deeply ingrained and deeply disturbing belief system. Again Janice, the female nature, took on the body on current day Earth. As usual, once she was born, she forgot the goal she set for herself. Janice steered clear of the medical/healing community. Having chosen parents who believed much along the same lines as she did, her gut level distrust was fostered and empowered her resistance even though nothing specifically negative had happened to her yet. She didn't realize why she carried such enmity and instead saw her dislike as a truth her parents had fortunately taught her.

She was easily persuaded that all doctors were greedy and the entire medical community was out for itself and had nothing to offer. She was on the Internet many times a week, sent out negative e-mails about the horrific nature of doctors, and thought she was helping to educate others. She didn't believe in or see any benefit with any of the alternative healing arts either. She became fanatical about eating the perfect diet and believed that one will never get sick or need any kind of healing if one just practiced the art of eating perfectly.

However, one day she was in a car accident and admitted to the ICU, unconscious with life-threatening injuries. She received good care and began to heal. She was at the edge of a new insight and an acceptance that the healing community could be a positive force. A few nights later, a nurse made an error with her medications. Janice experienced convulsions and nearly died. Janice now became completely certain that her viewpoint about the medical community had been justified once more, even though, again, it was the mistake of one individual.

This event again empowered all the distrust, hatred, rage, fear, blame, and victim patterns that she already carried regarding the medical/healing community. Despite her determination at the soul level to heal her belief system, her thought forms, habit imprints, and emotional blueprints were in charge. She was unaware while in body that she had created this horrible event in her life from the belief systems she herself carried and that the resulting patterns perpetuated themselves. This new event confirmed for her that nothing good could *ever* come out of the medical community.

What we manifest in our lives, the events, experiences, and people reflect perfectly on the outside what we believe on the inside.

Janice left the hospital against the doctors' urging despite the continuing need to get skin grafts, to have antibiotic treatments intravenously, and to have the burned areas treated continuously. As a result, she ended up with disfiguring scars, chronic pain, and illness patterns for the rest of her short, bitterness-filled life. And upon the return to the Heavens, she was hit by despair that she yet again replayed the same pattern.

Our beliefs and our self-identities are powerful. They determine many of our decisions and lead us down paths that are not in our best interests and can even do harm. Do we understand now how this can happen? Do we have great empathy and concern for someone like Janice/Jack? Of course we do. But can't we also see that by living with these beliefs, *without question*, we doom ourselves to continually repeat cycles of our scrambles that keep us prisoner?

Remember, too, that this is a partially fictional example and one that ended with the Jack/Janice soul conglomerate having failed to break through their scramble in this life. However, as I've mentioned before, here on Earth right now, we all have a huge opportunity to be successful at breaking through our scrambles. I ended the story badly because of the impact the difficult ending would have on the reader. I wanted you to fully understand how we can just repeat the cycles over and over and why we have so many thousands and tens of thousands of lifetimes. This is a long journey—a journey that has brought many of us in this life to a place (here on Earth now) where there is a clear opportunity to change course and avoid the repeated, upsetting, difficult patterns. Why? Because now we have the information available about the soul's journey *as well as* the techniques to heal the patterns. In most of our past lives, the concepts were too limited, and we didn't have access to the higher frequency levels of information that we do now. Now we know we can neutralize and dissolve these old scrambles and create new, powerful viewpoints that disconnect us from the repetitive cycles we have followed.

The story of Jack and Janice would seem logical and reasonable to most of you, as much of what I have said here is part of the psychological understanding of what makes us all tick. The only difference is that psychologists have us look at our current life here and do not address the whole of the soul's journey. This life is what they have to work with and what they understand. And the psychologist's work is powerful and important. They know much about the human psyche and without the field of psychology, we would not have the benefit of that expanded viewpoint and all that it gives us. Since we are exposed to the psychological ideas from all media—books, television, movies, news—it facilitates one's ability to understand this book.

Most of this book has a psychological gestalt as well. The exposure to the whole journey of the soul shows us general reasons why we are going through the overall experiences we have in this life. This understanding frees us from feelings that we are either fated or simply unlucky to have such terrible parents or such a tough life or any of our miseries. I hope you now understand that we have made our own choices to bring in these issues as at a deep level; we want to evolve and heal.

The next example of an individual's problems—someone who is alive and currently in body—also resulted from personal experiences (rather than cultural ones). Although she lives half a world away from me, she could be a neighbor who lives down the street because of our common humanity. This enlightening, though extreme example, explains the soul psychology behind this woman's current life pattern. This example of a Soul Scramble doesn't unfold like Charlie's from the scramble onset life through to the current life. Instead, it starts with what is happening in the current life, where most of us would start. The Higher Self explanations then illustrate how present life problems are the result of past experiences.

CHAPTER 8
Soul Fracture: Sofia's Story

Introduction

What is worse than a Soul Scramble? A *Soul Fracture*. Fortunately this is not as universal as a Soul Scramble though it is much more severe. This is a true story about Sofia (her name was altered to protect her privacy) who lives with the severe mental problems of a paranoid schizophrenic. When I came to know her, she lived in Europe with her parents and two siblings and was unable to work. She had spent weeks or months at a time in a mental institution almost every year for most of her adult life to both prevent her from killing herself and/or to stabilize her delusions. She would then be released to her home on medication. Sofia was in her mid-40s and had this condition for over 20 years.

Unlike Charlie's story, we don't learn from the Higher Selves how the pattern started and became so severe. There would have been a more normal Soul Scramble pattern that led up to her taking on the lifetimes of great cruelty discussed below that resulted in the Soul Fracture. But knowing the origins is not important or necessary. What we do know is that she needs help, and we begin where we are now.

Sofia contacted me when she heard me on my web-radio show. She used the Internet to find help for herself, and since she didn't work, she spent time trolling the Internet for answers, especially during her times of lucidity. At first, Sofia and I had a brief contact where I offered to work with her pro bono (she earned no money). I knew from what she said and how she said it that she had serious mental problems (her delusions were rampant and severe) and though I had not had another client with such serious issues, I knew that using the techniques provided by and being directed by the Higher Selves could absolutely make a difference. When our scheduled session on video chat came up, Sofia wasn't there and I didn't hear from her until three months later.

Sofia had been in an institution during those three months and while there, she kept thinking she had to contact me when she got out. Our connection seemed valuable to her on a gut level. I was glad of that and when we did begin, the almost weekly sessions lasted for a long period via video chat.

Her initial complaints and problems were massive. I've listed quite a few below (taken from my session notes and from the e-mails she sent me). She suffered from delusions that were for her devastatingly real. As the Higher Selves suggested, I stood in the center and did not judge what she said. As outrageous as things seemed at times, there could always be elements of reality.

Therefore, I chose not to dismiss anything, though I didn't lock into anything either.

- Her soul was lost from her right side.

- She was always full of anger.

- She was disconnected from and hated God.

- Her house was and continued to be invaded by people who came in to violate her every night when she was asleep.

- Her father was involved and took money from the violators.

- Her father paid off the police so they would allow her to be raped.

- She has had and continued to have black magic done on her and on her whole house.

- There were evil beings in her womb.

- Her neighbors constantly observed her, and she could not talk openly as listening ears were everywhere. Her e-mail was being spied on as well.

- She needed to be punished and to atone.

- She had a negative spirit (a disincarnate) taunting her at night and violating her as well.

- Often times she wanted to kill herself and actually tried to do it more than once.

- She had multiple physical problems from itchy skin, aches and pains all over, and was pre-diabetic.

- She needed money to escape from the situation where her family abetted the violators.

Due to the massive list of problems that Sofia presented, I took it slowly. She had been and still was under a doctor's care. My focus was to address the energetic causes of her problems coming from her soul's experiences. Sofia's Higher Selves led me step-by-step, addressing problems in the order they deemed best. Words in italics are quotes from the Higher Selves from the sessions when I was in frequency.

Soul Fracture Explained

Early on, just after I finished a session with Sofia and signed off-line, the Higher Selves sent me a powerful visual symbol regarding the state of her soul energy. The symbolic picture of her energetic field looked similar to an eggshell surrounding her body. Throughout the symbolic shell, there were crisscrossed black jagged lines 360 degrees around. The Higher Selves explained that Sofia didn't have a Soul Scramble but a Soul Fracture, a scramble gone so dark and deep that it resulted in the soul choosing insanity. It was an intense moment, and I was glad to get a preview before the next session. The next week, the Higher Selves came in during the session and gave Sofia the Soul Fracture information along with what had caused this pattern.

Mental illness is a complicated problem for which I have no medical expertise. What I do know is that each individual's difficulties manifest based on the experiences from his or her own unique journey through eons of lifetimes. Therefore, assumptions *should not be made* about another individual based on Sofia's story.

During the next session, I was shown one life that Sofia experienced. She was being held captive within a small room—closet-sized— with walls of stone and a dirt floor. Her wrists were chained to the lower part of the wall, and it was dark inside. She had little food. Most days she would be taken from the room and raped repeatedly by her captors, leaving her bleeding and in pain. As bad as the dark prison room was to her, compared to the constant rapes, it was her piece of Heaven.

Then the Higher Selves gave me a flipbook symbol (like those books where you see a small scene unfold when you quickly flip the pages). This symbol was used by Higher Selves to symbolically show that this life was only one of many along the same lines. Though different in detail (location, planet, culture), many of Sofia's lives were similar in cruelty, hunger, helplessness, hopelessness, great suffering, and total despair. For Sofia, there were no avenues (defense mechanisms) to escape this horrific reality. She couldn't get drunk or take drugs or become obsessive compulsive or run away or kill herself. Her only option to remove herself from this reality was the insanity pattern. The Higher Selves explained that all souls who suffer severe mental problems do not necessarily have Soul Fractures, but some do. Sofia, at the soul level, had decided to address her fracture pattern in this life.

The Higher Selves addressed Sofia during a session:

> In many of these lifetimes, you've had patterns where you were held prisoner with minimal lack of ability to move, unable to speak, and/or when you did speak, no one heard your screams of agony or requests for help. There has been great suffering in the neck and throat arena that is

now being processed. As the energy moves up, it is being released out of the top of the head. This energy is carrying many of your misunderstandings and misconceptions, for in those lifetimes (where there was great abandonment and betrayal and cruelty), you took on ideas and concepts that were your attempt to explain and to reason through why this was happening to you.

These ideas and concepts were based on what limited information you had, much of which was blaming yourself or blaming others or society. And when these misguided misconceptions no longer gave you solace or allowed you to tolerate the brutality, you simply gave yourself over to the insanity pattern. The pattern took you away from the brutality and allowed you to exist without having to face the reality that you lived. It was the only arena of help that you could find, for you didn't have the knowledge and understanding that you carried all the help you needed within. In this life now, you made the determination before birth to begin to heal the Soul Fracture and to release this insanity pattern.

Over the course of many sessions, we worked on neutralizing her insanity as well as other belief systems such as victim patterns, lack of self-worth, lack of support, lack of resources, and lack of love. Cruelty was the norm for Sophia and much deep healing would be needed. The following are a few specific issues within Sofia's Soul Fracture.

The Sexual Attacks as a Delusion

As part of the Soul Fracture, the problem of the sexual violation had to be addressed. Sofia believed she was being violated and raped every night while she slept. She continually avoided going to sleep, staying awake as long as she could to avoid the attacks. She believed that her father not only received money from the violators, but also then used the money to bribe the authorities/police to look the other way. I felt this complaint was part of her delusional system. For example, one time she said she needed money to fix the broken bolt on the window grate so that the violators could no longer enter the apartment by this back window. However, because the father in her delusion was helping them, he could have just as easily loosened the bolt again. Also, I had met her father over video chat twice when he wanted to thank me for helping Sofia and ask a question. Not only was it his idea to speak with me, but he also teared-up while speaking, for he could see the positive changes in Sofia as time passed. He did not seem like a man who profited from her abuse, though of course it was an impression and not a known fact. Having a strong feeling but not being a psychologist or knowing the reality, I was not sure how to approach such a sensitive issue. But the Higher Selves handled it perfectly.

For many weeks, Sofia talked with me, but the Higher Selves took their time to address it. Then, in one session, Sofia asked me a key question for the first time.

"Why don't I wake up when they rape me at night?"

I responded, "If you don't wake up, how do you know you have been raped every night?"

"Because I show the marks, cuts, and scratches all over my body each time," she answered.

Sofia's insight and courage to ask the question allowed the Higher Selves to address this delusion.

You are standing within the center of the focused thought in the now moment, loved and supported by us, your Higher Selves, and by your depth soul, who have watched this painful journey for you. Today our focus will be on the violations that you currently experience on a nightly basis.

In the lifetimes, where you have been violated sexually over and over again to the point where your womb tore into shreds or you gave birth to babies that were taken away from you, the effect of these repeated attacks was that you came to distrust and hate your sexual center, your womanhood, feeling that it betrayed you. You came to believe there was nothing but evil attached to this part of you. You found it repulsive, for you believed it to be the cause of the brutality. And you were determined to disconnect with that part of the body.

The reproductive and sexual nature of every woman in the Human Kingdom is a powerful part of who they are. For you, however, it was nothing but a source of victimhood. And you, over the lifetimes, turned more and more upon yourself, believing that part of you was evil and bad. You could not relate to it. You tried to even destroy it at times. In your insanity patterns, you were so disgusted and repulsed by your own sexual nature that you attacked it, even as others had attacked it.

This disgust, self-attack, self-loathing, and self-repulsion is something you have carried forward into this life pattern and has been part of the concepts and ideas that you have brought into this reality. At night when you sleep, you move into this pattern of self-attack, denying this beautiful part of your existence, trying to remove it in any way you can.

At times, the attacks upon yourself at night within the dream state are severe. It's as if you want to obliterate any feelings in the sexual nature. At the unconscious level, you trigger a shame that is so powerful you cannot deal with it. This is the shame of being a woman. This is the shame of feeling even an inkling of sexuality. You blame yourself and blame your body for the cruelty and the violations you experienced. This shame, once triggered (and it is a deep well), brings forward the need to cut yourself in order to release it. In your mind's eye, cutting the self and hurting the self (whether in the imagination or in the actuality) is something that brings relief, for you are convinced that you deserve to be hurt and that you need to spill your own blood. That is the belief system.

The Higher Selves led her through a healing to neutralize some of the deep issues she carried.

We ask you now to release the sadness, grief, fear, and belief that you are helpless, hopeless, and powerless. This fear comes from the very real experiences in lifetimes where you had no hope, but this fear has no place here and we ask that you release it: the fear of the unknown, the fear of being the continual victim, the fear of self-betrayal, the fear of being a woman, the fear of being a sexual woman, the fear of being a reproductive woman, the fear of violation, and the need to recreate the attacks over and over in order to punish yourself, all the misunderstandings and lack of forgiveness of the self, all the self-blame, the guilt, the shame. We ask you to let go of the endless despair, the need to avoid looking at reality; for in this life you are not in the situations where cruelty has license.

Like Charlie, we can see that there is a serious conflict within Sofia's Soul/Mind. Though not exactly the same type of conflict that Charlie had—his being the male nature versus female nature—Sofia's conflict, the hatred of her own female nature, is also profoundly crippling. What adds difficulty to her situation is the co-created decision made with the current father before Sofia was born.

The Father Connection

In the next session, the Higher Selves addressed Sofia's delusion that her father was a party to and profiting from the nightly violations she believed happened to her.

The father, in this life, triggers much of this fear for you, for many lifetimes ago he was one of your brutalizers. He has carried great shame for this pattern and has come forward as a way to atone for his past with you. It is not easy for him, for he now lacks (since he is in body) the conscious knowledge of his role in the prior life and of his role in this life. But the two of you have co-created the father/ daughter situation. He has agreed to care for and support you as you experience the insanity pattern. In so doing, he believes he is atoning for his past treatment of you. You have come into this life also to begin the healing of your misunderstandings with the father.

This is a difficult journey for both of you because there is little understanding at the conscious level about the agreement. Like you, the father has rejected much of who he is. For he cannot conceive of how he ever could have allowed himself to be the one that violated you (or anyone) so brutally. You both carry the lack of self-love, self-blame, shame, guilt, lack of self-acceptance, and lack of self-respect. We ask that you neutralize these patterns along with the heartache, the misunderstandings, the rage, and the isolation that have held you prisoner. And we ask that you also neutralize the fear of your father, of those around you, and of the unknown.

We bring to your awareness the idea that both of you are extremely wounded and have suffered greatly. Both of you are here to heal. Both of you have committed to each other to help with this healing. We do not expect you to fully grasp or understand all of what we have said today or to fully let go of all of these patterns that have been entrenched and part of your foundation for so long. We do, however, wish you to know that you have taken some very important steps forward today by allowing us to bring you these words.

Here is a good example of the idea that we choose the parents, many friends, and significant others before we take on the body. Some of the most difficult people in our lives are there for a reason. Because we are unconscious and unaware as to what the reason is, we can miss the opportunity the difficulties can bring. Sofia and her father chose to be together in this life to become aware of and to heal their issues. Sofia's delusions about the father were based in part upon the *unremembered remembrances* of him as one of her brutalizers. The Higher Selves brought the reasons for their relationship into Sofia's consciousness for a reason. *With knowledge comes power. With understanding comes forgiveness.* Most of us will never know for sure what our purpose is. However, I suggest we assume there *is* a purpose, at least that there *may be* a positive purpose to our problematic situations. By allowing the possibility, we are taking that first step to healing something that we have found so difficult.

Relationship with the Divine

In another session, the Higher Selves also addressed the origins of Sofia's disconnection from and the hatred of God.

> *At the end of the day, there was no ability to reason with the horror that you had experienced lifetime after lifetime. In these many lifetimes, when you prayed to a god or to the universe for help, your prayers were never answered. This led to the hatred of the system of gods and worship and religion. There was no resolution or solution from outside humans or from the spiritual community in the societies you were being tortured in. Thus, a disgust and hatred for the Divine Energy fields resulted. This intensified your despair and deep hopelessness.*

The disconnection or discontent from the source of the Divine Energies is something that all human souls carry to some extent. In general, it affects us more than we might realize. For Sofia, the disconnection and rage were so severe that she found it difficult in session after session with me to allow in the Divine Energies without feeling actual pain, panic, or believing that either she or the

Originating Source was being harmed. Moving through her blocks against the Divine Energies and her resistance to healing her Soul Fracture itself was a major undertaking. On the conscious mind level, Sofia wanted to heal, but at the soul level, she was afraid.

Resistance to Wellness

We all have developed ways of handling our pain and suffering with our own unique defense and coping mechanisms. The Higher Selves explained that we become comfortable and secure with our belief systems just the way they are.

One of Sofia's deeply held beliefs was that her family, neighbors, people on the street, food, the furniture—everything—controlled her and placed spells on her. She was at the mercy of her environment. These beliefs were part of her Soul Fracture pattern. The Higher Selves addressed the idea that her belief system created her own resistance to wellness.

There are no negative energies that control you. It is a misunderstanding that there is something outside of you in control that forces the negativity upon you and violates you. Instead, it is the powerful belief systems (taken on from the many life patterns) born during your pain and suffering that are triggered.

When you amalgamate in order to "become one with" your Pure Soul Essence, you are requesting that the balanced Divine Energies become active in your life pattern. However, for you, their activation threatens the parts of your belief system at the soul level that enabled you to deal with the horror that was happening. So your reaching toward the healing of your Soul Fracture triggers a powerful feeling (a misunderstanding) that you may lose your escape mechanism (the insanity) if you dissolve and neutralize these beliefs. This misunderstanding prevents you from realizing that it is your own belief systems keeping you prisoner and in a state of self-abuse.

You were ready last week to learn that the violating attacks were delusions being perpetuated from your own belief system. Until you, as the directing identity, made the decision to hear those words consciously, we would not have been able to bring that information to you. Now, the fear of loss of your belief system has been again triggered, and you feel threatened by the idea of emotional and mental health. It is a battle between the part of you that wishes to be healthy on all levels and the part of you afraid to leave the known security points. It is this fear we wish to address today. You are aware as a result of prior sessions you are no longer regularly threatening to end your life. Now, not neutralizing these additional fears would continue to hold you prisoner to the other battles going on within the soul.

We wish to work on the misconceptions that there is safety and security in the insanity pattern, and it is others who abuse you. Moving into that mental health and mental balance is what you, at the inner level, desire to reach.

Having more than one conflict is normal for all of us. We have developed belief systems in lives that conflict with belief systems from other lives. So we carry a myriad of conflicts, some more serious than others, but most of which are held at the unconscious level. And we carry resistance based on our own unique belief patterns. Resistance itself is a good place to start neutralizing when we work to dissolve the old unwanted patterns.

Results of the Work

When my sessions with Sofia ended, I knew that she was not yet totally mentally healthy since her delusions continued. Thankfully, during our time working together, her despair lessened significantly and she moved away from the suicide pattern and stayed away. Also, she was institutionalized less and now rarely returns.

I reconnected with her about a year and a half later. We talked about her father. Although I observed that her beliefs in her nightly attacks remained, there was a new understanding and forgiveness present about her father. There were times when she was angry with him, but she also said to me more than once that she understood he had his own patterns and wounds to deal with. This was quite a statement from someone so clinically paranoid as Sofia. She had come to see that what her father did/said/didn't do/didn't say wasn't always about her, and that sometimes it was just who he was. However, at other times, she fell into the victim viewpoint and continued to blame the external forces (the neighbors, negative energies, black magic, etc.,) for her plight.

Sofia had also believed there was an entity that raped her along with the men who broke in to violate her every night. Early in our work and before the sessions were recorded, the Higher Selves helped us address the disincarnate issue by calling in Jane & Company to assist me. (Jane & Company is a group of disincarnate souls educated by the Higher Selves who help other disincarnates stuck in a Soul Set to return to their own evolutionary movement forward.) In Sofia's case, it was not a delusion; there had been a disincarnate entity that was attached to Sofia. Jane worked with this disincarnate soul that bothered Sofia (though didn't rape her), and the soul chose to detach and move into its own evolutionary movement forward. Up to now, the disincarnate has not returned. (More on Jane & Company in Appendix III.)

When I asked her directly how she thought she had changed, she said with conviction that she wasn't a drama queen any more. And indeed, when speaking with her, there was a new sense of maturity and awareness that had not been there before.

The emphasis has moved toward her taking charge of her healing. She still waits for the magic bullet, someone else to change her life for her instantly. I have realized that our sessions reinforced her belief that she has no ability to help herself. Thus, the sessions are fewer, and I continually encourage her to be the directing identity for her own life.

Sofia was well enough to work—an exciting step forward. She started part-time in data entry or as a stock clerk when a job came up that she could handle. She was still afraid that the people around her may want to harm her and didn't take every job offered. In a year, however, she was able to move into an administrative assistant job that was full-time.

She still lives at home and due to her mental status, she has a long way to go to be fully independent. However, even if moving out of her fracture pattern takes years, this lifetime or a few more lives, any improvement while in body is significant. She has had the

Soul Fracture for thousands of years, so we can appreciate all the movement she has made and will still make in this life.

In conclusion, Sofia's story illustrates how far we can go at the soul level to protect ourselves. We have had so many lives and taken on so many beliefs that often they are at war within, a point Charlie makes. Sofia's inner wars illustrate, too, the intense and alarming way in which a soul can fight with itself, even going so far as to be a major factor working against its own healing.

Luckily, most of us do not have a Soul Fracture. Hopefully, the comparison to Sofia's difficulties might give us more of a half-full perspective toward our own problems. The good news is that if neutralizing and empowering can help someone like Sofia, we can certainly shift our difficult patterns to a better place.

CHAPTER 9
Death and Dying

Death and dying greatly affect us at a soul level. Though the dying arena may be part of the current field of psychological study, the death experience is not since most of us don't remember those death events in our past lives.

Death and dying are events that each and every soul has experienced throughout their journey with each lifetime—some more eventful than others. These events in one's life can and do significantly affect our Soul Scrambles. They often color our belief systems not only about death and dying itself but also about life leading up to the death. The misinterpretations and limited truths taken in at those times fold into our energetic fields and provide a significant part of our limited viewpoints and self-identities. Here are three examples:

1. Princess Lifetime Example
    I learned of a past life I had as a princess in a small kingdom

over 500 years ago. My parents (the king and queen) both died when I was in my late teens, and I took on the role of queen at a young age. I was surrounded by many advisors and took my job seriously. Over the next few years, I managed to do well and garner respect. In my early 20s, a noble of the realm wooed me in order to become king. He assumed that I would be his puppet, and he would have access and control of the monarchy. I was unaware of his true motives and fell deeply in love with him. After we married, he realized I would never be his puppet as he saw the deep respect I had gained. Then one day while we walked through the woods, he shot me in the back with an arrow. He buried me in secret and told everyone that I had run off. He had wanted the status of wealth and power for himself.

At the time I died I took on two indelible and deep convictions. The first was that I would never again have wealth and power because it made me a target! And the second was to never again trust intimate love. Of course, both misunderstandings had long-term (lifetimes long) consequences for me up to and including this life as well. Imagine never trusting wealth and how great the effect such an unconscious belief could have on one's financial pattern! Also, I now understood yet another part of my relationship issues with significant others. Once I learned about that life, I added both of these beliefs to my neutralizing efforts.

Even with no conscious knowledge about this death experience, I was already aware of and neutralizing both my relationship and financial imbalance patterns, and I also knew that they were connected. Knowing about this life explained to me what I had sensed and also further motivated me to work more on it.

These types of belief system links are common for all of us and sometimes clearing one simultaneously clears the other or at least moves the healing along more quickly. We don't need to know about our past lives to heal a pattern but due to the work I do, knowing about some past lives has helped me expand my understanding of the process that affects all of humanity.

Clearly, the death experience can lead to misguided truths in many lifetimes though it can become particularly entrenched when one dies a violent death (as I did as the princess). Think about how many wars and conflicts we have all been involved with over time. Man's inhumanity to man throughout man's existence is part of the journey of all human souls on any planet. It takes time to move up the evolutionary ladder as we progress past the more animal nature, which moves from the survival of the fittest (at the early levels in the Human Kingdom) to the full development of the expanded human awareness.

2. Death in War Example

HIGHER SELF QUOTE

In order to go through the self-healing process, it's important to understand that you are not to blame. You are only playing out (from a very unconscious level) whatever is imprinted within the soul, and you do not fully understand it at this point in time. Remember that painful experiences are often the soul's way of attempting to right wrongs. This means that so many of the painful experiences anyone is involved in are based on some misinterpreted emotional attachment that could be related to guilt.

When I took contact classes with Joan Culpepper the Higher

Selves gave us exercises each week to expand our psychic abilities. As part of our homework, we had a weekly exercise, and I would bug my friends to let me practice on them. One week we were to move our hands around a person's body without touching and find areas of energy that felt warm or cool or energetically different in some way. Then we were to "tune in" to find out why. When I felt around the body of my friend Greg, a willing guinea pig, I felt a very warm area around his left shoulder. Being shy at the time, I went home to see what I could pick up. Unexpectedly (as I was a novice), a life Greg had in the Civil War came to me. He had been an officer in the Confederate States Army and what I saw were the circumstances of his death.

Early one spring morning, the sun came up and reflected off the dew on the grass. Most of the camp's soldiers still slept. Suddenly, a shot rang out, waking the troops. The officer (Greg in this past life) ran out of his tent toward the direction of the shot near where the sentry he had posted was located. The officer was in his uniform pants (with suspenders that hung down off his shoulders) and a white undergarment that covered his chest.

Greg ran bootless toward the soldier, someone he knew well and cared about. Within ten yards of the soldier (who had indeed been shot and was now lying in a pool of his own blood), the officer was hit by the same lone gunman. The bullet went into his left shoulder area and he died of his wound, but not immediately. Frustrated because he had been unable to help the soldier, he believed he had failed him. He was convinced of his own stupidity to have not taken better precautions.

Greg left that life devastated by these circumstances.
Now 150 years later, he still carried this guilt pattern,
wearing it so strongly in his energy field that I (a novice
at the time) was able to pick it up.

When I let Greg know what I had found, I discovered two different professional past-life readers had told him about this life. He had even been given the officer's name. He was able to verify through history books the officer's existence and his death by a shot to the shoulder. What Greg hadn't known at the time (because it was before he met Joan Culpepper and discovered neutralizing) was how to interpret and utilize the information. He hadn't understood he needed to do something with it; it was just interesting to him. This was the third time Greg chose to have this life brought to his attention. Now my friend was aware of the importance of neutralizing. He knew he didn't want that guilt anymore and dove into clearing it. With his expanded awareness, he worked to neutralize this powerful emotional blueprint.

3. Annie's Dying Experience

HIGHER SELF QUOTE

Past-life exploration, while it can be phenomenally interesting
and can satisfy curiosity, is not necessary. Every past life (and all
of the experiences and thoughts related to them) lives in the now
in your Thought Form Body.

In a life from 300 plus years ago in Ireland, I had a significant *dying* experience where I locked into two unyielding beliefs. The negative consequences affected my behavior up to and in this current life. I was an apprentice maid named Annie in a house of a wealthy man and his family. It was a loveless and joyless lifetime where I worked my fingers to the bone and in my old age (which was probably in my 40s or 50s then), I had become so crippled by arthritis that I could no longer work. The family gave me a room on the fifth floor to live out my days but often forgot to feed me, and I was too crippled to go downstairs for food. I do not know the direct cause of my death, but the dying experience involved great emotional and physical suffering, pain, and chronic hunger. Dying took time, and I had little to do but think. And over the long, lonely, agonizing months, I decided that there was no God. I had been brought up Catholic and had always believed. But these conditions were so horrific that I could not understand a God that would bring so much suffering to someone. By the time I died, I was a complete atheist, believing that the loving God I had been taught about could not possibly exist.

By the time I learned of this prior lifetime, I had already been aware of my conflict about a higher power. I neutralized my confusions and misunderstandings in the early days of being in Joan's group. The belief that there was no God had played itself out early in my life. At a young age, I was very spiritual and got involved in the church. Then at 18, while walking across my college campus, I had what might be thought of as a vision. It lasted for maybe five seconds but within 20 minutes, I became a staunch atheist. (Now, decades later, I can only vaguely recall the vision though at that time it was intense.) Years later, after I learned the Higher Self information, I realized I had misinterpreted the vision and came to understand, too, that the emotional blueprint from the Annie life (and others) had been triggered by the vision and led me to the early atheism in this life. I understand now that believing I would be saved by something external to me had been the stumbling block because no amount of praying to God brought Annie any salvation.

Over time after the vision, I moved to a more agnostic system allowing for the possibility of God. And when I was introduced to the Higher Self material, I was able to see the Divine Energies as the powerful frequencies of All There Is. This perspective took the idea of God from the limited, unsettling concept (in my mind) of a wise man in Heaven, to something much more expanded, more impersonal, and more inclusive with the Pure Soul Essence that all souls carried inside. The Higher Self viewpoint clarified the role of the Divine Energies, which allowed and encouraged me to be in the driver's seat as the directing identity for my own growth and unfoldment. It brought me the empowerment I had been looking for.

Annie's dying experience created the deep belief system within me that I had to address and neutralize. The belief system had held me back and closed me to knowing and living out of the Divine Nature that I (and all of us) am/are.

This is part of my journey and does not mean it is the same for anyone else. We are all snowflakes and we are all where we are, taking in the higher frequencies of energy in our own timing and with our own process.

The death and dying process is significant and has had its effects on us all. If you consider life on this planet in the last 2,000 years (let alone the millions of years you have lived), you may be aware that the majority of deaths would be traumatic—death in warfare, from starvation, natural disaster, betrayal, or attack. Do we ever have a gentle and uneventful death? Yes, we have all had the dying in our sleep, the mostly painless death surrounded by our loved ones, and the quick deaths that ended our suffering. But the tough, painful deaths are much more prevalent. It is the unremembered remembrances of these that are the foundation of the common fear of death. Moving into the dying process especially triggers these fears and can be part of the fight we put forth to avoid it. It can also be behind the strength to fight a serious disease or even the locking into the belief that it is better to suffer than to die. Also, there are some people who, despite a difficult journey, are more connected to the sense that the soul does continue and may feel little fear at all.

The death and dying experiences may also play a big role in the soul's decision as to what life it will take on in the next reincarnation. Death is *the last event* in one's lifetime and if it carries with it great emotion and/or overpowering beliefs; the soul could choose the next life based on that event. It could return to a loved one lost or to get revenge or to a culture at peace to avoid warfare or to a place with great resources to avoid starvation. The possibilities are infinite. Because death and dying are so significant and at the same time unremembered, I recommend strongly that we neutralize all that we can think of around them.

CHAPTER 10
Illness Patterns as Part of a Soul Scramble

HIGHER SELF QUOTE

Within the Thought Form Body of the mind, the conglomerate thought form of illness attracts to it additional thought that relates to illness. Thus, illness empowers itself in a consistent manner from lifetime to lifetime.

Introduction

Other than death and dying, there are an infinite number of individual experiences that have a powerful effect on a soul by bringing in misunderstandings that become part of a Soul Scramble. Illness is often a significant pattern for every soul, though it would play out for every individual in his/her own unique ways. In general, in our current lives some of us are relatively healthy and rarely ever are sick, others are ill all the time with either a chronic illness or a series of major problems such as cancer. Most of us, however, are somewhere in between.

How would illness create or be part of or a result of a Soul Scramble? Why would anyone bring in a major illness pattern? It isn't just fate or bad luck or the unfortunate parental genes that caused it? We know from Charlie's example that he purposely took on a lethal illness in order to atone for what he believed he had "done wrong." However, he did not carry an illness pattern per se that was part of the Soul Scramble we learned of. Illness, in his case, was a solution to a problem for him, the only way (he believed) to atone. So let's look at someone else who has illness as a part of a Soul Scramble. I will call her Erin.

Erin's Example: Illness as a Soul Scramble

<hr/>

HIGHER SELF QUOTE

<hr/>

If each individual unraveled the mysteries of the soul, each individual would find originating lifetimes wherein these various misconceptions took place. Again, it is the complex and individual soul misinterpretations that go into the outward end result (in this lifetime or in any lifetime past), bringing the past forward and building on it in each new lifetime.

Erin's lifetime illness pattern was related to a serious Soul Scramble, which she told to all of us in Joan's Wednesday group one day back in the 1980s. Usually Joan led every group, bringing in the Higher Self information, but she also encouraged us to lead the group and to share our experiences or insights. Erin opened up her heart. It was the first time I fully grasped the concept that emotions and beliefs do fully impact our past and current lives.

Erin Quote: August 1985

I am here today to tell you that I <u>only</u> have brain cancer.

Erin was in her 60s at the time she came forward. She had had a long history of illness throughout her life and shared the timeline with us:

- In 1964, she hurt her back at work, which resulted in back surgery.

- In 1965, she had open-heart surgery because of an obstruction in the heart.

- In 1968, the heart valve was obstructed again so an artificial valve was put in.

- In 1974, the artificial valves then had to be replaced.

- The illness pattern also included mental issues that lead to a five-month stay in an institution where Erin had a series of 20 shock treatments.

- In 1981, Erin had breast cancer, requiring a mastectomy and the removal of her lymph nodes. She went through a year of chemotherapy.

- In 1983, her breast cancer recurred in the incision. This time she went through six weeks of radiation.

She explained that at this point, every ache and pain scared her. She handled it by ignoring any physical symptoms. She didn't go to the doctor to have anything checked out even as she was losing the control of her left hand. She had spasms, which she eventually found out, were actually seizures in the hand because there was a brain tumor.

She only decided to go to the doctor when she found another lump in the incision at the breast. That's when she showed him her hand, and he immediately said brain tumor. Because of concern that her breast cancer could have metastasized, she went for a full body scan. When she got the results of the test, there was nothing else there. She breathed a sign of complete relief knowing that *all she had was a brain tumor*, a brand new cancer, and as such, it was much better news than having metastases.

Surgery was scheduled for six weeks later and during the wait time, Erin had a series of five healings over five weeks from three people who did Higher Self healing work together. One was gifted at going into frequency and pulling in the Higher Self information. At the first healing, the Higher Selves came in and told Erin that she had not yet made the decision to live through the surgery. Of course she wanted to live at the conscious mind level, but at the soul level, where these decisions are made, she was undecided. From then on, with each healing, a major part of her emotional and psychological issues that were behind her illness pattern were uncovered, released, and neutralized.

In the first healing session, Erin spent most of the healing sobbing. The emotional upheaval involved great *guilt and shame* related to lifetimes she had shared with her current husband. In these lifetimes, over and over when things got rough, she would lay aside the body, and her husband would be left there stuck with all the problems on his own. Out of body, she understood how she abandoned him but once in body, she was unaware of the determination not to do it again. Thus, she continued to do it again and again. So much guilt. So much shame. These were released and neutralized (as was done for each part of the scramble in all five healings).

In the second healing, she was reminded of the feeling she had in some fashion all of her life. If she had the choice to stay here in body or die, she would prefer to die. This feeling was not one of wanting to commit suicide but at some foundational yet mostly unconscious level, she felt *the futility and frustration* of being trapped in a body. She discovered during the healing that she had felt this from the beginning of her sojourn in the Human Kingdom. And it played out in almost all her lifetimes. When things got rough and she hurt (emotionally) too much, she would lay aside the body with some type of illness. That was her way of "escape." This pattern built the foundation of the Soul Scramble that developed the timeworn habit of using illness and death as a way to avoid and evade pain, heartache, despair, fear, and suffering.

In the third week, the main emotional release was the intense *fear of being alone.* So when she felt alone, she took on a serious illness and laid aside the body as a way to avoid the loneliness. Unfortunately, after death, she was still alone because all her friends were still in body. So it didn't help and only kept the pattern going. There was also great *anger* that she had repressed during this life as well as in so many other lives. So the healing this week revolved around anger and fear of loneliness.

Just when Erin thought she had uncovered everything, the fourth healing brought an unexpected emotional issue—the *frustration of waiting* for help to come. (Annie and Sofia also carried this waiting pattern.) When there were rough times in many lives, at first Erin waited for the help to come from authorities, God, the universe, family, or friends. The help didn't come. She came to believe that when something happened, she would not be saved. She often chose to die rather than wait any more. This belief system also carried the feeling of complete *abandonment and hopelessness.* Though at the conscious level she was unaware specifically of these two emotional issues, she related to both of them in this way. When watching a movie or a TV program or documentary about starving children or wartime suffering, she became overwrought with emotion, sobbing as she watched the suffering while no one came to help. All of us have experienced help not arriving in many lifetimes, though with an infinite variety of situations and conditions.

With the fifth and final healing, Erin understood and then released and neutralized her *need to control her emotions*. Up until this healing, she had never allowed herself to show any emotion in all of her personal and work situations. She bottled herself up and never shared with anyone. This concept was the final major breakthrough for her and she realized she needed to also neutralize this pattern. The Higher Selves explained during this last healing session that this group of healers had helped her go from the darkness of misunderstanding into the light of awareness and had also empowered her desire to live. By the end of the session, the Higher Selves said she had now *chosen to live* through the surgery.

The following week when she went into the hospital, she was completely calm and had no fear. Of course, Erin did indeed make it through surgery (since she was telling us her story). Now with a personal and deeper understanding of how prior lifetime experiences and beliefs can have such negative effects on us, she continued to work on the process of neutralizing and on the proper releasing of emotions. She lived well for almost another decade.

I came away from that night's session completely overwhelmed and inspired. I thought, "I don't want to wait until I have brain cancer or something else equally horrific before I do the deeper work on myself." I had been neutralizing before that night, but Erin was the one who started me on the more determined and proactive approach to this form of self-help. And I will be eternally grateful that she shared her story. I hope it has the same effect on those reading this book!

The Higher Self Viewpoint on Illness (or Any Difficult Condition in Our Lives)

HIGHER SELF QUOTE

In this physical reality where each of you live and dwell and have your beingness, you are absolutely and totally responsible for your own reality. The attitude each individual carries is extremely important to the physical well-being of the individual. All distortions within the body manifest first through a state of mind or through an attitude carried by each individual.

All of us are going through forms of Soul/Mind detoxification. We manifest situations and conditions that trigger our patterns in order to become aware of them and heal them. We are often born into and raised in a family where major patterns play themselves out. We chose our parents, situations, and conditions for our lives before birth just as Charlie did. If a genetic inheritance means a serious health problem, that condition was pre-chosen and there would be a reason why we chose it. However, we would not be conscious of the whole plan we had for ourselves, at least not at first.

The usual viewpoint when we get sick is to look outside ourselves for the answers. When we get a cold, we look to find out who gave it to us. When we get a more serious illness we ask, "Why me?

What did I do to deserve this?" Often we go to the "blame" place or to the place where we are not responsible for our illness. We may think we got diabetes or cancer because it was genetically determined from our parents. In general, we most often look externally for the causes in one way or another even if we call it fate or karma. What is less common is to see the great opportunity that illness (of any kind) can give us. Illness has the potential to open the door to insight. If we look to be more aware and focused, we can use the manifesting physical pattern to discover and understand the belief systems we carry that created the illness in the first place. Remember Charlie got the HIV virus, but he chose to bring that illness into his life in order to atone. So even when we legitimately do get an illness from someone else or something else, the question becomes, "Why did we make that choice?"

If indeed one or both of our parents have diabetes, we would most likely inherit the genetic predisposition for it. Of course, if we feel it is our fate to get it, we may approach our lifestyle and diet as things that don't matter since we will get the disease anyway. Or, and many are like this, we may decide to do everything we can to avoid getting it (or to stay as healthy as possible if we have it already). Every soul would have a different viewpoint about the situation, and the viewpoints can also change as the circumstances shift and years pass.

The Higher Selves recommend that we also look at the soul level for reasons that are behind it. We might think, "I must have chosen these parents and thus have chosen this predisposition" (or the disease if it is already manifested). So the questions become: "What am I carrying at the belief level that would lead me to this choice? What can I learn and what can I neutralize to make sure I don't manifest the disease? If I do manifest it, how can I make sure its effects are as mild as possible or to even render it harmless?"

This is the option that the Higher Selves show us. And it is this added approach that will bring us the most rewards and changes. This encourages us to look at the reasons behind the direction our lives take. Unfortunately, the soul can't pick up the phone and call the mind to say, "Hey, you need to bring this belief into the Light and neutralize it."

Disease, upheavals, or chronic problems are often our soul's way to ask us to pay attention to the energies/beliefs/misunderstandings it carries and wants to heal. The potential for or the manifestation of the disease can (I hope) motivate us to do the neutralizing in order to heal.

Based on the Higher Self information, I see value in all the healing approaches—medical, dietary, alternative, neutralizing, and empowering—to improve all body imbalances and problems. I call it the shotgun approach.

I'd like to share two examples from my life. In my late 30s, I experienced early signs of arthritis (arthritis runs in my family), and once I knew what it was, I started neutralizing it. Neutralizing opened up a stepping-stone process for me, which often happens. We are first led to a door that helps and then to another door that continues the progress. My first door of help to improve happened at the chiropractor. After doing the adjustments for my sore neck, he recommended a supplement—glucosamine chondroitin. I agreed to try it and within weeks my symptoms disappeared; it became a standard supplement for me. The neutralizing had brought me the awareness of a supplement that slowed and minimized the condition. In time, as I continued to neutralize arthritis and all effects of aging, the arthritis itself seemed to have mostly disappeared.

The second and more significant example concerned a congenital deformity in my biliary tree, the system that connects the gallbladder and liver to the intestines. As a result, I had gallstones when I was two or three and required two major surgeries, one at 13 and one at 26. This resulted in the "plumbing" of my digestive system looking like an eggbeater got loose there. Early on, I didn't know the Higher Self philosophy and handled the pattern medically. But once I found the Higher Self information, I worked on this pattern. Up until then, my digestive system had issues: gallstones, chronic stomach aches, severe pain, constipation, diarrhea, distention, and food sensitivities.

Neutralizing has eliminated almost everything. I discovered many beliefs and traumatic events that I carried at the abdomen level: powerlessness (helplessness), betrayal (murdered many times by a spear or hatchet or arrow to the stomach), abandonment (waiting for the external authorities to save me but they did not or could not or were the cause of my suffering), and the search for external approval. At the soul level, I had chosen to have my stomach issues come in as a relatively serious genetic problem *that would not be fixed in one go*. Why? Because the chronic condition gave me many chances (opportunities!) to learn about and use this new approach to my medical problem.

With neutralizing, I cleared up different problematic areas. I was able to go years between symptoms once I started clearing the beliefs, hurts, and wounds that were part of it. When a symptom arose, I knew I still had neutralizing to do on the area and did more work. Each event was an opportunity to become aware, to focus, and to do deeper healing.

Did I still have to go to the doctor since the second surgery? Yes, of course, as some of the issues were difficult and kept returning. But now, I have healed even the transient and minor issues I had with food sensitivities—the last bastion of my digestive issues—as I continued to discover and neutralize the deepest and most hidden beliefs. Has this taken me a couple of decades? Yes, but there was continual improvement along the way, plus no more surgery and an increase in energy and revitalization. Much better to be 20 years down the road and 180 degrees healthier than before. And everyone can be successful with this approach!

Some belief systems posit that alternative health-related treatments (such as energy work or supplements) are more important than or can even replace a medical solution. (This approach is evident in the story of Jack/Janice.) And of course, there are many doctors who disparage the alternative approaches to health. However, there is room for and need for both. The Higher Selves have explained that once a pattern (a belief system, a negative energy stream) manifests in the physical body, then that pattern is running at a higher rate of speed than the energy work or alternative-healing systems can catch up with. They explained that the medical field addresses the disease/illness in the body in the moment, slowing down the progression of the problem and allowing the time needed by the body to manifest the energetic and/or alternative treatment healing. For example, my abdominal surgeries gave me time to discover and learn what else I needed to do. For cancer, the chemo or radiation can slow down the disease while the individual works to heal the energetic side in order to move into remission.

The Higher Selves do not take sides as to which approaches are the best but assert that all of them have their place and help in different ways. When I have a problem, I address it from more than one angle. I always do the energy work, but I also go to the doctor if I have an infection or something chronic and to the alternative healers when it feels appropriate to do so. Individuals will handle their illness patterns in their own unique way. With the Internet, we get a myriad of information and advice. Follow what resonates with you and if you see any kind of pattern relating to illness, think about neutralizing all the underlying beliefs. This opens up the viewpoints *and* the options for treatment.

Although all souls have an infinite number of personal experiences as they make their way through the learning curve of the Human Kingdom, it is clear that our experiences leading up to this life have significant impact on who we think we are, what our interests are, and what our problems are. But we must also look at the wider picture for our souls that include the cultural and societal beliefs.

CHAPTER 11

Culturally Based Beliefs

HIGHER SELF QUOTE

It is unfortunate that the conditions set up by society, whether they are for the "good" of the humanities or not, are conditions that deprive each individual of taking full responsibility for the self. Instead, they create within the individual the idea that the externals are conditions to be met. And when these conditions are not met to the satisfaction of the society the individual is made to feel that he or she is in the wrong.

The Relative Nature of Right and Wrong

When I was a little girl, I heard my friends and family talk about someone and make judgments or be critical. This bothered me. I thought, "If we only understood more about why those people did certain things, then maybe we would see that they were not stupid or silly or irresponsible. Maybe we would understand why a neighbor (who someone may have complained about) watered his lawn at the 'wrong' time of day (the gardener had instructed him as to the timing), or why some parent allowed their child a privilege when the child didn't deserve it (the child had made a mistake in one area but had done something outstanding in another so deserved the privilege for that)."

I don't remember any actual instances, as I was young—six or seven—when this idea first came to me. As I got older, however, I ended up developing a theory that much of right and wrong was determined at the *individual* level, and it was necessary to understand more about the motives and reasons for people's actions. I felt we often mistakenly and falsely judged others because we didn't know and couldn't know all the reasons why someone did something.

Did I understand this at a great depth? No. At the time, the concept was limited to why someone let their dog out too early or parked their car on the road instead of in their driveway. This concept expanded as I grew up. Then, when I was a junior in college, I took an introductory anthropology class because it was the only one available in the time slot I wanted to use.

The science is based on the premise that most of right and wrong, good and bad concepts are not rigid, but are relative to one's language and culture. Although this was culturally based and not individually based, the idea of the relative nature of ethical belief systems was exactly the same. I was stunned. It was the first time I had "officially" heard the idea that beliefs were relative to one's culture. I felt so connected with this viewpoint that I ended up majoring in the subject!

The anthropological viewpoint is significant. It means that cultures and societies have an overall viewpoint and perspective about life, people, and the world around them. Each culture and its language help define the world for the people born into it. The Buddhist in India would have a specific gestalt view of the world that would be very different from the Maori tribes from New Zealand.

Anthropologists have studied cultures around the world. They learn the local language and live and dress like the locals. They learn how to think and interpret the overall views of the people around them.

Many years ago, while working for Save the Children Federation (a worldwide organization) in Arizona, I had the opportunity to experience firsthand the different viewpoints of the tribes in the area. The Papago Indians (as they were called at that time but now they use their tribal name, the Tohono O'odham Nation) made decisions by consensus rather than by majority. Everyone in the community had to agree before a tribal decision could be made. This entailed many meetings and much discussion throughout the reservation. Most times, making decisions took much longer than the majority vote approach, which is so common in the Western world. Though their process was slow it created a close-knit society, one that considered the bigger picture—what would be best for all— rather than of individual or a small group's own particular needs.

Today, billions of people live in cosmopolitan environments where different viewpoints and ideas coexist. Also, with television and the Internet, we have greatly expanded opportunities to think differently than previous generations did no matter where we are from. However, we most likely still carry the foundation of beliefs that we grew up with whether we are Hispanic, Caucasian, Korean, Buddhist, Indian, or Aboriginal, even if we are living in a large city such as Los Angeles, New York, Tokyo, Sydney, Houston, or Miami that exposes us to the many different groups in surrounding neighborhoods. The cultural foundation for all of us is built as we grow up, and despite the exposure to other ideas, viewpoints and beliefs, much remains underneath.

Not only does the foundation of our belief systems come from the cultures and societies in which we now live (the anthropological viewpoint), but also from the belief systems of every culture in which we have lived in the Human Kingdom Universe (the Higher Self viewpoint)! *And we carry all those belief systems around in our energetic field, even if we are not conscious that we retain them while in the life we currently live!* Wow! That is big.

For example, we may have lived as a Hindu in one life, a Jesuit priest in another, and a tribal leader in a society that worshipped multiple gods. Yet now we might find ourselves born into a quiet commune that teaches God is a female and reproduction is the highest reward in life. The prior lives may seem like they have no connection to this life at all, but they do.

Each culture has its own set of judgments, beliefs, and truths based on the evolutionary frequency levels that the humanities had reached within those same cultures. There are many varieties of cultures on this planet now and over the course of human history. We have lived on thousands of planets during our sojourns and have all experienced thousands of different types of societies.

Mind-boggling.

How We Become Conditioned by Societies We Have Lived In

HIGHER SELF QUOTE

Who you are has nothing to do with any other person, situation, condition, idea, or concept. You are a pure, perfect, and absolute expression of Originating Source (that gave birth to the Totality of all the creations). You do not recognize this pure expression because it is buried under layers and layers of past conditions you have brought with you into this reality.

My childhood theory, though limited in understanding, was basically what the Higher Selves have shared with us. The motivations and beliefs are relative to each individual's experiences, not just from this life, but from all our lifetimes. Will we ever know and understand all of what makes us tick? No, but it makes no difference. We need to understand that judging someone else from our own viewpoints of right and wrong and good and bad means that we are most likely *mis*judging them. We all have our own unique misperceptions, misunderstandings, and false beliefs with all the resulting motivations carried in our unique way.

While on our journey through the Human Kingdom Universe, we also have created those difficult and often deeply entrenched Soul Scrambles from many lifetimes accumulated together. Today on this planet, we are fortunate to have expanded intellectual, scientific, and spiritual concepts available to us as we attempt to sort out our lives and our world. This was usually *not* the case in our previous lives. For example, a psychological viewpoint is the norm for most of us and strongly colors how we see ourselves, other individuals, and social groupings. But even as recently as the 1700s and early 1800s—pre-psychology—a child whose parent had blamed and beaten him could grow up feeling unimportant, bad, miserable, and "less than" for his entire life. He could die holding on to the deep belief that he was worthless and take on the self-blame for many of the events/conditions in that lifetime. Now multiply that type of experience by the eons of lifetimes we have all had! Fortunately, today in this society, with psychology and many other avenues of help that are available, there is a good possibility that if the same abuse happens now, an individual will find ways to heal despair, self-blame, and deep worthlessness.

Basically, consciously and unconsciously we take on these belief systems about ourselves (our self-identities) and about the world around us from each life. Some ideas come in by the role modeling from others, almost like osmosis. Other beliefs we are expressly taught by those around us: our parents, teachers, bosses, mentors, peer groups, intimate partners, and experts in various fields. In this way, layers of understanding and belief are laid down as we grow up and these not only enable us to exist in the particular society we live in but are also carried forward and affect us in our future lives. The Higher Selves indicate that there are several common (or generic) areas in our Human Kingdom existence that are a part of the complex foundation of human belief systems. Two of these general conditions are:

1. The role of the external authorities in our lives

2. The spiritual environments pervasive within the societies

CHAPTER 12
External Authorities and Spiritual Practices

In the Human Kingdom, the idea of Free Will is a valid idea. It allows the individual the expression to do what it wants to do, to make decisions that it wants to make, to choose or not to choose.

Introduction

Once man evolves out of the Animal Kingdom and into the human dimension, the soul brings with it an increase in consciousness. The Human Kingdom Universe is the Free Will Kingdom that brings with it (as for all souls) an innate curiosity and a desire to learn and grow. The three lower kingdoms—Mineral, Plant, and Animal—have no Free Will choice. They are guided by the connection of the Pure Soul Essence, and as a result, there is no resistance to evolution at these levels. The souls instinctively move through the levels as part of the *Divine Will* frequency. The Human Kingdom gives all souls the chance to develop consciousness and puts the responsibility for their evolution into their own hands. Our evolution, therefore, is more complex. We create resistance, blocks, and problems for ourselves without being aware of it. And more often than not, we make a mess of it. But we are never lost and never without hope. We go through lifetime after lifetime making and learning from our mistakes.

Two arenas of our common human experience—*external authorities* and *spiritual practices* create viewpoints and beliefs that most of us carry, which result in common *conditioned responses.* Our ideas and concepts are comprised of attitudes, judgments, misunderstandings, and emotional blueprints we have taken in over eons of lives. This is significant because the conditioned responses (derived from these commonalities) drive what we manifest in our lives. Understanding these two arenas is significant and relevant for all the humanities, even though specific situations and conditions are completely unique for each individual. This will not be a study that includes the detail of the photo, but it will be more like the gentle and light strokes of the watercolor.

External Authorities

HIGHER SELF QUOTE:

If we fall into the trap of placing anyone or anything on a pedestal that is higher than we are, we allow whatever or whomever to become a shadow over our own light.

There are many different types of authority in the vast number of different cultures experienced by any human soul over time. There could be a council of elders or a culture dominated by clans. The cultural authority could also be the spiritual leaders who not only dictate the rules and interpretations about the spiritual world but also control the secular one. There could be royalty or elected officials or a situation that is so primitive the leadership falls to those who are the strongest and best hunters. Any type of authority figure adds weight to the messages and interpretations of the world. If a doctor tells you that you are prone to heart disease, you may pay more attention and work harder to take care of yourself than if your neighbor told you the same thing after seeing a sitcom on TV about heart trouble.

We are all groomed from the youngest age to listen and pay attention to authority figures—and for good reason. We come into this world as helpless infants and are taken care of by our parents. They are the authority for us from day one and we learn the authority paradigm from that moment and have it enforced throughout this life and in all lives.

At the root of most of our belief systems are the footprints of the authorities we have had in each life pattern. Some may be benevolent and well-meaning and others may be malevolent and manipulative. We all have experienced many permutations and combinations and carry an incredibly complex interwoven series of ideas and feelings—good, bad, and indifferent—toward authority figures and to the information they have given us. The secular authority in a culture can make a significant impact on a soul depending on how it plays out. Let's look at three learned responses held by many of the humanities as a result of lifetimes of everyday exposure to the pervasive authority systems in every culture.

1. Conditioned Response:
    There Is an Automatic Reliance on Authority Figures

HIGHER SELF QUOTE

As tiny children in this reality, we were all involved in looking to the authority figure (the mother and/or father) to guide and direct us. We were conditioned early on to look outward for guidance and authority. In many instances that guidance was not geared toward creating self-confidence, self-worth, and proper self-image.

Reliance on external authorities is natural to us from the first moment in our lives because we learn at birth that others are responsible for us. We are helpless, and if we aren't cared for, we die. The external focus is inherent from childhood and becomes foundational in our belief systems. As we mature, we come into the hierarchy of society learning from and being supervised by our schoolteachers and then our bosses when we go to work. And all along the way we also deal with, listen to, take in, believe in, and give ourselves over to other authorities such as doctors, lawmakers, governments and/or spiritual leaders. So the external focus toward those who are seen as experts—more knowledgeable and more powerful—is a viewpoint inherent in most every society. It is so much a part of it, we either don't question authority or question all authority. Either way, it can be a knee-jerk reaction that keeps us from focusing on self-reliance and self-awareness.

2. Conditioned Response:
   Others Are Responsible for Our Lives

External authority isn't inherently bad or detrimental. Sometimes in the complex societies of today, it is essential to look to outside experts to discover answers and solutions for yourself. Yet finding answers or solutions is not the same as believing *that others are responsible for your life.* Many of us have taken on that belief because we have been conditioned to do so.

Most of us have come to believe (if not in this life, then in other lives) that those external authorities are responsible for how our lives unfold. We blame the government if there is a bad economy and we cannot get a job. We blame our significant others if our relationship is strained, stressed, or inadequate. We blame our parents if our lives go out of control. And though everyone understands the feelings, it is this placement onto the shoulders of others outside of us that brings us to a place of *powerlessness* and *hopelessness.* Why? We are powerless because we can't control the economy, the government, the parents, the significant other, or the past. We become the eternal victims, waiting for someone or something to change in order to fix our lives. Until we move to the place where we understand that we already have everything within that we need in order to be happy, balanced, healthy, fulfilled, and/or successful and that *we are the directing identities in our lives,* we will be stuck in the ever-spinning wheel of repetition of our misery, loneliness, helplessness, and blame.

Powerlessness is a strong belief. It is powerlessness that gives birth to fear. As we sojourned through the Human Kingdom, we were part of millions of situations and conditions where it seemed that there were no options. We were part of droughts, wars, epidemics, cruelty, abuse, accidents, natural disasters, and many more events where we prayed to a god for deliverance. Or we were part of an unsuccessful coup to overturn the political leader. Or we were betrayed or abandoned by a spouse. Or were beaten by hoodlums or hung as heretics or witches. Or. Or. Or. In those lives, we usually had no expanded understanding as to why the things happened to us, and as a result, we felt powerless to change the circumstances. We didn't know at the conscious mind level that we chose to experience many of the events for some reason before we took on that life or while in the life.

If we believe that we have no say over our lives, we continuously live with the anxiety of when the next shoe will drop, when the next accident will come, when the next disease will hit us. We would carry this fear both consciously and unconsciously, and it would play into our lives in many ways, even disguising itself as something else from time to time. We avoid looking at the fear. We put up many kinds of coping styles and defense mechanisms to deal with the fear-generated patterns. Yet, we can't escape it until we deal directly with it. And at this time, in this life, everyone has access to the knowledge of how to do just that. We neutralize.

One of the most significant steps for all the humanities is to become aware that no one is responsible for us because we are the pilots of our journey. Many here on Earth are headed to that way now. In time, we will move into the knowing that we are the true expression of Originating Source, that we carry all its purity and perfection, and that we already are all we need to be. We don't have to earn it, sacrifice for it, or become someone else to get it. We only need to dissolve away the layers of misunderstanding, which have become the basis for our belief systems and our viewpoints—*the fuel that creates the unwanted conditions in our lives.*

3. Conditioned Response:
   Self-Worth Is Based on the Opinions of Others
   Another common response is to take in and believe what others say about us to determine who we are and how much value we have. It is not that we cannot listen to others because learning and understanding can evolve in this way. However, the conditioning is there for all of us that others know best and carry the truth as to who we are. Each individual has to grapple with this issue, maybe intensely or maybe peripherally. Each journey would be unique to him or her. Each of us will continue with this journey over time and will get to where we are going. Here are a couple of the traps that result when we look to others as being responsible for how we feel about ourselves:

   - We often base our feelings of self-worth on external approval or lack thereof. And we may feel anxiety and worry about the reactions of others toward us. This external validation can be the determining factor to our moods and whether we are happy and feel we have value. In addition, we may put our own needs and feelings last on our priority list or maybe not at all.

   - We may honor external rules, shoulds and shouldn'ts at the expense of ourselves. We can compromise our hopes and dreams by following the paths others determine are right for us, even when we are unhappy about it. For example, we might take in that we are losers and failures from our parents who had their own difficulties in life. Or maybe they believe that to be a successful adult we need to be a doctor/lawyer/candlestick maker instead of a dancer/writer/baseball player. If we give up on ourselves or our dreams, we may find ourselves to be wounded, unhappy, unfulfilled, miserable, angry, resentful, or believing that we don't deserve happiness, fulfillment, material good, etc.

What we often miss is the perspective that we are our own best friend and our own best support. When we make the shift to take responsibility for how we function and how we feel, *we free ourselves from waiting for others to make us happy.* We move from the place of powerlessness to one of connection to ourselves as our own directing identity.

Once we are old enough to see the world through our own eyes, not just as the world defined by our parents, teachers, and government, we begin the journey of self-discovery to find out who we are as individuals, what our viewpoints are, and how we want to live our lives. Neutralizing can be a powerful and effective tool to help with this. It facilitates clarity and an expanded viewpoint when looking at your life. It helps remove the layers of "shoulds," "nevers," "musts," false obligations, misconceptions, shame, fears, etc., that stand in the way of having balance and health in all areas of our lives.

Spiritual Practices

HIGHER SELF QUOTE

In the majority of philosophical organizations (both orthodox and unorthodox), great emphasis is given to the externals as they pertain to seeking help, seeking assistance, having faith in, and having belief in. The individuals believe that they are helpless within their own right to affect changes. Yet, it is this philosophical belief (that the source of help is to be found in the outward reality) that literally imprisons the individual and holds them in place, creating conditions that do not allow the individual to live a happy, joyful, loving existence.

From the days of the Neanderthals, there is evidence humanity has always had a spiritual viewpoint, a belief in something greater than itself. The Neanderthals had special burial practices that indicated they believed there was something more after death. And no matter what cultures we look at on the planet now or as manifested in the past, we see heavy evidence of our spiritual nature. This is not an attempt to prove there is a God but instead to emphasize the eons of time we have been exposed to spiritual belief systems. These would range from a belief in one god or many gods, a belief in the intrinsic goodness of god with a forgiving and loving nature, or the intrinsic badness of god with a judgmental, punishing, and controlling nature. There are the female gods, the in-the image-of-man gods, the animal gods, and more. In addition, the spiritual belief systems would be dominated by those who are in charge or are the expert in the ways of the god as defined in those societies.

Many of the belief systems in many societies were born or used as a way to explain the unexplainable. A few of those questions could be: "What happens at death? Why did the earth move and eat up most of our village? Why did the food sources dry up? Why did a seemingly friendly village attack us?"

In the millennia when there were illnesses before the germ theory of disease was discovered, often the explanation as to why someone got sick was because he or she did something to upset the gods. Or maybe a superstition would be born, such as the village was attacked because we walked in front of a black cat or broke a mirror. The humanities were and still are always trying to understand and answer the bigger questions. And it was the frequency level of thought (the frequency level of truth in that moment) in each society that determined the answers.

We have absorbed truths—many of them harsh—from every society, and we carry all of them at the energetic level. For example, because the Inquisition was in place to ferret out heresies against the Catholic Church, it was a tough time for any kind of religious freedom. The church mandated what was to be believed and if its dictates were not followed and/or there was any resistance to the rules, persecution resulted, which could include torture and even death. Religion was often dictated by men in the name of God, setting themselves up as not only the experts but also the judge, jury, and executioner all in one. This type of approach resulted in a plethora of negative spiritual experiences and belief systems that we folded into our energetic field. Although there are many conditioned responses that could be discussed, I present two from the Higher Self perspectives.

1. Conditioned Response: There Is an External Savior

HIGHER SELF QUOTE

The human community carries a tremendous need at the unconscious level to find a power outside itself to lead it out of darkness. This need to find God externally is one of those habits carried at an unconscious level—unconscious because even though in consciousness, it is intellectually understood that you are your own responsibility. Often there is still this outward focus of attention that sees a separate eternal power that will lead you out of the darkness.

Many religions over the millennia carry the belief that God, Jesus, Allah, etc., is an external (more powerful) force in our lives and will lead us to Heaven and to our salvation. Even if we have moved out of that viewpoint in this life and have firmly connected to the idea of self-responsibility, we have taken in the idea in many other lives that someone/something else will save us. Not only is this idea still in religions today, but it is also behind some of the more metaphysical ideas, which believe that there are souls on other planets or aliens or angels (depending on the philosophy) who will rescue us. Even if we are fully connected to the idea of self-responsibility and are not looking for someone/something to save us we still carry all the teachings from eons of time with us at the soul level. These beliefs affect our lives whether we are aware of them or not. They hold us at the unconscious level to a "waiting game," looking externally for the salvation and help to come. And this orientation keeps us in a powerless place. It can result in our being more complacent about our lives or to shut off ideas and concepts that we might notice if not conditioned otherwise.

Whether known or unknown, the beliefs around an external savior are a good place to neutralize. We carry the Originating Source *within* and thus have access through that connection to the Totality of All There Is. Each of us is responsible for our evolutionary process.

2. Conditioned Response: Fear of God

Of course, in this life, if you suffer no persecution as a result of your religious beliefs, you may never imagine that you have an issue with any of the spiritual practices from your past lives. But one that I had came as a complete surprise. I carried (and was not aware at all) the *fear of God.* Not just that I had no respect for God; I was actually afraid. This is a *common and even dominant theme* for all of the humanities and was brought to my attention a few years ago. (Note: There is no intent in the discussion below to disparage anyone's religion or belief in God.)

All of us have experienced, during many tribal lifetimes and many other limited spiritual religious experiences, the concept of a god that was mean, cruel, vengeful, and judgmental. There were lifetimes, too, when the religious authorities required regular human sacrifice to the gods. Also, much of man's inhumanity to man and brutality to others was done in the name of God. Therefore, over these lifetimes, we have built up a powerful "fear" of God that was complex, entrenched, and operated underneath.

Once I was given this information I released and then neutralized this pervasive fear. Even though I could not relate to it consciously it made logical sense. There are infinite experiences, beliefs, etc., that we carry as part of our unconscious energy world. They often come from life experiences completely out of the range of normalcy for what we have today. But conscious or unconscious, they still exist and still have an effect on us. And in this case, I experienced a major shift in my life as a result of neutralizing.

Here's what changed immediately. The next morning, as I walked through my living room, the Higher Selves indicated that I was going to be reflecting them in my next private session for the first time since I began doing this work. I had been getting Higher Self information for a long time but had always been given it at a conceptual level that just was "downloaded" into my mind, which I then explained in my own words. It was effective but not a word-for-word situation. I was nervous and knew it was a big step forward for me.

I did it and it went well. After that, in many of my private sessions and my meet-up groups, I would move into frequency to get pertinent information when necessary. That belief, that fear of God, long-forgotten and not part of my conscious mind in this life, had been a limiter that had held me back.

Our conditioned responses, no matter what they are or how they manifest in our life, hold us back. The spiritual authorities and their teachings often have wrapped up the idea of the Divine in rigid and negative terms. Fortunately, the Higher Selves don't try to convince us to believe anything. They clearly lay out the seating at any table so no soul is more important than any other. No one gets to sit at the "head" while others sit far away in the back or at another table near the kitchen noise. We are all expressions of the Originating Source, each of us as pure and perfect as the next.

Conclusion of Part II

We are responsible for what we have created because what we process in this life is the end result of what has been experienced and deeply misunderstood in other lifetimes. There is much layering as result of all of the experiences from tens of thousands of lives compiled together. You get great complexity and great *intensification* of previous energy identities as new experiences occur in future lifetimes. Unraveling deep-seated beliefs is a doable process, and we don't need to know where and how the beliefs happened. Even though what we carry has taken eons of time to develop, the neutralizing technique begins its effectiveness immediately and with each time, the energy field we carry is permanently shifted to a higher frequency. With consistent use of neutralizing, the shifts add up quickly, leading to major results within a few weeks or months.

The soul's journey through the Human Kingdom Universe is long and fraught with misunderstandings, false beliefs, and misinterpretations. Our experiences in body, as we reincarnate over and over from both the individual level and the societal level, create the foundation of who we are, how we define ourselves, and how we see the world around us.

So what do we look at next?

PART III

The Human Kingdom Heavens: Home for the Disincarnate (Out Of Body)

The words from the Higher Selves should not be seen as absolute authority but should be seen openly and evaluated from your highest level of Consciousness and then taken in, or held to one side, or let fall away, as you are directed by your own highest nature or Higher Self.

Introduction

We need to include the totality of the human journey exploring both the times we are in body as well as the times we are out of body. We turn now to the out-of-body arena, where we spend much of our journey through the Human Kingdom. The disincarnate state that we move into at the end of our physical lives is also part of the Human Kingdom (the 4ᵗʰ Dimension). It is not some different dimension or a place that has little to do with us as humans. The place where we all go when out of body is *Heaven*. The Higher Selves call it the Human Kingdom Heavens. What is it like there? What happens there? Is it all we thought it to be? The Higher Selves have provided much information about Heaven that is both fascinating and provocative.

We will not debate about what is right or wrong, what is truth or untruth. This book provides a viewpoint, with information coming from one source—the Higher Selves. There is no intention to offend anyone, but due to a person's unique belief systems and upbringing, some of the concepts presented in this section may trigger certain reactions. It would be normal. Even though I have come to respect the information, it is up to each person to decide for him or herself if it is relevant or helpful. Whether you think of yourself as religious, spiritual, or neither, the Higher Self viewpoint could be surprising or upsetting. I'm not here to convince.

Please stand in the center of belief and disbelief and allow the information to come in and be what it is without judgment. After it has processed at the neutral level, you will determine if you resonate with it or not.

CHAPTER 13
Heaven Unveiled

HIGHER SELF QUOTE

The 4th Dimensional Realm is the totality of the Human Kingdom. It contains humans in the formed state and the disincarnate humans in the Heavenly state. A soul once released from the body in the form of death moves into the Heavens and carries with it into its own hereafter whatever conditions exist within its Soul/Mind at the point in time the death takes place.

General Overview

Because Heaven is a place that few can sense or see when we are in body, it is normal that we all have many questions and confusions about it. Between each lifetime, we return to Heaven and stay there until we incarnate into our next body. And the humanities in place in Heaven are from all the planets within the Human Kingdom Universe, not just Earth. There are an infinite number of souls in Heaven beyond our comprehension. There is no requirement that you be a good person to get in. There is no Saint Peter at the gates letting some through and keeping others out. All human souls go to Heaven between lives and the few that don't go immediately upon death do get there at some point. (See Part IV.)

Whether a human soul is in Heaven or in body (disincarnate or incarnate), it exists within the Human Kingdom. And because the Human Kingdom operates under Free Will, no soul is forced to follow any type of path or to get help or advice while in Heaven any more than someone would while in body. Instead, each soul makes its own choices. If you have a problem while you are in a physical body, you may choose (or not) to go to therapy or to a doctor or to a spiritual mentor to get help. It is the same in Heaven. Each soul decides to get help, and if not, they are sometimes completely on their own.

Heaven is a learning ground. There are schools of all types throughout the Human Kingdom Heavens. Souls can go to any school, though they are not forced to go. There is no rote memorization or rapping on the knuckles of an unruly student. And if students want to play hooky, they can do so.

There is guidance provided for souls related to their evolutionary progress if a soul chooses to pursue this option. The help focuses specifically on the individual issues carried by each soul based on the level of awareness of that individual. The educators guide them to process the past life they have just experienced and/or a series of lifetimes related to the same issue. The intent is to help souls figure out what they are misunderstanding, what they still need to experience, where to reincarnate, and under what circumstances. While going through this process, the elements of soul scrambles would be on the table. Souls at a very early frequency level of human awareness would not realize that help for their evolutionary process was possible or available. As each soul moves up the human ladder to higher frequency levels of understanding, interest in this option increases.

Once awareness has reached a certain level, souls often do seek out guidance. In the area of choosing a new life, educators help with a soul's decision, as to which planet in the Human Kingdom Universe would best serve it next. Depending on which issue or concept a soul may be working on, there is a planet that carries the Divine Energy particularly needed by that soul. For example, Earth carries *Divine Material Balance*. This means most souls on our planet need help with this evolutionary concept in some way and have chosen to be here for that energy. (My book, *CHOICES*, is a good resource to learn more about this Divine Energy.) Also, planets themselves are souls and go through their own evolutionary process moving up in frequency levels. Thus, human souls would also be directed by the educators to specific planets based on whether the planet matches the human's own evolutionary frequency.

As a planet evolves, it moves up in frequency levels, which parallel the frequencies of the life forms it houses. When it carries just the Mineral Kingdom, a planet also moves at a very low frequency rate. In time, the planet's frequency reaches the level where it can carry the Planet Kingdom, then the Animal Kingdom, etc. Within each kingdom too, there are many different frequency levels. Currently, our planet is carrying a frequency level that allows and invites reincarnating humans who have reached the higher levels of human awareness.

Once a soul is ready for the help, many other decisions evolve from discussions with the educators about the lesson/concept a soul wishes to learn. The return to the physical state gives a soul the opportunity to practice what it has learned in the disincarnate state. However, because we have no memory of why we have chosen the life we are in, we often repeat the same patterns we carry at the etheric level. (Charlie is a clear example of this.) When a soul is determined to learn or experience something specific when it reincarnates, it could take a lot of time to set up that next life. This means the soul would carefully put together a plan, which includes finding others who agree to work with it and together they would co-create certain situations and conditions. These are the conditions that would activate the issues the soul wants to heal so that it will be motivated to get help. The soul would also want there to be opportunities present for it to find the help it needs once it sets out to find it.

We all know learning something in school doesn't necessarily mean we will use it or remember it when we leave school and move out into real-life experiences. It is the same with the learning that goes on in Heaven. Learning in Heaven is a start and as significant as it can be, the lesson may take time to take hold and allow us to overcome the knee-jerk patterns we carry at the etheric level. As we have also learned from Charlie, it may take several dozens of lifetimes (or many more) to figure out even one major issue.

The practical experience in the body is essential because evolution is orderly. Even though we often perceive our world as chaotic, there is no backsliding in evolution. It is essential that we don't skip over some level of understanding as we climb up the evolutionary frequency scale. It would be problematic to discover at some point that the learning on a previous level was not truly assimilated. Backsliding then would happen on a regular basis to all souls, which would create a true chaos. Therefore, the building process of our evolutionary energies is slow but sure, and we test ourselves on every level to guarantee our learning is set. Once we arrive at the frequency level in our evolutionary process where we consciously care about our own journey's unfoldment, we do spend the time needed to plan each next life.

Common Misconceptions about Heaven

The evolutionary dimensions are made up of 7 levels: the Mineral, Plant, Animal, Human, 5th, 6th, and 7th Dimensions. The Originating Source of energy is the capstone of the evolutionary dimensions and does not exist (as is misunderstood by many individuals) in the Human Kingdom Heavens. The Human Kingdom Heavens are part of the 4th Dimensional Realm.

Below are a few common misconceptions about Heaven according to the Higher Selves:

MISCONCEPTION 1: Heaven Is Where God Resides

Many spiritual belief systems put God in residence in Heaven. According to the Higher Selves, the human level in the evolutionary process is only the halfway point of the return journey to the Originating Source. And even after that, souls continue the journey in what the Higher Selves call the *outer realities*, so different from ours that we cannot even begin to fathom what they would be like. (More on outer realities in Expanded Perceptions: The Divine Paradox)

Instead of placing this Divine Energy field in any one spot, whether in Heaven or anywhere else, we can view the Originating Source as a powerful energy field that exists everywhere. Originating Source is *All There Is*. We, too, are expressions of it. Originating Source does not have a special seat or throne in Heaven or in any other dimension or kingdom.

MISCONCEPTION 2: Souls Are Automatically Infused with Super-Wisdom the Moment They Lay Aside the Body

Souls still struggle with the same issues in Heaven that they have while in body. Every soul there still carries the etheric bodies providing the same viewpoints, which are based on the judgments and beliefs it had while in body. There is but a thin veil between both parts of the human arena. If you are caring in this life, you will be caring when you cross over. If you are a jerk in this life, you are a jerk when you cross over. You hold onto your self-identities even without the body, though if you spend time learning more while in Heaven, you could certainly begin to change while there.

MISCONCEPTION 3: Heaven Is Our Final Destination

Soul evolution is an ongoing process. Commonly, it is believed that when we die, we will go to Heaven and will finally be at peace. The Higher Selves have clearly dismantled the end-game notion that Heaven is where all souls will end up. Evolution takes us not just through the Human Kingdom, but also into and beyond the next three higher dimensions. The journey is immense and ongoing. It never ends.

MISCONCEPTION 4: Heaven Is a Utopia and a Better Place to Be Than Here on the Earth Plane

The expanded understanding around this concept from the Higher Selves is actually a difficult one for me to put in this book. So often people believe that Heaven is beautiful in every way and that their loved one (who has or is dying) will be in a better place than they had been in Earthly life. This concept gives great solace for those left behind. If someone had suffered with a long illness or was living from a place of despair, then death can be seen as hopeful and freeing to the individual. However, though the laying aside of the body can mean that the physical suffering is over, Heaven is not the utopia many are expecting. It is not about going to a better place. Instead, what a soul finds in Heaven is what the soul believes to be there. If a soul believes it will go to hell, it will find the hell it expects, which can literally be the devil's place, rife with all the fire and misery it feels it deserves. If the soul believes that God sits on a throne with streets paved of gold, then that is what the soul will find. If Heaven means a beautiful meadow and all the serenity of nature, the soul finds exactly that. Our belief systems are the root of what we manifest both in body and in Heaven.

Of course there are some souls not locked into a belief system about Heaven and those souls may be more open to discovering the opportunities for evolutionary advancement. They may seek out sooner than others the help needed to continue the steps of their evolutionary journey. But Heaven is not a utopia. The choices are endless.

One idea that may bring solace to those losing a loved one is to replace the thought that Heaven is a better place with the thought that when a soul lays aside the body, it is taking the next step in its evolutionary journey. The current body may be gone, but the soul continues forever. There is only a temporary loss for those left behind as souls connect and reconnect over and over again throughout their journey. Also, for this life, we can rejoice for the time, the learning, and the love that our loved one brought into our lives, and in turn, what we brought into theirs. This connection would never be lost as it is carried in the soul banks forever.

MISCONCEPTION 5: God Is in Charge in Heaven

God is not in charge in Heaven or on any planet in the Human Kingdom Universe because Heaven is in the Free Will arena. Just as the Higher Selves have shown that in body we are the directing identities of our life patterns, the same is true while we are in Heaven. Nothing can happen to us unless, in our souls, we have allowed it to happen both in body and/or out. There are no victims. We are not puppets of a male or female God. We are not puppets of Originating Source. Often we "stand" there as our lives unfold with our etheric energy identities leading the way. Often *our soul gives consent to this non-action simply because it believes this is what should happen since it is God's will.*

Originating Source is an androgynous creative vibration—totally impersonal. It knows no gender and makes no decisions. God is sometimes viewed in philosophies and religions as the agent that controls all it creates. In reality, it does nothing to you *except* what you will for yourself within the soul pattern. In the Free Will Kingdom, it is the human soul that makes the decisions, not the conscious mind or Originating Source.

I'll use natural gas as an analogy. It is a neutral energy. It is up to each of us to choose how we use it. We can use it to heat our homes and/or to cook our food. Or we can choose to use it to kill ourselves or burn a structure down. We are the directing identity. It is the same with the Divine Energy of Originating Source. The Originating Source energy is available to us in every part of the universe including within ourselves as the Pure Soul Essence. But at the Free Will level, it cannot trespass and it does not control us. Each soul has to choose to use the energy, and the Originating Source does not determine how or when we do it. We are the directing identity. One significant difference between natural gas and the Originating Source (besides the obvious) is that the Divine Energies of Originating Source cannot ever be used to hurt or harm either yourself or others.

Divine Will is different from Free Will and because there are some powerful misunderstandings about *Will*, the next chapter will clarify.

CHAPTER 14
Will

HIGHER SELF QUOTE

In the seven major levels of evolution, you have the three lower kingdoms which evolve on an Instinctive Will, and you have the higher dimensions above Human that operate on the Spiritual Will frequency. This connection to Divine Will allows evolution to take place effortlessly. It is only in the Free Will Kingdom (the humanities) where you have the evolutionary resistance based on decisions and experiences that any individual soul undertakes at any point in time.

Will is a concept that is a large part of our mental gestalt. We often use it in the following contexts:

- The willful child who is stubborn and won't do as directed.

- The idea of "where there's a Will there is a way" as if Will is the only motivator for us to do things and the only thing that carries the energy to enable us to get it done.

- The term "willpower," which usually means that we find the strength to resist something that isn't good for us such as desserts, drugs, or those bad relationships that end up hurting us.

What do these concepts related to Will have in common? They carry the idea of being controlled or controlling, being overpowered or overpowering, and/or being dominated or domineering. The concepts of control, domination, or victimhood are often part of the concept of Will as we see it, but the Higher Selves offer an expanded viewpoint. They clarify five concepts of Will: Instinctive Will, Free Will, God's Will, Divine Will, and Spiritual Will.

1. Instinctive Will

   The three lower kingdoms (Mineral, Plant and Animal) evolve differently than we do in the Free Will Kingdom. At those early levels, there is no resistance to evolution. The 1st, 2nd, and 3rd Dimensions are on a Divine Will frequency that is operational at an unconscious level. It works because the Pure Soul Essence within each soul is connected to the Originating Source. This connection enables the evolutionary movement of each soul (at these levels) to be divinely guided up the evolutionary frequency ladder through an instinctive process in a smooth manner. There is no decision-making at the soul level. All life can be viewed in these three lower levels as moving along on cue based on this evolutionary guidance by the Originating Source at the Pure Soul Essence level. This does not mean that the three lower kingdoms evolve at higher rates of speed than the Human Kingdom. However, they do evolve without question and efficiently because in the three lower kingdoms, there is no Free Will and no thought to interfere.

2. Free Will

   Humans operate on Free Will in the 4th Dimensional Human Kingdom. It is the platform between the three lower instinctive kingdoms and the three higher Spiritual Will Kingdoms. The

Free Will vibration is where each soul's journey eventually leads to the consciousness that it is the directing identity for its own life and is truly an expression of Originating Source. It is only in the Free Will Kingdom that we have *resistance* to moving toward this awareness due to all the misunderstandings, misconceptions, and misinterpretations taken on during the almost infinite experiences any individual soul goes through.

One of the misunderstandings is that we believe Free Will exists in the conscious mind. As the Higher Selves explain, Free Will exists at the soul level and not at the mind level. Of course, we have choices at the mind level: Do we eat at this restaurant or that one? Who do we chose to be on our soccer team? What color outfit should I wear today? But the major decisions are willed at the soul level. For example, you are in a plane that is about to crash. Everyone on the plane spends their last minutes willing themselves at the mind level to live. However, all souls on the plane may die. Clearly, death is not a mind level decision but a decision made at the soul level based on the beliefs we carry. All souls choose their own death. It's only an illusion that we have Free Will in our conscious, everyday lives.

Because of the misunderstanding about Free Will, some people will interpret events being caused by fate or God's Will or even deciding that there is no Free Will after all. When our choices from the mind level don't pan out, we often turn to these other reasons to explain it. This can lead to despair and hopelessness because we feel we have no control. This is a misinterpretation.

3. God's Will

There are many philosophies that promote the idea that the individual soul must "give up" its own Will to a higher Will in order for the soul to make progress in the right and proper way. This promotes the idea that the individual is not responsible for his or her life. The belief is that this higher being is the one establishing the soul's lessons that have to be learned in order for the soul to then be saved by this higher being.

The following ideas about God's Will carry an element of familiarity and similarity for many of us. These ideas are so basic to many belief systems that they are often not questioned. However, there are some misunderstandings according to the Higher Selves. This presentation is not about right and wrong. It is never about finding fault. Looking at beliefs is a healthy practice because it is an essential part of the journey we are on. Here are some common concepts (or misconceptions) about God's Will followed by the Higher Self perspective.

I.   There is a higher power that leads us. If we follow what it directs, we will be all right. For those who are familiar with the Lord's Prayer, one of its phrases is "Thy Will be done."

The idea that it is the Will of a higher being that rules our lives in some way has been and continues to be a pattern of belief on this planet. This concept has created confusion as well as a veil of darkness—darkness not in a sense of evil or bad but in areas that deal with the mind itself—confusion and blindness from misunderstanding. The confusion promotes the idea that the individual is not responsible for his or her life. Whether the belief is that a higher being or a Karmic pattern controls the life, the viewpoints are limited in nature. Though we move through the Free Will Kingdom to learn, grow, and expand at the soul level, we do *not* do so to get to the point where we deserve to be "saved" by this higher being.

Another way to look at this is by understanding that when we think/believe that something external calls the shots, we make ourselves puppets or we ask to be puppets. Our concept often is that God is in charge of everything, directing us in mysterious ways. It is almost as if God is like the spiritual Santa Claus who knows if we've been bad or good and then decides whether we manifest problems in our life or good in our life. We had better "watch out" or the "Will of God" won't be pretty. The fear is maybe we will get coal in our life's stockings.

II. If we keep praying to God, doing for others, and asking for help and forgiveness, we will be saved.

Again, this reminds me of the popular Santa Claus myth. Didn't many of us as children try to behave extra good before St. Nick was due? Didn't we want to convince him that we deserved great gifts? I don't mean to draw the analogy out too much for fear that it may seem to belittle one's faith in God, which is not my intent. In reality, it isn't Santa Claus that gives the gifts in the stockings and in the same way it isn't really an external God who is going to save us.

For example, Charlie made the choices in his life patterns and *he* had to find his way through the morass of his confusion and misconception. *He* is still on a journey of self-discovery and growth, and it is *he* who will finally forgive himself and be able to fully resolve the Soul Scramble.

III. We will find bliss and fulfillment and the right to be in Heaven by following God's Will.

This is a tricky belief because what is God's Will exactly? This is one of the mysteries of all time. There are many interpretations of God's Will in the various religions and often those religions feel they have the best answers if not the only answers. There is a sincere intent to figure this out because often, from this viewpoint, our salvation is at stake. Yet, often the answers are vague or conflicting.

How do we explain why bad things happen to good people? One of the mysteries of all times is why there are so many horrible, cruel, and destructive things in this world. Even the most giving and loving people have difficulties in life that many outsiders cannot understand. How, too, can innocent babies and children get illnesses or be kidnapped or become disabled? Because we haven't understood up until now that it is the individual souls that choose what happens to them, we have instead put the responsibility into the hands of the Almighty. The feeling is we need to have faith that God works in mysterious ways and even the bad things have a purpose if we only could know what God thought. However, if bad things can happen, how do we avoid the things we cannot understand? How do we know when we could be the recipients of these bad things that happen for some unknowable reason? According to this belief system, we don't.

Also, when something negative happens to some people, they may assume that the god or a higher being is punishing them. If people devote their lives to following God's Will as interpreted in their particular spiritual practice, they either blame the higher being or blame themselves when something bad happens. Following this concept of God's Will leaves little wiggle room for success and lots of room for judgment and feelings of fault because we all have difficult things that we have chosen (at the soul level) to happen to us.

There is also an unspoken corollary to this belief. If bad things exist, wouldn't it mean that God can do harm, that He can be seemingly cruel and unjust? It is hard for most of us to conceive that God can do harm. But whether it is held consciously or unconsciously, this corollary leads to the empowerment of the "fear of God."

IV. We need to subjugate any kind of Will we may have to God's Will, as our Will most likely comes from ego or other baser motivations.

There are many philosophies, both orthodox and alternate spirituality, that promote the idea that the Will of some higher entity (some people call it God, the Will of Allah, the Will of Divine Mind, whatever the term may happen to be) is what we need to follow rather than have any Will of our own. The general idea is often an individual soul must give up its Will in order to give over to a Higher Will so that its soul can progress in the right and proper way.

We all have heard from many sources the pros of humility and the cons of ego. There is a general consensus within the religious and metaphysical communities around the idea that ego is a bad thing and ties us to the mundane, baser motivations and that humility and self-sacrifice are the most altruistic of orientations. If one takes this idea on as a belief, then the individual will live out of that belief system. Yet the Higher Self viewpoint states that locking into belief systems creates limitations in our lives. With every judgment comes another ceiling we cannot go past, and most of these judgments have already been in place for eons of time.

In addition, the belief centered on the requirement that we give up our will is in direct conflict with the concept that we are the directing identities of our own lives. We are in the Free Will Kingdom for an important reason, and by believing that our will is untrustworthy or negative in some general way is another layer of misunderstanding adding to and supporting the idea that we are not worthy and that our humanity is somehow impure and imperfect.

Finally, giving up our own will continues the empowerment of the belief that we are powerless and have no choice. If we see God's Will directing the whole or part of our lives or if we believe there are times when we have no choice, then we would move along our journeys as puppets *even when there is no puppeteer!* When we believe there is a puppeteer—our God—then we act as if we have strings attached.

Thus, we often have the idea that in some ways we have choice in our lives but on the other hand, God's Will is present and making the decisions. This inherent conflict tends to be vague and is not clear as to where the boundary is between being self-responsible about our own decisions and where God's Will is making the decisions. So mostly we gloss over it, do not think about it, or assume the answer is another one of life's mysteries.

4. Divine Will

In lieu of the term "God's Will," which carries old and biased connotations, Divine Will is the term the Higher Selves use. Divine Will is part of the Totality of Originating Source of All There Is. What makes up the Totality of Originating Source and where does Divine Will fit in?

When light is shown through a prism, it comes out the other side as a range of colors that make up its whole. Light has many aspects or parts to it—those parts being the many colors of the rainbow. We don't see them without using the prism, but they are there whether visible or invisible. In the same way, the Totality of Originating Source has an infinite range of aspects that make up its whole. There is Divine Mind, Divine Soul, Divine Heart, Divine Word, Divine Love, Divine Vision, etc. Divine Will, then, is but one powerful aspect that makes up the conglomerate of All There Is. We already carry Divine Will within our Pure Soul Essence. Every soul carries this within and every other powerful Divine Energy as well.

The Divine Will aspect is the energy flow that moves us along our soul's evolutionary path. It is not imposed upon us in the Human Kingdom but offered if we are *willing* to take it in. There is no force, no control or coercion in this concept. When we choose to stand in the center of the Divine Will Energy and act from that place, we will manifest in our own Highest Ideal facilitating our life's evolutionary journey. When making that choice at the Free Will level, we allow our Free Will to become one with Divine Will. Because Divine Will is part of the all-knowing, all-balanced, all-pure, and all-powerful Originating Source, becoming one with this energy (as with all Divine Energies) will aid our unfoldment from within, instead of our needing to figure out what God's Will is from the mind level.

Being a Divine Energy, Divine Will is available to us but cannot trespass. We can call on it anytime we wish, and it will be there for us. However, usually we are unaware of its existence and what it can do for us. Until we access it (or any of the Divine Energies), it is only potential power. It is as if we have the most super-duper powerful computer in the world on our desk. It is able to do anything we ask it, even clone the kitchen sink, but until we turn it on and type out an instruction, it does nothing! Instead of using our inner super-duper computer, the Pure Soul Essence, what we usually do is to allow our unconscious energies to direct our lives.

When the Human Kingdom comes to the point where we are aware of the Divine Energies, we can then give them permission to move into our life pattern to help us. For example, how we awaken, how fast we awaken, and how our journey to awareness unfolds, is part of the Free Will process. But awaken we will. No soul is lost. Until you awaken, your soul gives consent to whatever happens to it based on its beliefs woven and locked in from its thousands and tens of thousands of lifetimes of built-up misunderstandings and misconceptions—in other words, its Soul Scrambles. Originating Source doesn't determine how we use its energy. We do. We decide when and how we are ready to use the Divine Energy of Originating Source.

5. Spiritual Will

Spiritual Will is the type of Will used in the 5th, 6th, and 7th Dimensions. Like the three lower kingdoms, Spiritual Will is also on the Divine Will frequency. The difference is that Divine Will in the lower dimensions is operational at the unconscious level (Instinctive Will) while in the three upper dimensions it is taken on at the conscious level (Spiritual Will). When one graduates from the Human Kingdom into the 5th Dimension, one has already come to the full understanding of the purity and perfection of its soul. A soul consciously agrees to accept the Spiritual Will principal to be operational at all times. (Note: Will at this level does *not* mean Originating Source forces any soul to do anything. It still has choice.)

Significance of Will

There can be resistance and possible confusion about some of the ideas about Divine Will, God's Will, etc. I had my own resistance to the idea of Divine Will for many years and refused to become one with it. Then one day the resistance was gone. When I asked the Higher Selves what was the reason for my resistance, it turned out to be because my concept of Will (as discussed above) was limited in nature due to unconscious conditioning. I felt Divine Will would force me to do something I didn't want to do. Fortunately, the active neutralizing of many different patterns, including the conditioning of looking to external authorities to save me, meant that at some point I neutralized enough layers (even though I didn't know this at the time) and allowed in Divine Will. And guess what? The sky didn't fall on me, and I'm still my own directing identity!

CHAPTER 15
Choosing Your Next Life

Understanding More of the Basics

Within the Human Kingdom, like every other kingdom, there are evolutionary levels that human souls move through, ones that begin at low frequency of awareness, moving up to higher and higher frequency levels.

When we begin our journey in the Human Kingdom, we have just finished moving through the Animal Kingdom and have barely touched on the enormity of information and knowledge that we will gain over the eons of lifetimes it takes to move up the human evolutionary frequencies. Therefore, early on, when a soul lays aside the body, there is little thought or concern about the next life. Choices for the next reincarnation that are made at this evolutionary level could be to return to the same area where one just lived, to be with another soul they cared about, to go back to get revenge, or anything else basic. To get to the point where a soul is concerned about its own evolutionary process means the soul has already experienced many eons of lifetimes and has made good progress up the evolutionary frequency ladder.

Earth, like all planets, has its own evolutionary process. It, too, as a planet that houses life-forms, evolves in its own right. And again, as its frequency rises, the evolution of all life upon it moves up. At the human level, this plays out in such a way that if a soul has a frequency level much lower than the planet's, it would most likely not reincarnate here. It would reincarnate on another planet with its same frequency or slightly higher. And if the planet's frequency increases while a soul is in body here and the soul could not keep up with its progression, the soul then would lay aside the body and incarnate on another planet that matches it in frequency. In this way, the soul doesn't lose anything as it gives itself another chance (as many chances as it needs) to move up the ladder of awareness. Souls that have a higher frequency than a planet can and do incarnate on a planet with lower frequency for various reasons, but the most common one is to be on the planet to help others in some way.

Frequency of souls is not something you determine by looking at a person. There are souls with very high frequency who are involved in primitive tribal societies on this planet (and others) or are involved in criminal activities. Yet, they could carry an equal or greater frequency than those who seem more evolved. They have chosen these primitive or difficult experiences for reasons unknown to us. This isn't about judging yourself or another as superior or inferior. We are all equal. We all are expressions of the Originating Source. We all are snowflakes with complex and complicated journeys, no two alike.

The frequency of Earth at this point in time is quite high (and expanding on a moment-to-moment basis), and as a result, most of the souls upon Earth have reached a higher frequency level, which has enabled many to touch greater levels of self-awareness, self-responsibility, and interest in self-help. It is these souls that, when out of body, are at a place in their journey where they make more consciously informed choices and decisions as to what situations and conditions they need to set up for its next life. Charlie was a great example. There were times early in his Soul Scramble when as long as he reincarnated as a male where he could exercise his dominance and power, he was happy. He didn't focus on developing his female nature for some time. It wasn't clear what brought in that motivation, but we see that his focus slowly changed. He moved more and more into a place of determination to learn and "get it right."

We have the lives we do because we choose it for ourselves. For the next example, I have taken elements of Soul Scrambles from clients (and from overall information from the Higher Selves) and created the story of "Sarah" and "Sam." This story illustrates in a simple way how our scrambles and soul misunderstandings create patterns and how a soul decides which situations and conditions to choose for its next life.

Sarah and Sam

HIGHER SELF QUOTE

Souls agree to come together to fulfill a specific dance that each believe must be participated in. It is important to understand that no one or no thing can do anything against you that you at the soul level have not agreed to. The patterns within the soul, even though they may be unconscious to your mind, are nevertheless being processed and carried out to the exact degree that the individual souls participating in that specific dance have so chosen.

Sarah had spent many of her lifetimes on Earth and had a giving nature. She believed that to be spiritual and godly, she needed to give to others. She dedicated herself in those lifetimes to self-sacrifice as the way to be as spiritual and saintly as possible. There was also the supporting concept around her that the material world was tantamount to the devil. As Sarah continued her reincarnations, she moved more and more into an imbalanced place in many of her lives, giving to others at her own expense. She had continually put aside her wants, needs, and desires and always put others first in those lifetimes with little joy for herself, no time for a family, and the barest of sustenance.

Her dedication brought her hardship and early deaths more than once. She carried guilt and shame because her difficult experiences early in some lifetimes caused her to fail at the particular job she did. In one life, she died young, leaving her disabled parents without her to care for them. In another, the orphans she provided for were left unable to fend for themselves. When she died prematurely in these lives, she left the physical life riddled with doubts, shame, and worthlessness. She took on the powerful misunderstanding over and over again that she needed to sacrifice herself even more to have any value at all.

What she learned from Heaven's educators (before the current lifetime) was that she carried the belief that goodness was *dependent* upon how much she suffered. And this belief was based on misunderstanding and limited in nature. The educators helped her to see that *balance* was the key, and suffering was not a defining or necessary element. The focus on the spiritual at the expense of the material world is as imbalanced as a focus on the material at the expense of the spiritual. She was shown that she had sacrificed herself based on the misconceptions taken on from cultural conditioning while in body. Although Sarah made progress with understanding the balance issue, she was still unable to allay the guilt she felt over what she saw as her great mistakes. And because the Soul Scramble was a deep and complex one, Sarah decided to tackle the balance issue first, beginning with her next life.

Sarah now prepared for her next life. She hoped to break her misery cycle by using all she had learned from the educators. She had to figure out what were the best circumstances and who were the best people to bring into her next life. Her goal was to have her patterns triggered, to bring in awareness and to motivate her to find the help needed to heal. This time she would take more care. This time she was determined to get the circumstances right.

She chose to return to Earth because she knew the false belief of the self-sacrifice ideal was pervasive there. It was where the Mother Teresas of the world were placed on pedestals and anyone in the corporate world was often seen as greedy and heartless. This way she knew that her own false beliefs would easily come into play. She also knew that she wouldn't be alone in her struggles. Earth itself carried the powerful energy of Divine Material Balance to help all souls to materialize from the abstract to the concrete in a perfectly balanced manner in the highest good.

Now Sarah had to pick the country, city, and basic situation of her birth and the people who would be part of her journey. She decided on the United States where there would be plenty of help available when she was ready to heal her pattern. She also decided to ask a lifetimes-long friend, Sam, to be a part of her journey. He had his own patterns to work on, and they had both been together before. This time, he was working on a Soul Scramble where he believed at a deep level that it was much better to do as little as possible and not fail than to try hard only to find it he couldn't make something work. On his own journey, he had come to believe he was a loser and a failure and found the best coping mechanism was not to try. As a result, after many lifetimes of holding true to his pattern of non-action, Sam believed he was a worthless human being.

Sarah understood his belief system held him back. She thought coming in together would be an opportunity for both of them to become aware and to heal. She explained the situation and he, too, thought it would work. Once they married (they theorized), they would begin or continue to play out their patterns. Sarah would struggle to care for Sam, the house, and eventually the kids and to bring home the money. Sam would likely become more and more passive and live from a place of non-action. This would lead Sarah to move fully into her self-sacrifice pattern where she wore all the hats, got no help, and took care of everything. They were sure that as their patterns became more extreme in their manifestation, the difficulty would wake them up and they would become aware of what they were doing to themselves.

Thus the co-created decisions were made from Heaven before they reincarnated. They made a contract soul-to-soul that would be played out unless one or the other or both decided for any reason they no longer needed to go through with it.

In an actual situation, a soul would choose more people other than a significant other (such as the parents, siblings, area of the country, etc.,) and would set up more situations (wealthy, poor, city, countryside, etc.,) but for the sake of this example, I kept it simple.

Sarah and Sam came into life following the general setup they had chosen and right from the start, Sarah felt drawn to the spiritual side of life and became involved in the spiritual practices she was exposed to. Sam, too, followed true to his basic fear of getting involved, fear of taking an active role in life, and did what he needed to do, but little else. When out of high school, Sam and Sarah met, fell in love, and got married. Because Sam was married to someone who was always out there, helping others and doing all she could to make Sam happy, he easily continued the non-action pattern. In time, they had two children and Sarah's work doubled. She worked, took care of the house and children, and maintained her volunteer work. Her stress was off the charts. Sam did little to help out. When he didn't have to work, he would sit on the couch and watch TV. Both Sarah and Sam became obese because they used food to self-medicate and to avoid looking deeper into their marriage and their problems. And one of their kids followed suit. Did the extremes of their patterns wake them up?

Each year, Sam and Sarah developed more physical problems related to obesity: high blood pressure, early onset adult diabetes, sleep apnea, and loss of mobility due to the great weight they carried. They found it difficult to be good parents to the kids. Because their problems became so challenging, they did indeed "wake up." From TV, they learned about the problems with obesity and the options that could help them. They could have fallen into the blame game. Sarah could have blamed Sam for all the work she had to do. Or Sam could have blamed Sarah for her constant volunteering and giving so much of her attention to others. But instead, in this case, the extreme nature of their predicament moved them to the place of awareness. It was exactly what they both had hoped for when they co-created this life pattern, even though there was no memory of their choice at the mind level.

They knew they needed help and something was deeply wrong. This led them to the decision to apply to the show, *The Biggest Loser.* (The show is used as an example because I've seen many on the show look at their fears or misconceptions and decide to change their lives.) Sarah and Sam were chosen as contestants (in this example, not in real life). Their time on the show was the opportunity to learn and understand their imbalances, fears, misunderstandings, and false beliefs. Sarah found that she needed to give to herself and to know that it was okay to receive help, support, and love from others.

Sam faced his fears of failure and realized if he didn't win a challenge or had a week of little weight loss, it didn't mean he was worthless. In time, with the help of all he learned, Sam shifted his life to one where he was active and involved. For Sarah and Sam, it was a successful journey. They lost a lot of weight and got in shape physically, mentally, and emotionally. They accomplished what they wanted to accomplish.

Sarah and Sam now stood firmly on the step of increased awareness and increased movement forward. Both became involved in giving back but in a balanced way. They spent more time actively involved with their kids. Sarah gave up some of the volunteer work she had taken on, and Sam let TV become a small part of his life—only something to watch while on the treadmill getting exercise. They moved closer together as a couple, and were positive role models for their kids. The co-creation in this example was well planned and worked!

Sarah and Sam choose the conditions they setup which propelled them to do exactly what they needed to do. Sometimes, no matter how much careful planning is done, the soul is so led around by the entrenched energetic pattern it came in with, it never comes to the place of understanding and learning that it initially intentioned for itself. But for all the times when we were not successful in changing our patterns, we also have had many lifetimes when we've been successful, like Sarah and Sam.

This teaches us to pay attention to our lives. Where are we unhappy? Where are we stuck? Where are we blaming ourselves or others? These are the areas where we have Soul Scrambles. These are what we can learn to resolve, to heal, and to bring to a state of balance and understanding. Let's change our viewpoint then, from one that sees our misery as something we cannot change and will always keep us prisoner, to the viewpoint that our misery is our biggest opportunity. Once we have this new viewpoint, we will understand that our misery (anxieties, suffering, pain, etc.,) is what we have set in motion in order to develop the motivation to move into a seek-and-search pattern to find help. Now, we can use the Divine Energies to neutralize and resolve these miseries and create what we had always hoped for.

As an aside, I would like to say that obesity is one of the last arenas that many feel they can make fun of without seeming like thoughtless and bigoted people. If we don't understand this yet, obesity is a tool of the soul just like alcoholism, drug addiction, hoarding, etc. These are coping mechanisms that souls have chosen to avoid the deep fear or sorrow or self-loathing or whatever is incredibly painful inside. There need be no blame here. The obese have chosen a difficult road for two reasons. First, unlike other addictions, being a "foodaholic" is visible to everyone from close friends to the passersby. The overweight can never hide. Second, the obese do not have the possibility to stop *all* eating in the same way that another type of addict can, for example, stop *all* drinking or stop doing *all* drugs. The overeater is tempted on a daily basis. This indicates that at the soul level, the obese are determined to get it right this time. We should help them get it right. We should have the same level of understanding for those who use food as a way to avoid their pain as we do for those who use alcohol or drugs. We are all on a journey and we all have Soul Scrambles and issues we need to work through and learn from. Let's not add more salt in the already deep wounds.

CHAPTER 16
Is This What Happens with Every Human Soul?

Any move forward in evolution is permanent. Once a soul has made a step forward and is firmly in place, that soul cannot regress or move backward. In the 4th Dimensional reality, it may appear many times that souls step back. But what you view as a soul regressing is really personality and psychological distortions an individual soul must work out. These distortions are unrelated to the soul evolutionary standing that is permanently in place. And when ready, the soul will move forward once more.

Basic Soul Evolution Related to Future Reincarnations

Each soul is unique and has its own journey. In describing what happens to souls in Heaven or in body, one should avoid the terms "never" or "always." Just when you think you have seen it all, something new pops up that was not even a seed in your imagination due to our infinite experiences while moving through our eternal evolution.

Every kingdom has seven levels that the souls pass through during their evolutionary movement. Then there are also the 8th and 9th levels, which are incubatory in nature and which prepare the soul to move into the next kingdom. The first kingdom, the Mineral Kingdom, moves so slowly that it seems as if it stands still. However, the Mineral Kingdom does and has evolved. There are levels within the Mineral Kingdom: igneous rocks, metamorphic rocks, and sedimentary rocks exist there as well as minerals, crystals, and gems. Though we may not understand which of the seven levels a particular rock is on, there is evidence everywhere that differences exist.

As a mineral soul moves upward, when ready, it will evolve into the Plant Kingdom. In the Plant Kingdom, there are increasing levels of complexity going from simple algae and grasses to the flowering and fruit-bearing plants—evidence that evolution has been at work here as well. A soul that moves in the Animal Kingdom also goes through the seven evolutionary levels. There are simple animals in the early evolutionary frequency levels such as amoebae, sponges, and coral. The higher evolutionary scale includes elephants, dolphins, dogs, and primates.

When a soul is ready for the transition into human, it goes into the 8th level of the Animal Kingdom, the level that amalgamates its soul's experience with the conglomerate experience of the total Animal Kingdom. What does this mean exactly? The soul is brought into a place where all of its experiences are shared with the conglomerate animal soul. And in return, the individual animal soul also learns from the experiences of all other animals on this and other planets that have evolved into human. Thus, individual animal souls take on the knowledge of all of the animals that have graduated before (from this and all other planets) that have made it through the Animal Kingdom. Think about that! This process guarantees the animal soul is brought up to the highest level of knowledge about the animal nature that it can reach, before it moves into the human arena.

The next level (the 9th), the second incubatory level, is the level where the soul goes to prepare for the entry into the next kingdom, in this case, the Human Kingdom. The souls are given information, energy, and knowledge about the next phase of their journey. And the information is taken in at a basic level and carried within the soul banks. At this point, the souls are still animal in nature and are completely inexperienced in the Human Kingdom.

When a soul moves into the Human Kingdom, it moves directly into the first level of the first level. Yes, there are levels within levels. The evolutionary process is complex and the learning and expansion of the human consciousness takes eons of time. At the first level, the soul would incarnate into a primitive type of life. (Primitive signifies lower frequency levels of awareness.) It could be on any planet but think what it was to be a Neanderthal on this planet. Neanderthals certainly had human characteristics as they had family groupings, some spiritual belief system (evidenced by the rituals they had when burying their dead), forms of art and tool use, and hunting and gathering skills. Here on Earth, our scientists consider Neanderthals not fully human. They hold somewhat of a transitional place in the evolution of man coming after apes but before Homo sapiens. From the Higher Self perspective, however, they are considered in the Human Kingdom, but would be living within the very low frequency levels.

So what happens to souls such as Neanderthals when they lay aside the body? Would they have a clue about the schools and educators in Heaven? Would they understand that becoming aware of their patterns and misunderstandings was important and essential to move forward in one's journey? No. When souls from lower frequency levels die, they have little understanding and their choices as to the next life are simplistic in nature. Even Charlie's focus in the beginning was to avoid being a woman at all costs and then, once having found an arena where he was successful and powerful, he spent lifetime after lifetime developing the expertise with germ warfare. And Charlie was much further along on the evolutionary frequency levels than that of a Neanderthal. It took a long while for him to get the idea he needed to address his feminine side.

As a human soul moves up the levels, there are countless choices as to what to focus on in the next reincarnation. Some may return to deal with unrequited love or to get revenge. Some may get caught up in a number of Soul Scrambles. There could be little thought and just emotion that plays into the choices of someone's return. And this, too, is part of the process. Learning and becoming aware is slow. All of the humanities have to go through the journey. Each soul finds its own way and every soul will make it to the place of awareness, the place of expanded viewpoints and understanding and to the top level of the 7th level of the Human Kingdom. There is no stopwatch, no time limit, and no one offering us a prize if we get there faster than someone else. We all move at our own rate.

At the top of the 7th level, the humanities are ready to graduate into the 5th Dimension. When they complete the graduation process, the souls move into the 8th level of the Human Kingdom. As with the Animal Kingdom, the 8th level is where a soul goes to amalgamate the conglomerate human soul containing all the knowledge and every experience of all humans of all time. Then finally, the soul will go to the 9th level, the level that prepares the human souls to move into the 5th Dimension (the Inner-Planetary Kingdom). This dimension is where *all* the humanities eventually go. Heaven is not the end point for us. Heaven is part of the Human Kingdom. Because graduation to the 5th Dimension has not happened on this planet, it could be difficult to conceptualize. The graduation occurs solar system-wide and will happen in our solar system in approximately 2000 years.

Can We Judge a Book by Its Cover?

You already know the answer to that one. What I would like to emphasize again is there is no way to judge on the surface what level a soul has evolved to. The souls on this planet at this point in time have already moved into the higher levels within the Human Kingdom. Sometimes, souls at higher frequency levels of awareness may come into a life to help in some way or to develop a skill set or a body of knowledge that is more easily done in a tribal society. Perhaps the simplicity of the culture means it would be easier for the soul to focus its experience on just one issue. There could also be those who may come into a society as part of a criminal environment to learn something or help someone. This person could be in prison or be a leader in a criminal group such as the Mafia or a gang.

It is not about trying to figure out where someone is in frequency and then treating that soul accordingly. We cannot know the level of someone's soul frequency based on a given life situation. Try not to fall into the comparison trap. Soul evolution is not about being superior to or better than someone else. To get here, every soul has taken eons of time. Every soul is on its journey and has its own complex reasons for the way the life unfolds. His or her issues and patterns may come up early in life, during mid-life, or in later life, or they may manifest throughout one's life. There is no way to tie level in with the behavior you see. There is no room for judgment. Every soul is equal. Every soul is an expression of the Originating Source of All There Is and carries the Pure Soul Essence. Every soul has its own Soul Scrambles and is playing them out in the ways it has chosen.

CHAPTER 17

Choosing Your Own Death

Introduction

As we learned from Charlie, it is the soul that chooses the situations and conditions of death. In his case, he chose his death before he took on a body (in this latest life) but that is not necessarily the case every time. *Always* and *never* again cannot be used to describe how or why souls make the choices they do. Many times, the choice is done before they return to body and many times, the decision is made after they return. Also possible is that the soul can change its mind, choosing one scenario ahead of time and then deciding later that it wants a different type of death or a different timing of death. The key element here is that the decision is done at the soul level and not the mind level. This holds true even in the situation of committing suicide. The suicide attempt would not succeed if the soul has not made the choice to die, even though the conscious mind may want to die.

There is also great variation as to why a soul chooses the how and when to die. We saw from Charlie that he chose his death to atone, to suffer with the same type of illness that he believed he inflicted upon others. He left it somewhat open-ended as to what germ and the timing of it in his life. Overall, the possible choices and the reasons for them are infinite.

When Death Is Chosen before Birth: Joe's Story

This is a real-life example of someone I will call Joe. Joe was born in the mid-1900s and was one of three children. He was patriotic, joined the marines when he came of age, and was sent to Vietnam, like most in the military at that time. He did two tours without a scratch and came home with his life. Three weeks later, he died unexpectedly in a small plane crash at age 27. From the outside, his death seemed senseless and frustrating. There was no understanding fate at this point. Family members could only ask why!

Now, almost 50 years later, Joe's sister asked me to help her understand Joe's death. She had not made peace with it after all these decades. She and Joe had been very close and some part of her had never gotten over it. Of course I offered to help, even though I couldn't guarantee that I would be able to tap into the answer she was looking for. Fortunately, I did this time. When I focused in, I discovered immediately that Joe had already returned to a new life in body and was now an eight- or nine year-old boy here in the United States. However, the mind of his life as this boy was unable to address my questions about his prior life. Thus, I asked his soul to come forward to help me. And at that point, a grown man was projected to me (symbolic of Joe at the soul level) and I "talked" with him.

"Joe" explained what happened. There were five individuals he had been with in past wars from different lifetimes that he felt he owed a debt to. One individual had saved his life, and he had never been able to repay the "favor," which was important to him. The other four men were cases when Joe had had opportunities to help in some way but had not stepped up (at least in his viewpoint). Joe carried shame and guilt. He believed if he had stepped up in each of those cases, he could have saved or helped these individuals in a significant way. I did not get details of each scenario, but the shame he felt was palpable. The issues relating to these five men burned Joe up inside. He wanted to heal and release this pain and the obligation he believed he owed them. He also felt he had to take care of this before he could move forward in his evolutionary progress.

What he decided to do in his next life—the one with the sister— was to die young. His longer-term goal was to heal this pattern for himself, die, and then to take on a life shortly afterward where he could focus on helping others in some greater way. Joe decided to handle his obligations with all five men at once. In planning his life here as Joe, he co-created with the men before incarnating an agreement where they all would be in the same military unit together, which they were. Of course, Joe got to know the men in his unit once he was in body, but he did not remember any of the plans he had made with any of them while out of body.

What Joe chose for himself was to volunteer for the position in the unit where he would be a point man. He chose this function even though and especially because being the point man could be very dangerous. A point man is the first to walk into possible booby-trapped areas, sniper fire, enemy territory, or an ambush. But if the job is done well, a point man can save the lives of the others in a unit.

He chose not to die in the war even before he was born. He wanted to live through the war so that he had every chance to make good on his goal to help these men. However, the plan was that he would die soon after so he could move quickly into his next life. He was able (through his great success as point man) to effectively help many in his unit survive—the five men he had wanted to help and others, as well. Joe came away from his time in the service having relieved much of the shame and guilt, knowing at the soul level he had done all he could. He had satisfied himself and his need to fulfill obligations and repay debts.

The need to atone is a common theme throughout the humanities. Though often it doesn't work to bring relief, such as with Charlie, in Joe's case, it was successful. He was able to forgive himself.

Now, 50 years later, one thing was still very important to him. His sister had known he was going to die young before either of them had taken on the body. However, because neither of them remembered the plan once in body, he regretted that he had left her bewildered and devastated. He was glad to speak with me so he could explain and put her mind at ease. He reassured her that he had accomplished what he had set out to do and greatly appreciated her support. For her, now that she understood why the death happened as it did, her grief and confusion was alleviated even though she was still sad not to have had her brother with her for more years.

When Death Is Not Chosen before Birth: Ned's Story

QUOTE FROM JOAN CULPEPPER, WHEN DECEASED,
AS TOLD TO JANET RICHMOND:

Ned has the potential to become a spiritual demonstrator. This is similar to a born-again Christian but instead of finding the seat of the divine without, a spiritual demonstrator has found (and will show others) that the seat of the divine is within.

Sometimes the soul doesn't always predetermine death before returning to the body. Perhaps a soul has a goal for what it wants to learn or to heal and depending on how it is going within the life pattern, it wants to decide later the how and when of its demise. A friend of mine, who I will call Ned, is an example of one such soul.

Ned had serious problems in his life—off and on unemployment, often on the verge of homelessness, and in the direst of times, he would turn away from those who cared and became a hermit of sorts. He gave in to his many dark and self-defeating inner voices and looked like a man who wanted to die. He was a diabetic who did not monitor what he ate and was inconsistent with taking his insulin. And over a two- to three-year period, he often went into diabetic comas and had to be resuscitated by paramedics when his landlord would find him unconscious.

Ned closed his ears to the pleas from those around him to take care, until one day his landlord found him in a comatose state. And this time, Ned was extremely close to death. He was rushed to the hospital and remained unconscious for three-plus weeks. The doctors weren't sure how well he would be able to function if he woke up. The diabetic coma had put all his organs at risk, and he was sustained by machines in the ICU on total life support.

Ned had been my friend for almost 30 years, and I was one of the friends who had tried to help for so long but he had pushed away. I always understood. We had worked together in a group for several years, and I knew his intractable patterns well. He had never fully stepped forward to take responsibility for his problems and relied on others to make them go away. As hard as we tried, we could not do it for him and understood that as the directing identity of his own life, there was some part of Ned at the soul level that would not accept the healings we did with him.

From the start of Ned's time in the ICU, I would "tune in" periodically to get information on him. I worked with him at the soul level, psychically communicating with him and/or going into frequency to get information from the Higher Selves. Unless stated specifically, Ned was not consciously involved during the sessions. Also, Ned had to agree at the soul level to come forward for a healing or to "talk" with me. I could not nor would not force him or any other soul. And when he was ready to leave or to end the session, he would.

I was reluctant to do a healing as the doctor had told me that if Ned woke up, his recovery would be long and grueling and it was unknown how much function would return to his vital organs. So before doing a healing, I wanted to first understand Ned's wishes at the soul level as to his future.

I then called Ned in while he was in the extended coma and talked with him and his Higher Selves even though he was unconscious. His choice as to whether to lay aside the body or not was important, for if he decided to stay, not only would he have a long journey to wellness but also he didn't have family in California to support him. He had no medical insurance and no money. In my mind, he would have to be a ward of the state. His elderly parents lived on the East Coast with financial and health issues of their own, so they would not be able to visit often. He would be alone.

When I first contacted Ned at the soul level (from a distance), he told me that he had decided to lay aside the body. So I was ready to hear from the doctors in real time that he had passed away. But I didn't. The days came and went and still he was in the coma. I contacted Ned again from a distance. He told me that the machines made it difficult to die, but he still wanted to. This answer seemed odd to me, so I asked his Higher Selves. They said he could choose at any time to die, as it was his decision and not dependent on whether he was on machines or not. They explained he was still conflicted about the decision, and therefore, the coma continued while he vacillated first one way and then another.

I decided to help by neutralizing his conflict and confusion about this choice in order to facilitate his process. I, thought at the time that laying aside the body was the best solution for him, but I did not want to influence his decision by my viewpoint. I am not him and could not know the deep-level issues he grappled with. I "called Ned in" to encourage him to release the confusion and anything else that kept him stuck in the waffling pattern. I worked with him for about 20 minutes. And then suddenly, Ned left the session!

This was unusual in my experience because normally there is a winding down process that I go through when the healing is done. I guessed that Ned's abrupt departure signaled he had made a firm decision. I just didn't know which way he was going to go. The next day, I found out. Ned woke up! He had decided to live. It was a shock to all of us, as we didn't understand why he would make that choice. Luckily, the Higher Selves were there to help us understand and within a few days, I went into frequency to inquire further.

They explained that Ned understood there was an advantage for him to live with serious disabilities. He knew he would be so physically restricted that he would have the time to concentrate on healing his inner demons—those voices he had battled with for so many lifetimes. His old repetitive behaviors—such as his addiction to the Internet—would no longer be possible. He would have the mental space and focus to do the inner work he had long avoided. It took courage and determination to make this decision. Ned decided to honor the value and power he had within in order to move beyond the victim pattern onto a road of self-responsibility.

Joan Culpepper also "came in" while I was in frequency and explained the deciding factor in Ned's decision. Both Ned and I were part of Joan's metaphysical group in the '80s, so Joan had known us both well. She explained to me that while Ned was in the coma, she had spent a lot of time with him at his unconscious level. Like me, she was very careful to stay neutral and not sway him one way or the other. She was there to talk with him about his questions and concerns in order to help facilitate his decision. However, she told me that a mutual friend of ours, Roger, who had also been a member of the group, had come to speak with Ned during the coma.

Roger has been out of body (and still was) for almost 25 years and his viewpoint was not neutral. He wanted to convince Ned to stay in body! It turned out that Roger had spent a lot of time preparing for his own return to the physical state, and he wanted to give Ned the benefit of some of his discoveries. He told Ned it was difficult to set up the next life in order to make sure all the factors were in place that would enable him to accomplish what he wanted. He said it was essential to find and make agreements with the people who would help trigger the patterns needing healing. And it was also important to set up the opportunities in that lifetime which would enable him to resolve them.

Because Roger was frustrated and worried about picking the perfect next life to accomplish what he wanted, he told Ned it would be best for him to stay alive. Ned already had in this current life the information, knowledge, techniques, and support group to get rid of his "demons," and he should take advantage of that! There was no guarantee he would get it right in the next life or the next. As it turned out, Roger's "talk" made a great impression on Ned and was one of the key factors in Ned's decision.

The demons of Ned's mind (and anyone else's in their own unique ways) are made up of those misunderstandings, false beliefs, fears, and self-loathing that had held him prisoner for so many lifetimes. By choosing to live, Ned would face these demons and release, neutralize, and get rid of as much of them as possible.

Even though it all made sense, I was still concerned because of the difficult physical road ahead for Ned. The Higher Selves reminded me of a book I had read about ten years ago titled *A Bed by the Window* by M. Scott Peck, MD. This book takes place in a nursing home where one of the characters is disabled and couldn't move or talk. Readers are inspired as they "hear" his thoughts and the richness of his inner world was described.

The isolation Ned was going to experience would make his inner world more fulfilling and would allow him to find all of his self-worth within *simply by being.* He would also have the time to connect with his Higher Selves. The Higher Selves did say, though, that Ned's journey would be difficult and he could change his mind at any time.

The Higher Selves related the conclusions and decisions Ned had made for himself. They were not directing him or decreeing the way things should be. Just as with Charlie, the soul could ask for as much assistance and guidance as it wants to take in, but all decisions at the human level are always up to the individual soul.

Now that he was awake, Ned was soon moved out of the hospital to a rehabilitation facility. After about three weeks, I went to see him. He greeted me with a big hug and said he had been worried that he would never see me again. (He had not remembered any of my previous visits.) He couldn't talk because he had a tracheotomy tube in his throat but was able to write his thoughts on paper. I told him what the Higher Selves and Joan had said. Though he didn't remember any of the communications while he was in the coma, he resonated with the information. He told me he had been working on himself everyday neutralizing, and he did healing exercises for others in need at the rehab center. In addition, he talked about the kind and competent staff. His focus on this warm and loving concept kept him motivated. He seemed a changed person.

Over the many months, Ned and I talked about many things. I found that Ned was healing on many levels. He took responsibility for himself in ways he just couldn't manage before. He was present and connected to his own life for the first time. From time to time, I saw the "old" Ned reappear so I knew he still had a way to go to heal all those voices and to change the patterns of many lives.

But whatever work he does on himself in this life will lessen the problems in the next.

Ideas to Consider:

1. When I work with the Higher Self healing techniques, I always amalgamate myself and the healee, joining us in the Highest Ideal with the Pure Soul Essence, the Higher Selves, and the Originating Source. The general principle is that because this is a Free Will Kingdom, no matter what the healer does, the individual being worked on may or may not agree at the soul level to be healed. The *amalgamation* guarantees that there can be no harm and no trespass. However, no healing is wasted because, even if the soul does not want to heal at that moment, the healing energy would be held in its soul bank until such time the soul was ready to use it.

2. Having gotten the Higher Self information about why Ned decided to live explains what would have been a mystery to all of us. We were of the mindset that it would be best if Ned died and at first were dismayed thinking about all of the physical limitations and suffering he would experience. Whether for Ned or anyone else, once we understand some of any soul's journey, it makes it easier to understand the individual choices.

3. Ned made a choice at the soul level. He chose to give himself one more chance in this life to turn himself around. He was and is determined to do what he needs to do in order to heal

the deep wounds in his soul. Although it may sound extreme for a person to make the decision to keep himself physically injured, the soul can often reach a point of desperation, much like Charlie did. At such times, the soul is more than willing to take drastic measures rather than watch yet another lifetime go by, still locked into a debilitating Soul Scramble.

4. Though Ned still struggles with the voices that had ruled him before, he sees the light at the end of the tunnel. He now knows he is not his condition, he is not his depression, he is not his old worthless self-image, and he is not his disabilities. He is learning to stand in the Light, his most perfect and most potent point of power. Whether he will become the Spiritual Demonstrator (per Joan's quote) is still unknown. However, Ned is making progress.

5. We have also heard that it can be difficult to set up the circumstances of our next life. Therefore, I would encourage all to take advantage of this life. If we don't become aware in this life, we will return again and again until we do. So let's get it right while we are here and already have the resources and knowledge of how to help ourselves.

As of the writing of this book, Ned has been moved out of the sub-acute area of the rehabilitation center and into a transition area. He has no tracheotomy tube, no dialysis, no catheter, and is eating regular food for every meal. He walks and talks and does more and more physical therapy to strengthen his body, though his organs are seriously compromised. But he takes each day as an opportunity to bring in healing, balance, and focus on what he needs to do to take care of himself. When a physical crisis arises and he is rushed back to the hospital, discouragement sets in and he seems to lose some of his motivation. However, all that he neutralizes is gone permanently. His decision to return to the body has borne fruit and even though all the "demons" of the mind might not be gone, he has made significant progress. What seemed to me such an odd choice from the outside looking in, Ned's decision to live was logical from his perspective and had positive results.

CHAPTER 18
Heaven's Educators

HIGHER SELF QUOTE
_____

There seems to be upon this planet much misunderstanding in areas that deal with the spirit entities. Those who consider spirit entities seem to group and classify them as good and high or as bad and low.

Introduction

There are four general categories of human souls in Heaven. They are:

1. Those who consciously try to move themselves forward on their evolutionary path

2. Those who hang out for some reason and don't focus on learning and evolutionary growth

3. Those who actively hold themselves and others back, whether they are consciously aware of it or not

4. Those who become Master Teachers, guides, or other educators

You have already seen examples of the first group of human souls in Heaven that consciously try to move themselves forward—Charlie, Sam, and Sarah. Many human souls pursue the path of awareness, go through the process of learning to understand their last life and/or their Soul Scrambles, and then plan what is needed for the next life. There is an intention to move away from judging themselves or others, though they may not always be successful. Heaven provides the opportunities, schools, and educators to help these souls through the process.

The second general category contains souls who hang out for some reason. Here are a few examples. Just as we know people in body who don't do much with their lives, so, too, do we find those types in Heaven. Perhaps these souls are caught up in some type of activity or arena that is not helping them. There are those souls mentioned earlier that are still at the lower levels of human and are not as yet aware of the meaning of their journey. They don't really care. Lastly, there are those souls who have strong belief systems that hold them in place. For example, there are those who believe Heaven is the last stop (the end goal of their existence) and now there is nothing more to do. There are even souls who have died in their sleep, and they are doing nothing because they still believe they are asleep! For the most part, the souls that hang out are relatively "stuck" in Heaven. But, there is no rush in the evolutionary process. No soul is lost. Every soul evolves. There is no stopwatch and no one looks for the winner. All souls win. And because the journey is freely Willed, no one, no thing, and no god pressures any soul to make a choice in any certain way or in a specific time frame.

The third category relates to souls who have become engaged in negative activities. Don't we have souls here in body getting involved in more problematic arenas, such as gangs, selling drugs, etc.? Yes, of course. The more negative arena in Heaven is different because it is the disincarnate state—no guns or drugs there. Yet, there are things these souls can do to get into "trouble." There are souls who are tricksters, acting more or less like teenagers getting into mischief. Some are involved in negative activities because they play out of the ideas of control and power. They may find ways to interact with other souls in order to manipulate them for their own reasons. This sometimes involves the process of *attachment*. Attachment is when a soul out of body follows a soul in body and directs that soul through thought. Of course, the *attachee* is agreeing to the manipulation at the soul level, though he or she would likely not be aware of that.

The attachment process is described in more detail in Appendix III on Jane & Company, the introduction to this group of disincarnate souls and the topic of my next book. Briefly, Jane & Company is a group of souls in Heaven that were once misguided and unaware and who could be viewed as destructive at times due to their attachment to others in body. In the early 1980s, Joan Culpepper (with the help of the Higher Selves) led the original group of disincarnates through an educational process whereby they voluntarily detached. In time, the group moved out of their stuck belief system and formed a grassroots organization helping others. These souls now work in the Heavens to guide others there that are misguided or stuck for multiple reasons. In so doing, they also help themselves in their own evolutionary movement forward.

The fourth category is those human souls who are conscious to the point where they have made the decision to become or have become Master Teachers, guides, educators, etc. There are training programs in Heaven to educate the souls who wish to prepare for a service commitment to help their fellow man. As with training here on Earth for many careers such as doctor or professor, there is also training for the educators. Just as we know that a medical student, an intern, a resident, and a full-fledged doctor reflect the level or expertise that has been reached in medical training, there are also levels of expertise that are reached by Heaven's educators. Master Teachers (trained by 5th Dimensionals) have reached the highest level of training possible. Spirit Guides are those who have had at least some training but have not yet reached the "PhD" level of the Master Teachers. Whether Master Teacher or Spirit Guide, these educators are highly evolved 4th Dimensional souls of the Human Kingdom who play out a valid supporting role helping the humanities (both in body and out of body) in their evolutionary process. They help disincarnate souls who attend Heaven's schools or who seek out counseling help. They also aid those in body by coming through the many and various channels providing helpful information.

Not everyone either in body or in Heaven uses the term guides in this way. Many souls in Heaven may call themselves guides or Spirit Guides who have had no training at all. And often many people in body who work with guides aren't aware their guides may or may not have had any training. Therefore, just as we would be careful about what we take in as valid when we see some media broadcast or read some internet article, we also need to be discerning as to the information we receive through the channeling process. Everything that exists in Heaven is exactly the same as everything else and only exists in a different form of energy and relates from a different direction. When one lays aside the body, one still carries the self-identities, the basic character type, the belief systems, and the etheric bodies that one had in body. If we look around on this planet today, at the souls in body, we see a huge variety. It is the same within the Human Kingdom Heavens. Laying aside the body does not create a master prophet, a Master Teacher, or a Spirit Guide. A disincarnate human can call itself whatever it wants whether it is true or not.

When working with those who call themselves guides within the Heavens, it is wise to consciously amalgamate with your Higher Selves and to remain conscious of that amalgamation, as they (when directed) will monitor who will come through. Many souls who act as guides are *not* coming from that place of purity. These masqueraders pretend to know, teach, guide, and direct. Other souls drift about looking for people, situations, and conditions that best suit their purpose, such as where they can manipulate and influence someone in their own best interests and not in yours. There are also other souls that believe they are helping, but because they have had little or no training, may impart more limited and skewed information that could result in significant misunderstandings and misinterpretations. This is why as recipients of this type of help, it is always best for us to be discerning.

Whether we talk about the lower realms of souls who may play games or attempt to use, dominate, and control others or whether we talk about souls that are well-meaning but untrained, I suggest we suspend judgment and instead activate understanding. Though some who call themselves guides may appear to be "bad" in so far as some of the pranks, manipulations, or mistakes made, these souls can be educated and assisted in moving into higher levels of evolutionary consciousness. However, it is still important to use discretion when you begin to tap into the disincarnate realm within the Human Kingdom Heavens.

Lastly, souls who are in training and who have made the decision to devote themselves to the service commitment do so in order to progress in their own soul's journey even while they help others. Their training gives them a boost in viewpoint and an expanded understanding that increases their frequency of awareness. The commitment is not done at the expense of themselves.

Communicating with Disincarnate Humans

I do not begin to list all the ways communication can happen with the disincarnate humans, only the three ways discussed by the Higher Selves. In general, when those in body work with those out of body, the process can happen in more than one way:

1. A disincarnate can come in through the channeling process, whereby a medium channels one of them by actually mixing his or her mind energy with the soul of the disincarnate human being channeled.

2. A psychic can receive an entity's communications by psychic means without direct channeling.

3. A disincarnate human can be connected in the manner the Higher Selves taught Joan—by *reflection—to mirror or act out what a disincarnate wishes to express or communicate.* The reflection process does not entail the mixing soul energy.

One of the many disincarnates that Joan Culpepper reflected went by the name Jerome. Joan reflected him during one of her class sessions. Jerome was an educator in the Human Kingdom Heavens—a Master Teacher—who came forward to explain in his own words the role he plays while out of body in the Human Kingdom Heavens. The following is Jerome's story as reflected by Joan Culpepper on 8/8/84—edited for purposes of this book.

Jerome in His Own Words

Good evening. My name, should you desire to call me something, is Jerome. I will tell you that I have not been in a body {he seems to be thinking or calculating} *for 50,000 years—calculated in your Earth terms. If I were appearing on some other planet in some other time and space dimension, the terminology would, of course, be different.*

When I last laid aside my body, it was not on this planet. My history was as predictable as the histories of almost any soul in bodily incarnations —some good times, some bad times, some lifetimes of learning, some lifetimes of play and dissipation. But I had reached a point within my own inner beingness where I wanted to move into higher levels of understanding. I had attained already a high level of understanding then, but I would not graduate into Mastership for many thousands of years.

We have noticed (from our viewpoint) that not only on this planet but on many other planets the conformity of the human mind creates ideas and concepts that could be read out as blanket statements. Those in body often assume Mastership is attained at the moment in time the soul desiring to become a guide moves into the Heavens. This is true in only a few cases, but most often, the soul has only reached a point of intention to attain Mastership and must continue in the disincarnate state in areas of education.

Now, as Jerome, in my own individual incarnational pattern, I have lived at many different levels and studied many different philosophies played out of many different roles while in the human form. For example, I had participated and been involved in many of the Atlantean patterns played out on many different planets. For a while, I was still in my evolutionary processing and was taking on that bodily form, I carried what could be viewed as an insatiable need to travel. Therefore, I incarnated on many different planets.

With the decision to move toward Mastership, I spent many years in study. Those of us who aspire for those higher levels of learning are tutored and assisted by the 5th Dimensionals (the Higher Selves) who have returned to the Human Kingdom . . . to work with us in these higher levels. {See Appendix II.}

In my continued study, I was given much assistance and have been taken into many different schools rooms and further educated. It could be viewed as a college of letters where I personally studied healing and many different arenas whereby healing could be accomplished. I studied 5th Dimensional philosophy, de-intensified to a degree that I could handle it. I studied communications, acting in those earlier years as an apprentice so that I would accompany Master Teachers and observe and watch how they handled situations. I am of the old school of Mastership, where long hard years of study and application are required. It was thousands of years before I was able to assist humans who were in the formed state by myself.

You may not know that when a spirit entity merges energies with someone in a bodily form, those energies are not merged at the body level. If you logically think about this process you will understand it is impossible for a disincarnate soul without a body to move into and take over a body in form. What you have, instead, is a merging of the soul (of the disincarnate) with the mind of the individual in body. And living individuals who are joined with those energies take on the flavor of the merging disincarnate.

There have been difficulties (in my Mastership) of reaching human individuals at the levels they need to be reached. It is difficult to impart information and knowledge in purity through an impure mind. This is not meant as a criticism. It is a statement of fact. The mind carries the totality of all the experiences and existences, and this creates a tremendous amount of "garbage" through which a Master Teacher must penetrate.

It is fairly common within the Human Kingdom for individuals to worship and place us in a state of idolatry, to be in awe of, to feel grateful and feel gratitude that we, as Masters, would stoop to a lower level. As a result, it creates an inner need for those individuals to look to us externally as some kind of god. We find ourselves at the Mastership level of being a teacher at more than one level. We have information to impart (when we can move it through the garbage in the mind of the individual we direct it toward) *and we are teachers in that each individual must learn there is no external source; all power lies **within** each individual.*

Mastership is not easy. Those that become awed or humbled that a Master is working with them are also not the most effective individual channels. The state of humility many times limits an individual's ability to reach into the higher levels we would impart. It is also hard to reach those who would lock into ego frames of reference for they, too, are unreachable. So while it may appear from the 4th Dimensional Reality that Mastership is something big and wonderful, let me assure you that the last 50,000 years have not been easy. What we attempt to provide when we are able to reach an individual (depending on the level of those we contact) is as much assistance as possible in areas that deal with moving into higher and higher levels of evolutionary awareness.

Also, similar to what you see unfolding on your own planet, the so-called generation gap between the young and the old or the old and the new, we experience in the spirit world as well. There are renegade disincarnates—renegade in that while they are sincerely motivated in their soul pattern, they are misguided and could rebel for the wrong reasons. In this rebellion, it is as if a teenager suddenly knows more than the parents and wants to create life based on what the teenager believes to be the right way of doing things. Many of the renegades find it difficult to deal with and honor the idea of not trespassing the Free Will patterns of individuals. Many of these renegades feel they have pertinent information and knowledge and should be shared when, in reality, they are not ready to play out the apprentice role, let alone as a Spirit Guide in a position of giving advice and assisting the humanities.

When we work with humans through the channeling process, it is a merging of the mind of the individual with the soul of the entity or Master Teacher. When someone opens to the merging of the mind with myself or with any other disincarnate entity, he or she opens the mind to be flavored by whatever I carry (or whatever another disincarnate entity carries), should it be one other than myself.

And so one must be cautious and careful, for when the disconnection occurs (of the entity soul and individual's mind), the flavor of the disincarnate gets left behind within the mind of the channel. If that disincarnate is a masquerader, a renegade, a mischievous playful entity, or of a low-level soul frequency, it would create schisms within that channel that would resist a positive and effortless movement into the higher levels of his or her unfoldment. There are instances, too, where an individual is open to receive, whether or not one is consciously "desiring" to merge with a disincarnate. If someone is open at the unconscious level, an invasion can also take place.

In time, I will return and take on a body form because I have reached the point in my conglomerate totality of being able to move into the 5th Dimension, and this can only be done from the incarnate state. I have planned to do so in about 1,500 years. I have not yet decided if I will incarnate on planet Earth, for there are other planets in *other parts of the Human Kingdom Universe also making their preparation to move into their evolutionary new age concept.*

Even though sometimes it is difficult to inner-penetrate pure information into the minds of individuals I work with, we do the best we can. And there are no words wasted or lost, even though they must be processed through the "garbage" contained within. They have been placed within the mind and we know in some time/space dimension, those words in their purity will manifest. Thus, we have performed a good work.

I am involved in working with this group that you refer to as Jane & Company. As a Master Teacher and because they have been introduced to the 5th Dimensional vibration, I am able to assist them in their own evolutionary understanding. Jane & Company will continue this work long after I have incarnated and have moved into the 5th Dimension. It should make each of you in this group {those attending the weekly group Joan held} *feel rewarded due to the good work accomplished with Jane & Company. Because of Joan's help, the results of that work will be long-reaching in its effect. Those disincarnate souls who are a part of Jane & Company work daily to assist souls in distress who cross over due to fatal accidents and who cross over in a state of incomprehension looking for their biblical Heaven or their biblical hell.*

They are a marvelous group of souls. They have grown, evolved, and expanded. We appreciate the work you have extended, for we need all the help we can get in areas that deal with the lower-level disincarnates. It is fitting that we blend our energies from the invisible realm with your energies in the visible realm in order to accomplish the evolutionary mission you have incarnated to fulfill and I will later incarnate in order to fulfill.

The reflection of Jerome ended but the Higher Selves briefly verified that Jerome has been a very vital part of the Jane & Company educational process as if he adopted them. He continues to expand their educational process, which Joan had started. Then the Higher Selves concluded:

A true Master Guide and a true Spirit Guide, those that are standing in the highest human evolutionary level, who are aware of and work with the highest levels of soul conduct are connected very closely to the 5th Dimensional Realm. And many of them will, in this coming New Age, return to this planet and take on bodies so that they can take that step into the 5th Dimensional level.

That was the end of session.

The Distinction between the Higher Selves and the Master Teachers

In the beginning, when the Higher Selves worked with the Wednesday group, they were clear about the difference between Higher Selves and Master Teachers—the Higher Selves' frequency comes from the 5th Dimension while Master Teachers are part of the 4th Dimension, humans who have reached a high frequency level in the human evolutionary arena.

It is important to distinguish between the Higher Selves and high-level human souls because the Higher Selves (from the 5th Dimensional frequency) instruct the Master Teachers (as Jerome mentioned). Many of us here in body often call on our guides for help, not understanding the difference, thinking we brought in our Higher Selves. If this occurs, you create a force field of energy that calls forth human souls. This then creates a smog frequency between you and your Higher Selves who will not trespass the 4th Dimensional Free Will of the human soul. In addition, despite a guide's desire to help, their information and help would be coming from a lower frequency (4th Dimensional in nature) rather than the Higher Selves (5th Dimensional in nature).

True Master Teachers do have much to offer for they have attained a high level within the human frequency. Their information is powerful and can bring effective help. Also, it can be easier at times to "hear" the information from the guides than to go into frequency (more on this in Appendix II) in order to learn from the 5th Dimensional Higher Selves. However, it is at least important to be discerning and conscious of the amalgamation with your Higher Selves even if calling in your guides. This way the Higher Selves can be in charge of which souls respond to your call (should you desire this type of help). The amalgamation is your guarantee that you will not connect with a masquerader or renegade. Masquerading is commonplace in the Heavens, as mentioned by Jerome. By giving your Higher Selves permission, they will make sure the masqueraders do not "get a seat."

When learning to make contact, Joan Culpepper always asked for information from the highest frequency that she could reach, not limiting it to a specific soul. (She hadn't known about the 5th Dimensional Realm then.) But by requesting the highest level information, she came to connect with the frequency of the Higher Self information—the information from the dimension above human. I, too, have followed this practice though it may not be for everyone.

Now that you understand the differences between the frequency levels, you at least have a choice. And there may be times when you choose a Master Teacher and other times when you choose the 5th Dimensional frequency. Each individual can decide.

CHAPTER 19
Angels

HIGHER SELF QUOTE

We have always promoted the idea that you neither believe nor disbelieve but stand within the center and allow the information to flow.

Much of what the Higher Selves have to say on angels may in some way feel odd, off, nonsensical, or just plain wrong for some of you. My goal is not to convince anyone but to present the information from the Higher Self perspective. The idea is to stand in the center of belief and disbelief and allow the information in without judgment. This allows its energy to come in at the highest level of understanding each of us can reach.

Two Schools of Thought

Generally there are two groups of people regarding ideas and viewpoints about angels:

1. Those who believe in the existence of angels from the religious standpoint, having been taught that there is a celestial hierarchy that includes angels. They perceive angels to be "spiritual beings believed to act as attendants, agents, or messengers of

God, conventionally represented in human form with wings and a long robe." From this perspective, angels by definition are not part of the evolutionary soul process as presented by the Higher Selves. Instead this describes them as a part of a Heavenly hierarchy including other angelic-like beings (seraphim and cherubim). These beings stand the closest to God and are there to help, support, and instruct the living.

2. Those whose belief systems are out of the religious arena (whether metaphysical or spiritual in some other way), often feel that angels guide and protect us. Even though this group may not fully understand what an angel is supposed to be, they still often believe in the idea that they are benevolent spirits. Either they have "seen" or experienced them in some way or have adopted the idea from cultural exposure. (For example, the TV show *Touched by an Angel* and the movie *Angels in the Outfield*.) As more people on the planet open up to spiritual viewpoints and look for answers, angels become more appealing to more people. It is reassuring to think that someone (some angel) looks out for us and will either keep us from harm or will be there to support us if we come to harm. And when potential problems are averted, we often say something like "something or someone up there is looking out for me!" Sometimes we even use the term angel.

Looking at the Angel Concept

There are many "angels" on the planet—all those who help others less fortunate. When I asked the Higher Selves about how to approach this topic, they indicated to acknowledge those in body on the planet who help the disadvantaged, homeless, hungry, sick, and the poverty-stricken. These incarnate living angels help move the world population into expanded awareness on a daily basis. When someone in body is ill or hungry or homeless, they have no time or energy to focus on matters of awareness, learning, or growth. For desperately unfortunate people, the total focus is on the need to fill the hungry stomach or to find shelter. These needs must be addressed. The human angels who give the jumpstart needed to build a state of security for them, we give gratitude and appreciation.

Now, what about etheric angels? According to the Higher Selves, there are no beings outside of the evolutionary pathway of minerals, plants, animals, humans, and 5th, 6th, and 7th Dimensionals. Thus, the Angelic Hierarchy in Heaven (as outlined in religious teachings) is outside of this paradigm described by the Higher Selves. In addition, Originating Source is All There Is. I have already presented the concept that the Seat of God is not in Heaven or in any other dimension. Thus, the idea that angels sit at the hand of God in Heaven is also not part of their paradigm. Yet, the idea of God and angels in Heaven is so ingrained in most of us that it may be difficult to adjust to this idea.

There are an amazing number of human souls who have laid aside the body (in Heaven) that could be viewed as angelic in nature in the same way as those in body are viewed. Many disincarnates in Heaven help others both in Heaven and in body (the Master Teachers, Spirit Guides, and the Jane & Company group of souls, to name a few).

Why has the idea of angels persisted and grown over the centuries? If there aren't any angels, what is it that people perceive when they sense or see angels with the classic look of a lighted being with wings? Is there any explanation? Is there any other reason for this deep belief many of us have come to accept? Could the concept of angels be part of a misunderstanding or misinterpretation?

The Eye of the Beholder

The Higher Selves reminded me when I went through my earlier visionary experiences and met my collective Higher Selves for the first time (who I perceived as individuals in body form as a group of entities), I identified them as Jesus and the disciples. At that point in time, 15-20 years ago {in the early 70s}, I was unable to go beyond the concepts and the beliefs held in my mind.

We all know that one person's trash is another person's treasure or that beauty is in the eye of the beholder. This idea directly relates to one major reason as to why the belief in angels is so strong today. Many have seen angels in different forms and at different times. But how can this happen if there are no angels as commonly accepted?

Over time, within Christianity as with most religions, there is the search for answers to the timeworn, seemingly unanswerable questions as to how and why and who and where. And over time, the perceptions of this realm developed the angel theme that began centuries ago. The idea moved into religious artwork and writings. Even though some of us in this life may not have been exposed to the rigid definition of angels through religion, most of us have lived past lives in religious circumstances. The beliefs then included the existence of angels and now we carry those belief systems at the soul level. Also, as the media on this planet went from town criers to local newspapers to radio to television to the Internet, the idea of angels moved out of the religious realm to all corners of the globe. When we encounter an entity that is loving and supportive, perhaps we see them as angels because it is what we expect.

There is another possibility:

> When Joan first got the Higher Self information, she saw an energy stream she knew was her Higher Self. He said to her, "My name is Urius." She saw a tall, blond figure, lighted and in robes. For Joan, Urius was the personification of her Higher Self. Then, a few years later, that energy flashed in (for a lack of a better description) and communicated, "You are placing far too much emphasis on a name. You are placing far too much emphasis on what we look like. We don't look anything like what you perceive us to look like. We don't have names. This is all your projection. Please do not lock it down."

Projecting our viewpoints onto an invisible energy stream of any kind or an individual out of body is something we all do. Fortunately, Joan did not lock down and was later able to pull in a more accurate concept of the Higher Self energy. However, all of us live in this five senses material world and relate to a symbol or picture more clearly than an energy stream. Sometimes the picture comes from what we expect and sometimes a disincarnate purposely projects what we expect or something to match our beliefs.

In a recent private session, a Master Teacher named Sarah stepped forward and explained that at times she would project herself as an angel when called in by a channel. She did so if this meant the receiver of her information, the channel, would be more predisposed to listen to what she wanted to impart. Sarah also explained that on other planets, the forms differ depending on what the humanities on the planet believe are the most sacred. She gave the example that on one planet, the holiest form was of certain mixtures of animals (like our griffins and harpies) that were considered gods. Here, on Earth, the form is that of angels. Sarah also showed me the image of her quickly changing from how she truly looked to the angelic form and back again many times.

The final reason for the angelic misinterpretations is related to the frequency of energy on Earth. The frequency on the planet and in the whole universe is increasing exponentially. The last 2,000 years have moved the equivalent of 10,000 years in evolutionary frequency terms—a large jump in evolutionary awareness. The energy on the planet in the early days of sensing and receiving information regarding angels was much denser than it is today. Thus, it was easier to misinterpret in some way what was being seen or experienced.

The probability was that what was seen as angels many centuries ago were instead Master Teachers or 5th Dimensional energy streams. In the Dark and Middle Ages, due to the much denser nature of the frequency, it was more difficult to pull in information from the invisible realm. The idea that human souls out of body would be trained to become teachers to provide information to those in body wasn't present in those earlier times. Soul Evolution was an unknown concept. Instead, there was the idea that once souls died, they returned to God and their journey was done. So another realm of beings was invented. It would have made sense at the time to place these "beings" as messengers and helpers of God.

Could there be yet another reason the belief in angels is so common today?

How Masqueraders Use Our Belief Systems

HIGHER SELF QUOTE

It is to be understood that any person involved with an entity (disincarnate human) is involved based on the unconsciousness of having given permission for such an involvement to take place.

There is a huge variation of souls here in body on the planet and that same variation exists in Heaven. This means, as Jerome pointed out, there are human souls in Heaven masquerading as guides for more manipulative or devious reasons, as well as those who want to help but want to do it their way as an inexperienced and willful teenager would do. In either case, these disincarnates are able to intentionally project to the receiver (us in body) the image that they are angels. This goes beyond our simply misunderstanding what we perceive. Instead, these masqueraders use the beliefs of the receiver, in this case, the belief in angels, to appear in that form on purpose. Unlike a Master teacher like Sarah, they would have more nefarious reasons. They would want to appear that they are here to work with the receivers in accordance with God's Will. This makes it easier for the masqueraders to manipulate and control because the receiver becomes willing to do whatever they say.

Thus, there are a vast number of reasons that so many firmly believe in the angelic realm. One very other significant reason is because there are Astral angels which will be discussed in Part IV (see Chapter 23).

Whether or not angels exist in the traditional sense, there are loving and caring souls both in and out of body that find joy and fulfillment in helping others. Yet, each of us is our own directing identity and whether from God or from angels, expecting something outside of ourselves to transform our lives means we can expect a long wait time. For as you now know, this is the nature of the Free Will Kingdom. We need to do it for ourselves.

Heaven Wrap-Up in Review

COMMON VIEWPOINT: Upon dying, we miraculously become benign and all-loving beings.

HIGHER SELF VIEWPOINT: Dying does not free us from the thought form, habit, and emotional bodies that we carry around with us both in and out of a body. In the disincarnate state, we still remain *prisoners* to the Altered Realities and belief systems that live within our etheric bodies. While it is true that, upon dying, we may be able to see things in a broader, big-picture perspective, we still reside in the Human Kingdom Universe and we view everything through the soul's unique etheric body viewpoint. In addition, this viewpoint is an amalgamation of beliefs from all the soul's experiences from all of its lifetimes, even if the soul is operating in Heaven as if from the mind level of the last life in body.

COMMON VIEWPOINT: Upon dying, we *automatically* gain help and compassionate understanding from a higher level.

HIGHER SELF VIEWPOINT: We cannot receive any type of assistance unless we first become aware there is help and then ask for it (thereby allowing it in). Also, Heaven is a part of the Human Kingdom and there can be no trespass of a person's Free Will there as well. Because the judgments and beliefs we held while in a body remain with us when we are out of body, and because they are often constrictive in nature, they may not allow us to have the open-minded state that is required to *hear* anything that is outside the limited viewpoint. This, of course, is true while we are in body, too.

COMMON VIEWPOINT: While in the disincarnate state, we have the power to decide how we will react and behave in our next lifetime.

HIGHER SELF VIEWPOINT: While in the disincarnate state, we only have the power to decide and determine what *situations* and *circumstances* we will find ourselves in; however, once in that lifetime, how we will react and behave will be determined largely by the Altered Realities within our etheric bodies *without regard to what our intentions were prior to coming in.* However, we are able to become aware of our patterns and can then change them.

Clearly Heaven is as complex and busy and with as much variety as the physical reality is. But we can't do without it. It is the other half of the Human Kingdom Universe, the invisible half, and it is as much a part of our journey as being in body.

Now, another layer of great complexity will be added—the Astral.

PART IV

The Astral

CHAPTER 20
The Astral Overview

Introduction

Wikipedia's definition of the Astral is the following: *It is the world of the planetary spheres, crossed by the soul in its Astral body on its way to being born and after laying aside the body and is generally said to be populated by angels, spirits, or other immaterial beings.* Below is the Higher Self information.

The Astral Defined

The energy field known as the Astral is symbolic of the Thought Form Body that surrounds the planet Earth. Just as you as an individual carry energy in the form of thought forms based on previous experience, so the planet carries energy, which could be seen symbolically as global thought forms.

The Astral is a part of the Human Kingdom Heavens though not the same as Heaven. It is energetic in nature (not perceived with our five senses), and exists within the physical realm and Heaven. And all human souls upon death move through the Astral planes to get to Heaven. So if it isn't Heaven, what is it? Symbolically, a picture of the Astral could be viewed as bands (layers) of energy that surround the planet.

Remember that there are energy bodies that surround our physical bodies. These other parts of our beingness are the invisible but very real etheric bodies that we carry with us at all times. Even when we lay aside the body, these energetic fields remain with us. In the same way, the layers of Astral energy could be viewed as the etheric bodies or the force fields of energy of the planet. These layers move upward from the lowest band that is comprised of dark swirls of negative energy and progress up from the darker to medium and then light-gray layers until the highest band filled with swirls of light is reached.

What type of energy do these layers contain? We know that when we think a thought, it creates a real energy that moves into our Thought Form Body and becomes a part of the etheric envelopes of energy around each of us. But thoughts also go somewhere else. Think of thoughts as being like radio waves. When we think (create thoughts), we send thought energy out over the airwaves in the same manner that a radio station sends its shows out. As the radio station broadcasts, a radio in the studio picks up the broadcast, as it is a receiver of the radio wave energy. In a similar manner, our thoughts move out and are received by our Thought Form Body. But radio waves can also be picked up by more than one radio once they are projected into the air. This happens with our thoughts as well. They are also broadcast outward and are received by more than our just our own Thought Form Body. Our thoughts also move into the Astral planes—the planet's thought receiver.

Unlike a radio, however, our Thought Form Body not only receives the thought energy but also then becomes the storage space for those energetic creations. In the same way, the Astral also becomes a storage facility. Because as thought energy once created cannot be destroyed, our Thought Form Body contains all of our thoughts from all times in this life and from *every life*. The Earth's Astral also contains the thought energy of *all of the humanities of all times* that have ever lived on Earth. The Astral is the Thought Form Body of our planet and our Thought Form Body is our personal Astral. There is also an Astral around every planet in the Human Kingdom Universe that houses humans. And together, all the planetary Astral bands make up the totality of the conglomerate Astral.

Earth has but a drop in the ocean of thought energy in relationship to the enormity and immensity of the Human Kingdom conglomerate Astral. For us, however, our Earth's Astral still carries almost unfathomable power. The power of the Astral comes from the enormous amount of accumulated energy that is magnetic in nature. Because all thought is magnetic and is the basis for the law of magnetic attraction, the Astral magnets have immense pull. Think of the powerfully huge magnets that operate within some of our industries. MRIs, for example, use very powerful magnets, as do the colliders that provide data for the study of atomic particles. There isn't a way of comparing the Astral thought magnets to these physical magnets but thought magnetic energy is no lightweight. This is significant because so much of the Astral is negative (as is true of our own etheric Thought Form Body).

The way the energetic magnets work is that like thoughts are attracted to like thoughts. So a thought of "Life is so much fun" is going to be magnetically drawn to join all the other like thoughts of fun within your own Thought Form Body. At the same time, the thought will also be magnetically drawn in and will join with the like thoughts of fun in the Astral. Because millions and billions of people over the eons have had thoughts of fun, the Astral fun energy identity is huge.

Now let's look at an example of negative thought energy, even something we might deem insignificant. Let's say we resent a loud, obnoxious, and inconsiderate person, and we'd like to teach that person a lesson. These thoughts empower our own revenge thought form whether or not we enact revenge. Simultaneously, we also are empowering the Astral revenge thought forms. Imagine just how common thoughts (and actions) of revenge have played out not only from the more primitive societies but also in more modern day cultures that hold an "eye for an eye" belief system. In modern day, perhaps, we don't act on the revenge thoughts as often as we would have in the more unenlightened times, but overall, revenge is almost as common as any basic instinct. The magnetic power of the Astral revenge is unimaginably large and dwarfs the magnetic power of fun.

The Astral bands or layers move symbolically from the densest, heaviest, and most negative layers to the highest, lightest, and most positive. The blackest level carries vast negative power and is the largest of the Astral planes. The more negative the thought, the heavier and denser the energy is. The positive is lighter in weight and in color. All thought energy (whether in our own Thought Form Body or in the Astral) is soulless, mindless, and will-less. This energy operates strictly through the magnetic process.

The Interaction between Both Astrals — Personal and Planetary

HIGHER SELF QUOTE

An individual soul's thought forms and the Astral work together in a cooperative manner. All human thoughts move into the Astral. Simultaneously, a soul's own thoughts magnetically attract to it like energies contained within the Astral band. Thus, there is a constant feeding back and forth of that particular vibration.

The accumulation of magnetic energy in our Thought Form Body and in the Astral means there are magnets everywhere. What is the effect? A continual dialogue occurs between these force fields of energy on a moment-to-moment basis, and they work together in a cooperative manner. "Like energies" are continually attracted to "like energies." The thoughts contained within one's Thought Form Body are magnetically attracted to and attract in the like energy in the Astral band. In this way, the energy an individual carries is empowered by the Astral energy, which in turn creates more similar thoughts from the individual, which then move back to the Astral. This is the dynamic of constant feeding back and forth of whatever particular vibration is active moment-to-moment. Usually, we are completely unaware of this interaction.

It is more difficult for us to move past our own entrenched patterns because the Astral is an endless reservoir of thought energy from all the humanities of all times. It is mostly negative and mostly carries limited belief systems. These energies work to further entrench our Soul Scrambles by continuously feeding our own energetic bodies. It is no wonder that it can be so hard to clear our patterns especially when we aren't aware of all that goes on!

Recap

- The moment a thought is in consciousness, it becomes a fact in the energetic state.

- Thought energy is magnetic in nature with each thought carrying its own magnetic signature.

- Each projected thought moves into our Thought Form Body and into the Astral. It is magnetically attached to thought energy like itself within both the personal and planetary Astrals.

- Earth's Astral could be viewed as the Thought Form Body of the Earth.

- The thought energy in the Astral has been created by all the humanities of all time.

- This process continues on a moment-to-moment basis continually empowering the Astral.

- Every planet that houses the four lower kingdoms has its own Astral and all of the Astrals are connected.

- Like our own Thought Forms Bodies, the predominance of thoughts in the Astral is negative in nature.

- The Astral is an immense reservoir of thought energy that interacts with and empowers our own thought energy.

CHAPTER 21
What Are Altered Realities?

HIGHER SELF QUOTE

The Thought Form Body is an invisible envelope of energy carried by each individual. It contains the Altered Realities of your thought processes in this lifetime and other lifetimes. In this Altered Reality there are many different versions of your self doing many different things. Once you have created a thought, it immediately becomes active in a manifested form within your Thought Form Body. That thought form then moves out into the universe of its own creation and builds energy and empowers itself with all that is like it.

The Basics of Etheric Energy

HIGHER SELF QUOTE

Within the Altered Realities you carry the thought, the emotional blueprint, and the habit; the Altered Reality carries the totality of all that experience.

As we have lived through many lives, at some point there never were any more new "events." Instead, the same types of events repeat with the blueprints, thought forms, and habit imprints becoming larger and more complex. The growth and empowerment of these energies is why we often have mixed feelings about situations, conditions, people, concepts, etc. As we move through our many lives, we experience the same type of event but under different circumstances. And in so doing, the blueprint around every event intensifies.

Let's revisit the snake example in Chapter 7 where the child went through three different snake events that built an emotional blueprint of caution and terror of snakes. What if his soul happened to choose a father in the next life (on another planet) that raised snakes for a living, breeding them for food much like the chicken farms we have here? The father was not afraid and valued the snakes as he used them to feed his family and to support his household. Even though the child would have an initial reaction of fear upon seeing the snakes as a toddler, with continual interaction with his father, the child could add interest, worth, and excitement to the snake event. The other response of fear is not lost nor does it disappear. Instead, the emotional blueprint is expanded and made even more complex and now has both anxiety and value attached to the same event. These mixed feelings are understandable. In our own journey, rarely is any event completely black and white for us.

Altered Realities contain not only the emotional blueprints but also the powerful thought forms and the habit imprints that have built up about the snake event (and all other events). They exist as a conglomerate within our energy field in a genuine state of being—though soulless and mindless. They each have their own dwelling place (that we have created through thought), their own social grouping, and their own philosophical beliefs. If you are able to sense at the energetic level, you can talk with them to find out when they were created and what they think, feel, and believe. Although they are soulless and mindless, they are still very real and reflect back to you the thoughts and feelings that make them up— that you gave them! Each individual has created his or her own individually unique Altered Realities. No two people have built the exact same ones, though there can be similarities.

Think about dreams. We wake up in the morning and dreams can seem very real, be simple or complex, have people and places in them. Some we recognize and some we don't. Our dreams clearly are soulless and mindless. They are scenarios that we have created in our sleep state. Altered Realities are very similar. We have created them in our waking state from our thoughts, habits, and emotional responses. Altered Realities carry the full weight of the magnetic attraction.

They have "lives" within the etheric world, and though will-less, they magnetically draw to them the situations and conditions that will empower them. They want to grow in power, not because they have consciousness but because they are magnetic in nature and *all they do* is attract. The strongest ones bring in our repetitive patterns. It is why, for example, some women find themselves drawn to the wrong guy again and again or some men hold onto and relive their high school or college football successes every chance they get. These energies are powerful, having been built up over eons of lifetimes and greatly limit our choices in life. They are our unconscious prison bars holding us stuck in situations and/or conditions where we often don't want to be or are unhappy with. They are made up of thought, emotional, and habitual energy.

Examples of Altered Realities and
How They Could Impact Our Lives

Remember that Altered Realities and the various thought forms that are part of them are aspects of you living in their reality. These thought forms living in their own reality "desire" always to manifest themselves into physical reality. And you are the vehicle of expression that gives birth to these Altered Realities into your physical reality outside of your consciousness.

Altered Realities are often picked up by psychics and can resemble a past life since they are formed as we go through each life. Energetically, these are actual and factual realities in the energetic state. I've provided a few examples from the hundreds I've discovered within my own etheric bodies or those of my friends and clients. Most are negative in nature because they are what I find when working to heal myself or someone else. The positive and joyful ones are not problematic and rarely come up.

ALTERED REALITY 1:
An old lady, hunched over, living in library bookshelves
or a large food storage pantry.
She was a hermit, lonely, fearful, and isolated. If someone came into her environment she scuttled around the shelves until she disappeared. She desired no personal interactions and no possible chance to be disappointed, hurt, or discounted by anyone. She carried with her a dark cloud of despair.

IMPACT: This type of energy identity could indicate why someone would grow up shy, fearful, have few friends, want to hide from the world, have an avoidance reaction to meeting new people, and stay away from all possibilities of being noticed. There would be sadness, loneliness, and, when older, even depression. There may be a weight problem and/or a deep feeling of social awkwardness.

ALTERED REALITY 2:

A court jester, a dwarf who found meaning while playing the fool. He took on a role of protector of the queen, a beautiful yet oppressed woman. He was determined to be of service and stayed within the close circles of the royal house. Yet, over and over he felt he let the queen down because either he couldn't prevent her abuse at the hands of the king or he couldn't do enough to help her in other ways. He carried senses of frustration and failure, and a determination to do it better the next time.

IMPACT: This Altered Reality could be part of someone interested in helping others. However, he may go overboard in his attempts to help while still believing he fell short. There could be a "rescuer" pattern or a quality of wanting to fix other people's lives. There would be an undercurrent of guilt. The person could also be funny and might play the role of the class clown or use humor in other ways to distract attention during difficult situations.

ALTERED REALITY 3:

A person living in a vast and deep hole or cavern. Covering and surrounding the human figure was complete darkness and a weight of misery so heavy the Altered Reality believed it could not stand up. Despairing and joyless, it didn't even remember what light was. I've seen many variations of this with numerous people, and it presented as male, female, and even gender neutral.

IMPACT: When deeply entrenched, this type of Altered Reality can occur in people dealing with real depression and despair. There would be a sense of hopelessness, deep worthlessness, and emotional pain, which could engender some sort of avoidance pattern involving drugs, gambling, OCD, alcohol, etc. There could also be emotional or physical abuse or both, a severe lack of self-love and self-value, and difficulty with maintaining jobs and good relationships.

ALTERED REALITY 4:
A small child on the side of a busy roadway.
Many people rushed past continually, and yet everyone ignored the child. She felt lost, unseen, confused, afraid, hungry, and hopeless.

IMPACT: Someone who felt invisible and unimportant could carry this type of energy identity. She may have grown up in a family with a sibling who was a prodigy or perhaps one who was severely disabled. Or perhaps the parents were absent physically or emotionally. The child would feel like an afterthought. As she moved into adulthood, she may be passed over for promotions and pay raises. She may feel like a victim and think, "If only this or that were different, then I would be happy." Most likely in relationships, the significant other would focus on himself and discount her wants and needs.

ALTERED REALITY 5:
A Mr. Fix-it type with a tool belt
living in a dwelling in constant need of repair.
He continually patched up the dwelling but it was never completely fixed. He was like Sisyphus, always rolling the boulder up the

hill only to have it roll down again. Frustrated, Mr. Fix-it felt he couldn't move on in life, like he was stuck and unable to get out. He knew there was more to existence, yet he knew that he had to take care of the problems here first before he could discover what else there was. Unhappily, he resigned himself to the boredom and repetition in his life.

IMPACT: This Altered Reality could cause a person to suffer and endure the situations and conditions manifested in his life pattern with a sense of hopelessness. The school, jobs, and relationships would be unrewarding. He would put his responsibilities first and self-nurturing last. He would feel great burdens from life but would believe he had no choices. He could bring in a parent and/or spouse that reminded him of his duties and obligations and would likely put chronic guilt trips on him or remind him that to be a "man" he had to endure.

ALTERED REALITY 6:
A person fighting a kind of guerilla warfare.
A man hiding behind huge boulders who would come out from time to time to take potshots at the enemy. He was afraid to confront the enemy directly. He was always in hiding and avoided contact with others. He was also completely unsure of himself and even did not know who the enemy was. Instead of figuring out what was really going on, out of fear, he used the potshot approach to keep the perceived enemy at bay. He was isolated and even kept others away that were friendly.

IMPACT: The Altered Reality may cause an individual to avoid conflict. There would not be an effort to communicate and talk things out. He would make little effort to understand the emotional reactions he had and would inappropriately attack someone out of misunderstanding or just as a way to express the emotions that needed an outlet. This would play out in relationships and in work patterns as passive-aggressive behavior, as the insecurities and fears would affect his interactions. He could also blame others for his own fear and confusion and most likely would avoid looking at his part in personal issues.

Altered Realities can be easy to dismiss like we often dismiss our dreams. We feel that most dreams are insignificant, or we forget them instantly. However, some dreams we pay great attention to; we know that on some level dreams are significant. Altered Realities are vitally important, too. We can dismiss or discount these realities because we tend to believe and give credit to the things we discern with our five senses. Yet, haven't we all accepted many things, such as the existence of ultraviolet rays and their harmful effects to our skin, even though we can't see these rays? And even though we might carry an altered reality that has a male orientation although we are female (or vice versa), it doesn't mean that it isn't as active and effective in our lives as any other one. It just means it was created in lifetimes when we played out of the opposite sex.

Altered Realities can also be harmful, even though scientists haven't been able to measure them. To ignore them is detrimental because Altered Realities, when they gain enough strength, *push* themselves (though not with consciousness) into the physical world when they gain strength enough to be manifested in our *physical reality*. These Altered Realities (and our ignorance of them) are the reason we get so bewildered when we try to figure out why certain unexplainable things occur in our lives.

Although Altered Realities (that live side by side within each of us) may be viewed as separate or secondary to our everyday physical lives, they are a significant force behind all we do.

Recap

- Altered Realities are made up of real energetic identities that live in our etheric bodies. They have their own state of beingness, even though they are soulless, mindless, and will-less.

- They are the conglomerate of the thought, habit, and emotional energies that each of us has created throughout our vast number of lifetimes.

- They are the energetic counterparts to our physical life, and everywhere we go, we have these companions.

- They are the foundation of the soul scrambles we carry and attract in the complex patterns we experience in life.

CHAPTER 22
Creating Our Own Astral Identities: The Astral You

HIGHER SELF QUOTE

Within the Astral dwell many different yous. For instance there is the "you" who lives there who is poor, and who has no money. This Altered Reality has been created by you based on every thought that you have projected in this and other lifetimes that deal with a state of financial lack.

Altered Realities are carried within our personal etheric bodies but also can be duplicated within the Astral. Each individual human soul creates its own specific and individual Astral Altered Realities. Consider that you have a thought within your mind, which is immediately replaced with another thought. One thought follows another thought, and we string these thoughts together throughout our lives. As these thoughts stream through our minds, they not only move into the individual's Thought Form Body but they also move into the Astral, creating within both your etheric bodies and within the Astral a conglomerate of your thoughts. There is in the Astral individual Altered Realities each of us have created from our individual mind that make up all the "thought facts" we have thought in this particular lifetime. These thoughts recreate the "energetic yous" in totality in the Astral. There are many different facets of each individual, which are very real and viable. There is a "you" in various stages as a child, teenager, student, single adult, married, divorced, parent, employee, boss, sibling, widower, etc.

Also, the Astral Altered Reality of the individual becomes greatly empowered through the additional like thought energy from within the Astral itself. The like thought energies from so many billions and billions of others that are carried within the Astral are magnetically drawn in by the magnetic power of the thoughts you have unconsciously placed there. In return, the thought forms and Altered Realities in our own etheric bodies are getting empowered by our own Astral identities! We are *partnered* with our Astral identities and together they facilitate the manifestations of the situations and conditions in our outer reality that are like what we have built within our etheric bodies and the Astral.

What this means is we have a reservoir of energy in the Astral that matches us exactly and is a continual source of energy for our Altered Realities. Here is an analogy: Malaria is a tough disease to conquer. One of the things that make it intractable is the human community is not the only source of the disease. The primate population—monkeys and apes—also carries the parasite. If by some miracle we cured the whole human population of malaria in one day, but we do not remove the additional source of the parasite (from the primate population), the disease would re-infect millions the next day (via the mosquito that is the vector). In the same way, the Astral becomes the reservoir that is continually supplied by the humanities' thoughts, and in return, continually supplies the humanities with magnetic energy that empowers their own etheric bodies. We are continually moving in, through, and around these bands, the energy fields around the Earth. The Astral, remember, is the etheric body of the planet. We and the Astral planes coexist in the same space at all times. This could easily seem very discouraging on the surface but when we become aware of the Astral and how it affects us, we can do something about it.

Let's look at a specific example of how the Astral affects us. You come from a dysfunctional family, and there was a lot of abuse, pain, suffering, and misunderstandings. During your childhood, you created by thought and action the Astral "you" who is equally suffering on multiple levels. You have emerged from childhood feeling and identifying yourself as a victim, a loser, worthless, and miserable. The adult in you, though, is determined to break through the misery and move out of this place. However, every step you take to clear up the confusion, to find other viewpoints and solutions to your problems, is like fighting an uphill battle. This difficulty with your struggle is in part because the energy identities you carry from both levels (your own etheric bodies and your Astral identity—let alone from all your prior lives) are entrenched and rooted in the belief systems you developed during childhood. And these belief systems continue to empower themselves over and over again. Thus, it is no wonder that it seems incredibly difficult to find your way out of a Soul Scramble into a place of understanding and enlightenment.

Every soul has had to find great courage and determination to get to wherever they are. Each individual deserves a round of applause and great support. It takes courage for all of us to step forward and move down that path. The journey through the Human Kingdom Universe from the first lifetime out of the Animal Kingdom to the point where one is ready to move into the 5th Dimensional level takes eons of time.

The great news for us (as I keep saying), here and now on this planet, is that the frequency of energy is high and expanding rapidly. This means not only that there are expanded concepts present that can help with your journey, but also the process of resolving your difficult patterns by unraveling the Soul Scrambles is happening at an ever-accelerated rate. There is hope and help and it is easy to use our inner powerful Light that will neutralize and demagnetize all of these disastrous energy identities. There is no reason to fear. There is only reason to be aware and excited by the opportunity for change.

CHAPTER 23
Solidified Astral Truths

The Astral and Truth

Contained within the Astral are *solidified* thought forms and Altered Realities that have crystallized over the time that the planet has housed the humanities. The Higher Selves call these *solidified truths.* To review briefly, even in the highest level of the Originating Source, *truth* does not exist because from moment-to-moment, what is seen as truth evolves and grows and experiences and becomes an *ever-evolving* truth. There is My Truth and Your Truth but no *"The Truth."*

However, contained within the Astral, there are various realities created that could be viewed as solidified truths. This means that the energies of some of these Altered Realities have been so heavily intensified over time, they are perceived as being hard facts. The beliefs in these truths are so powerful that they have become *absolute and unquestionable.* Let's look at examples to illustrate some of these solidified truths, keeping in mind there is no attempt to convince and/or upset anyone.

- There are some very orthodox Christian religions, past and present that emphasize the idea of the devil and satan. Therefore, there is a very real devil Altered Reality in the Astral, with horns and pitchfork. He's been created through thought.

- There is also the Astral Jesus, in fact, more than one. One Astral Jesus suffers, weeps, and hurts and has a pattern of betrayal and martyrdom because he's been placed there on that cross daily by centuries of religionists and metaphysicians who perceive him as such. Another is the Astral Jesus who is the Son of God, who sacrificed himself for all humanity and who asks for belief in him to gain salvation and a place in Heaven. This is not meant to upset anyone who has a deep and caring connection to Jesus. It is only one of many types of solidified truths that the Higher Selves described to us. It is not meant to be a description of the true nature of Christ.

- There are Astral gods as well. We have a god that is male, a god that is female, and a god that carries the vibrations of revenge, the punisher, and the judgment maker. There is a god that sits on the throne in Heaven, determining who will be allowed into Heaven and who will not. There are many gods in the Astral from every religion and every spiritual practice. Some, of course, have positive traits and others have the more negative aspects because it took eons of time for the humanities to ascribe the higher concepts to the god(s) they worshipped.

The more time the Astral Altered Reality was empowered, the more solidified it became and the more intensely it would empower any belief systems we may have carried in our own etheric bodies. This makes it difficult for individuals to question their own belief systems as their own truths may have become solidified and intractable.

How Do the Solidified Truths Affect Us?

HIGHER SELF QUOTE:

When an individual (who was raised in a culture that believed God is an all-punishing God) prays to God, that individual unleashes the Astral thought form of the revengeful/punishing God into the unconscious of all the souls on the planet that carry the like belief.

We already know that the individual etheric bodies and the Astral planes continually empower each other. But how else does the Astral and its entrenched solidified truths affect us? Because the solidified truth energy is so powerful and is in literature, lore, cultures, and surrounds us everywhere, we tend to go along with it, not questioning its validity. Even if the question comes up, the idea is present everywhere and we would think, "Who are we to doubt?" This unquestioning acceptance holds us stuck. It slows our process of growing awareness and our movement up the frequency levels of conscious thought.

Let's say we have been brought up in the hellfire-and-damnation type of culture. Our parents were very religious, and we took on their church's beliefs and all the fear that it instilled in us. We carry those thoughts and feelings in our etheric bodies. Now, when we call on God, this "big bad god" from the Astral floats down because it magnetically matches what we are carrying and calling on. This further empowers our energetic field and makes the belief structure we carry stronger and harder to shift away from. It holds us stuck on one of our stepping-stones because we have built our house there. And it is not a good thing to enhance a fear blueprint as we all carry enough fear to last a lifetime. Also, these Altered Realities work well with each other so that fear in one helps empower the fear of another.

Not only would this energy empower your energies that carry the belief in the punishing god, but it also would empower the energy identities of others that carry the same beliefs. Fortunately, the Astral god of punishment can only affect those humans with that particular form of god already present in their thought form bodies. Energy of an Astral punishing god would not (could not) affect a Buddhist who was never involved in that vibration. Except, here's the kicker. An individual who is a Buddhist in this lifetime could have in lifetimes past been in one or several cultural patterns with a belief in a punishing god. Remember, we all carry forward all of our energy identities from all the previous lifetimes and that type of god would still be in that individual's Thought Form Body. Thus, most every soul could be affected by this unleashing of the Astral god because at some point in time the individual probably has worshipped such a God.

We need to understand that the terms we choose to use are important because of the heavy-duty influence they carry at the Astral level. Consciously, we are not trying to call in negative god energy, so there is no intent. However, it happens when we put out that fervent call for God. (This is **not** a dissertation against God and is not meant to offend or upset anyone. It's only to indicate the terms we use and the thoughts we think can open us to these Astral energies.) This is the primary reason the Higher Selves asked Joan Culpepper many years ago to start using the term Originating Source instead of the term God or other alternative terms. They did not want us to unleash any of the negative Astral god energy and the term Originating Source was not a solidified, rigidified Astral truth. The secondary reasons—that this "new" term carried no cultural or spiritual bias (such as the terms Allah, Buddha, Jehovah, and God would) and no preconceived images (such as god in man's image, god sitting on the throne, god in Heaven, etc.,)—were very important, as well, but not as important as the problems with the Astral energies.

Now that the Astral has been explained, we may better understand the wisdom of being careful with our words.

Other Astral Solidified Truths

What else do we see in the Astral? There are many Astral demons, for in the minds and thoughts of many of the humanities over time, demons were used to explain the evil in the world. There are dragons and unicorns and gargoyles. Even Old Saint Nick (Santa Claus) has a large place in the Astral energy world.

Also, the Astral energies are active around institutions—both religious and mental. These operate from the unconscious level. For example, a minister that preaches hellfire and damnation calls on these Astral entities from a millennium of thought energy without realizing it. People who come to this kind of institutional gathering are getting a lot of energy from the Astral and they're "taking these energies home with them" in their etheric bodies.

These Astral energies are added to their own force field of energy, empowering what they already carry.

We also have Astral wars going on. When we get angry and fight with someone, we call in the warring frequencies that are in place in the Astral and draw them magnetically into our own Thought Form Body. Those in actual wars call in these energies on a continual basis. Many times, it is at the unconscious level but sometimes, with war rallies for example, there is a conscious call out. Sometimes those at war sporadically ritualize the calling forth of these Astral energies, though they may not understand exactly what they are doing. When a war rally uses negative words such as hate, hate, revenge, revenge, war, war, kill, kill (whoever the enemy may be), the Astral Altered Realities move into the space of those calling and could be viewed symbolically like the killer dogs a police force may use.

We know what can happen when there is a mob. Whether it is a lynch mob, a riot, or any negative mass grouping, the Astral energies of anger, rage, self-righteousness, and revenge are activated. Often, people in mobs take actions they would never do in other circumstances. Afterward, they may feel shame, guilt, or confusion. The Astral is why. The additional power of the Astral energy that is brought in by so many simultaneously is combined with the like energy that the mob individuals carry themselves. This combined energy can be so strong, it propels the individuals in the mob to act in a cohesive manner—the mob mentality. The Astral is a powerful energy source that affects us all whether we believe it exists or not.

These Astral Altered Realities can do nothing to us that we do not allow. Even though we give permission at the soul level, we still have our reason and conscious mind to make decisions. In some cases, it is as if our reason is weak and it is. But we aren't helpless or powerless. We have the incredible ability to neutralize our own energy identities and hopefully, by the end of the book, every reader will be motivated to do it for more than one reason.

What about the Positive Astral?

Since there are also positive Astral bands, it would be normal to surmise that positive Astral Altered Realities could be as helpful as the negative ones are harmful. In some ways they can, although there is much less of the positive Astral and those energies will only help if we carry like energies. The good news is, on the planet at this point in time, most people have some matching energy. So invoking the positive Astral energy could empower the like. Would the positive Astral have solidified truths?

Yes, whether positive or negative, we find these entrenched truths where we don't even question. This is the situation with Astral angels. In the same way that we have so many solidified truths in the dark Astral, we also, over the millennia, have created intensely beautiful Astral angels in one or more of the positive Astral bands. And when we call on angels, we invoke these energy streams that move down and into our energy fields. We might pray or call in that which we believe are actual beings, but we are also calling on the Astral Altered Realities of angels. Though soulless and mindless, they would seem very real and loving. This energy confirms our belief in angels as we see, sense, and feel at some gut level they are there for us. It conforms to what we have been taught for centuries; it fits because all of our thoughts have gone into creating these angels in all the forms that we have believed exist.

QUOTE FROM JEROME

*It is fairly common within the Human Kingdom for individuals to worship and place us in a state of idolatry, to be in awe of, to feel grateful and feel gratitude that we, as Masters, would stoop to a lower level. As a result, **it creates an inner need for those individuals to look to us externally as some kind of god.***

The question is: Are Astral Truths from the positive Astral planes as problematic for us in the same way the negative Astral truths are? The answer is yes. Any solidified truth holds us stuck. Be careful about looking to externals as saviors, as answers, and/or as the ones that are going to fix your life. If we invoke the angels to give us answers to tell us what to do, we may get an answer, as angel Altered Realities have been given thought energy that includes answers. However, the answers are coming from the vast thought processes of the humanities of all times and are not relevant to your life and where you are in the moment. It is like asking a question of a recorder that has recorded random people's responses to the same question and then hitting the play button for your answer. The auto response from the Astral angels would be based on what has been programmed into it from the accumulation of thought energy over the millennia. It will be mindless and soulless. For that reason, if we have a question, it is best to look within. If we have the question, we also have the answer.

In addition, and perhaps even more importantly, if we are looking to angels for salvation and to be saved, this too could trap us. Only we can save ourselves. We feel like the Astral angels will save us because we sense the loving energy they carry. But instead, these Altered Realities could give us a false sense of security, holding us firm to the idea that we need to wait for someone, something else to do it for us. Looking to the externals distracts us from acknowledging and using our true power—our Pure Soul Essence. It is who we truly are and we carry it within. Counting on angels to fix your life, to save you from difficult times, and to heal your hurts and wounds would mean a very long wait.

Fortunately, with time, humanity does get past some of the Astral solidified truths and make progress. It is never hopeless. An example would be the idea that the Earth was flat. For a long time, the humanities on the planet believed this to be true. Fortunately, with Columbus, other explorers, and space travel, this truth was dispelled. However, this idea is still present in the Astral as an Altered Reality and within our personal etheric bodies! And, despite the preponderance of evidence from all corners of the globe, there are some that still believe this concept. They belong to the Flat Earth Society and are greatly affected by this Astral solidified truth. Perhaps these people played an authoritative role in multiple past lives within the scientific or spiritual communities that fought for this flat view of the world in all earnestness and genuine belief. They may carry much stronger altered realities along this view within their etheric bodies than most of us. However, it is important not to judge them (or anyone for that matter) by thinking they are illogical or stupid or dismiss them in any way.

How the Astral Truths Are Part of Our Journey to Awareness

As the individuals upon this planet (and every planet) open to higher and higher levels of understanding (higher frequencies of thought), many times they come face-to-face with these solidified realities—the truths that are defined based on what the Astral of the planet is carrying. As explained, in the Astral of Earth, there are solidified truths as they pertain to every philosophy, religion, and process that have gone into the idea of higher levels of philosophical seeking and searching. Every philosophy, regardless of the level upon which it has processed, lives within the Astral of Earth as a very real, solidified and unquestionable truth. As individuals awaken to higher and higher concept levels, they often reach and lock into whatever truths the philosophy or belief systems they are processing which are contained in the Astral. Because solidified truths are the most entrenched and foundational Astral Thought Forms, they make it more problematic for the seeker and searcher to move past a truth they have locked into.

It is difficult for many individuals to disengage from these powerful truths. And as awakening proceeds and the individual questions these entrenched truths, there can be great confusion, unease, frustration, and anxiety. This is an extremely important activity and one that is the heart of the evolutionary process of every human. Each individual, in order to expand and grow, needs to discern what truths it believes and follows. As the soul moves through the Human Kingdom, its ideas of truth will expand, leading it further up the human evolutionary scale as its limiting belief systems fall away. Again, the Astral truths make this more difficult. They have great power and feed our own belief systems, which can hold us strongly to whatever limited truths we carry. It makes our limited truth feel comfortable, right, and secure.

The Higher Selves always encourage individuals to pursue any path they desire to pursue. And they never promote the idea that what they say is the "be all and end all." Nor do they promote the idea that we should attempt to sway individuals at any level from the path they happen to be on at any point in time. It is important that each individual explore their truths to see what they feel or don't feel about the truth. **This is our journey** and if we change our minds about the truth we focus on, we need to be certain. We need to know at the heart level that when we decide a truth is no longer right for us, we don't make that decision because someone else told us it is so. Then, our move to the next level of truth is on the firmest of foundations.

The Battle Within

As with all types of frequency levels, the Astral planes have layers within layers. The very bottom layer of the black Astral band is the savage level of the human community. This means it carries the stone-age mentality. Energy streams that are more animal than human in nature predominately govern this band. All the humanities evolve from the Animal Kingdom, and the complete human nature takes many eons of time to come to full flower within the human soul.

It is these savage Astral personalities in the darkest of the Astral levels that could be called the "legions of darkness" named in modern day scripture. They are the enemy battling for the soul of the humanities in the coming age of enlightenment. Every soul has to deal with its thought forms, empowered by the Astral energies. The battle is *within* each individual as each person finds his or her way through the misunderstandings, solidified truths, and false realities while moving through the journey to higher and higher frequencies of awareness. It is not about a massive planetary war with man against man. Could there be wars? Yes. But *the war* is within. We each have to deal with our own internal demons of the mind—those beliefs that hold us stuck and are empowered and entrenched — with the help of Astral energies. It is a difficult road, but we come equipped with all that we need in order to be successful.

The more we neutralize, the weaker our magnets become, lessening the magnetic attraction energy that draws from the Astral. We need to neutralize, neutralize, and neutralize. As long as we have energy identities, we have magnets bringing in more energy to empower them. In addition, we are not limited to neutralizing the energy identities within our own etheric bodies. *We also need to neutralize our own Astral identities.* Of course, it would also be beneficial if we helped neutralize the Astral itself to reduce the endless reservoir that magnetically supplies the food empowering what we carry. Working on the complete Astral is best accomplished in a group setting, but we can easily address our own Astral identities.

CHAPTER 24
Soul Transition at Death from Body to Heaven

What Happens to a Soul upon Death?

When an individual dies, the soul begins its journey to Heaven by moving through the chakra system (energy exchange points) of the Astral planes. It is this movement that creates the effect of the tunnel of white light that so many with near-death experiences have reported.

The Astral bands—from the darkest to the lightest and all levels in between—contains the equivalent of nine chakra centers. The seven major chakras that we know of relate to the body (plus the two that are located on either side of the crown chakra) are also present within the Astral levels just as they are carried by every other state or condition. (An example of another state of being is that each mineral, animal, and plant particle has its own chakras as well.)

Within the Astral, there are nine main levels. And within each of the levels, there are nine levels. The 8th and 9th levels are the birth canal into the next highest level of understanding. It is the 8th and 9th level of the Astral that is the entryway into what we consider to be Heaven. When a human lays aside the body, it moves through the Astral chakras (the tunnel of Light) in order to reach Heaven. This is what happens to the great majority of souls.

A common viewpoint is one that says when a soul stays attached to someone or some condition on Earth, once it lays aside the body, the soul is not yet in Heaven. There is much attention paid to helping these souls "go to the Light," when in fact many have already gone through the tunnel and are already in the Human Kingdom Heavens. Even if a soul stays around a person or a place in the physical world, this is not an indicator that the soul has not moved into Heaven. Instead, it is often an example of a Soul Set, which was described in Chapter 1:

> *There are times when someone gives up the body (dies) when that soul is overwrought with distress, jealousy, rage, vengeance, obsessive love, or other emotional blueprints. These powerful emotions are usually directed at other people (or situations and conditions) from the experiences, events, or people of that life. They may take on what is called a Soul Set—the body is laid aside and the soul continues to live through and play out of the mind level of the prior life. The individuals who play out of a Soul Set would be "stuck" in their own evolutionary movement forward. Because they maintain their emotional focus on various situations, places, or people from their prior lives, they aren't continuing to learn and expand their own*

awareness. These souls may or may not be already in the Human Kingdom Heavens. However, either way, they are intently focused on what they have left behind.

This type of Soul Set process is common with many different scenarios. It is the basis for hauntings and ghosts. The idea that all such souls are not yet in Heaven could be viewed as one of the solidified truths. One of the reasons for this misunderstanding is that we think of Heaven as being up in the sky or out there in the galaxy somewhere. When we think of souls who hang around people and places on Earth, we could believe they are not yet in Heaven. If we keep in mind that there is but a thin veil between the disincarnate world of Heaven and physical world here on Earth, it may be easier to understand a soul could process into Heaven and could still keep its immediate focus on what it left behind. When a stuck soul is ready to move into the *light of understanding,* it signifies that it has acquired a willingness to continue on its soul's journey forward.

There are also times when a soul dies and moves upward through the various levels of the Astral that a partial aspect of a soul containing heavily weighted negativity can be pulled out and separated from the whole soul. The magnetic energy of the mindless and soulless Altered Realities within the dark Astral has a pull so strong that a detachment can result. When separation occurs, the fragment of a soul's beingness, now disconnected from its conglomerate, stays in place in the lower Astral. Of course, that partial soul fragment has to agree to the disconnection. This leaching out or separation process could only be done if the soul's energy identities had a very heavy strain of matching negative energies. Most souls on this planet now would not be carrying a predominant darkness in their Soul/Mind. Therefore, most of the soul fragments trapped in the dark Astral have already been there for a long, long time.

The soul fragments caught within that magnetic band of the blackest Astral may think they are in the burning fires of hell, or depending on their belief system, somewhere else as horrible. When a fragment of a soul gets trapped there, the remaining soul energy of the conglomerate soul continues to move upward and stops at a higher plane of the Astral, the one that best matches the remainder of its being. No soul is able to move into Heaven without the totality of the soul process. These two parts of the soul would remain in the Astral until they are reunited. When this occurs, the soul will move into the Human Kingdom Heavens whole and complete in its conglomerate beingness.

While these soul fragments live within the dark Astral (because they are actual souls and not just energy identities with magnetic energy), they are actively empowering the negative Astral with their thoughts. They feed the Astral on a moment-to-moment basis just as the humanities in body would be doing, and it happens with the darkest, most negative level. Therefore the savage levels of the Astral are getting empowered even though most of the humanities on our planet are no longer at the savage frequency level. (Note: Living in primitive or traditional tribal societies does *not* mean that a human is at the lower frequency levels of human.)

When souls are stuck in the Astral and are not yet in Heaven, they are not able to go to Heaven's schools, see the counselors or educators, or go through the reincarnation process. They are not evolving. Does this mean that they are lost? No. They can be stuck for centuries and millennia. But there is no timetable for any soul to meet. And there is help for them all.

The Astral Clean-Up Process

The freeing of the soul energies within the Astral is greatly beneficial in that it lessens the power of the Altered Realities that permeate it, thereby rendering those energy identities less potent.

There are highly evolved souls in the Human Kingdom Heavens—both 5th Dimensional Higher Selves and those that work with and under the supervision of the Higher Selves—that help with neutralizing the Astral planes. These Astral workers work on two levels: they neutralize the Altered Realities within the dark Astral bands and they free the fragmented souls from the dark Astral.

First, working from within the lighter Astral bands, the Astral workers take the light and love infused there and direct it to the darker levels to bring in healing (by neutralizing) to the dark Astral bands. This process has been ongoing in recent decades as a way to lessen the magnetic pressures on the planet and the humanities as we move toward the New Age infusion. Because this is a significant time on the planet now, the group of Astral workers has been increasing with more and more volunteers. There is a large planet-wide cleanup process that is ongoing.

The Astral plane Altered Realities have no mind and no soul—it is energy. Astral workers can project this light and love into the dark Astral to neutralize it without the need to worry about trespassing Free Will. When it comes to the soul fragments in the Astral, the process is now one that must deal with the Free Will pattern. Those Astral workers are not able to trespass and must wait for any soul fragment *to choose* to move into the Light.

There is a process where the workers provide the opportunity for the fragmented souls to choose freedom. What the Astral workers do for the soul fragments (and I am simplifying it here) is to create a large tunnel moving through the chakra centers from the lightest level of the Astral down into the heaviest level. The light of the highest level is then sent down through the tunnel. When it is projected through, it is directed toward those Astral soul fragments in the dark bands. In this way, the beautiful and loving energy can and does attract those that are stuck there.

A vortex motion is created by working these energy streams through the nine chakra centers. The hope is that the soul fragments in place would be attracted to the vortex and would allow themselves to be pulled in and then shot upward into the higher Astral levels. This shoot-up process deals only with those entities in a fragmented soul pattern. Due to the Free Will process, the soul fragments must volunteer to move into the light. They cannot be forced or pushed. Once these fragmented souls choose to move into the vortex of light, they move up and rejoin the rest of their soul process at the higher levels of the Astral. They become a conglomerate soul once more and are able to move into Heaven proper. When the fragmented soul has successfully moved into the vortex of light, become whole, and reached Heaven, the fragmented soul views the experience as if it has reached salvation. It requires an enormous amount of group energy for the Astral workers to process the Astral facet personalities into their proper form as a total soul process.

In addition to the powerful reconnection of a soul process, its return to Heaven, and its ability to now move forward in evolutionary movement, there is another powerful effect as a result of the removal of those stuck in the Astral. The mindless and soulless Astral Altered Realities in place there are also greatly weakened when these soul fragments are vortexed up and out. Why? Because it deprives the black Astral energies from the consistent feeding of thoughts from these soul fragments. Simultaneously, the vortexes also bathe the dark Astral Altered Realities in powerful light energy, further lessening their power and helping to bring the dark Astral to a higher frequency rate.

What Can We Do?

There are things that we can do in the formed state (in body) which lessens the powerful thought energy from the humanities.

The darkness of the Astral has not been completely removed, but because of the Astral workers neutralizing the thought energy and because the continual seeding process from the fragmented souls has been reduced, the blacker Astral levels have begun to move from a dark to medium gray. Divine Light can easily neutralize the dark energy identities created from human thought. But the massive energy of the dark Astral level needs massive Divine Light to lessen its power, particularly because of the moment-to-moment feeding of the Astral by the thoughts of the billions of humans on the planet and by the remaining soul fragments.

One way we can assist those in place in the light Astral is simply to send our light to them when we are in an amalgamated state. With the help of the Astral workers and with our help in the formed state the planet will have an easier, more accelerated movement (as it is also going through its own evolution) as will those humans upon it who struggle to expand, change, balance, heal, understand, and forgive as the power of the Astral Altered Realities are reduced.

Conclusion

These concepts are not meant to challenge or disparage anyone's beliefs. It doesn't matter what you believe in this life, if you carry a matching energy from any life, you will attract in the like energy from the Astral. You may or may not be thinking about global warming or angels or famine or God or anything, and yet you could still be vulnerable to Astral energy that is called in by others. When you pray, think about, concentrate on, talk about, or dwell on anything, you are unaware that there is a whole unconscious exchange going on that can sabotage what we are consciously intending. This is not a good thing. And this is why neutralizing needs to be done! The Astral is one reason why it can be hard to change and why we need to support all those, including ourselves, who are struggling to do so.

We all come into our lives with Souls Scrambles and often our goal at the soul level is to resolve these. To facilitate that process, this Astral energy has to be addressed. Otherwise, the scrambles can be more difficult to break out of. It is not that it cannot be done as we have seen countless examples of successes. With more understanding however, there can be a huge increase in the success rate.

Much of the emphasis in this book is on the disincarnate state as a significant part of the journey through the eons of time in the Human Kingdom. For this reason, the Astral is an important topic to cover. And while it may appear on reading this section that our sole focus should be on neutralizing our Astral imprints, using the neutralizing process on our own etheric bodies is of *utmost importance*.

You may be wondering now how to connect all you have learned to your own life and how it applies to you. Part V, "Connecting the Dots," offers a personalized example of one of my own major Soul Scrambles. From there, guidance is offered as to how to apply it to your own life.

PART V

Connecting the Dots

CHAPTER 25

A Personal Example of a Soul Scramble: Mom and I

Souls involved in conflicts together are in agreement (at the unconscious level through the Altered Reality). The agreement will be carried out unless one or both souls involved make a decision (out of the Free Will pattern) to recreate and move away from that specific situation.

Most of us, when beginning or even when in the middle of our journey toward awareness, have not and would not understand our scrambles—where they originated or how we pre-planned to figure them out. We all have begun or will begin at ground zero—a place where we are unhappy for some reason. That is where I began, in my childhood where the manifestation of my scramble started to unfold in this life.

Mom and I—The Circumstances

HIGHER SELF QUOTE
(GIVEN TO JANET IN A PERSONAL READING FOR A CLIENT)

In the process of change and purification, the energy will move out and remove toxic conditions from your life. These changes can be viewed as upheavals. If you will stand within the center of the removal and be calm like the eye of a hurricane, you will see that your life is being re-sculpted in order to make it a work of art. You will then be able to move out more easily, freely, and happily into the changes of the total destiny pattern.

This is not a "Mommy Dearest" type of story. Not only am I not here to hammer my mother as a bad parent, I have also received her blanket permission to write this story, as she is proud to have been part of my healing. She wants this story told for the help it will provide to others. Also, both of us are fortunate that we successfully followed through on all we had hoped and planned by choosing to be together in this lifetime. The hopes and plans were made prior to birth, and I portray the difficulties and struggles as they felt to me at the time but not for the purpose of denigrating my mother. It is to illustrate how wounded I was, how deep the misunderstandings were, and to help others grasp the powerful healing that occurred.

I was an only child growing up in Connecticut when both parents were killed instantly in a car accident. I was 18 months old. Living nearby were an aunt and uncle who took me in immediately and adopted me five years later. It is the second mom that I talk about here whenever I use the term Mom. My two moms were sisters.

Of course, losing my parents was extremely traumatic for me. This very personal experience (rather than societal conditioning) made a serious impact upon and greatly empowered my belief systems. I had hoped this would happen at the soul level pre-birth, though I was so young at the time, I didn't understand any of it. One day my parents just didn't come home. I would have had little conscious awareness and certainly no concept as to what death was. In a state of complete confusion, I was moved into a very busy home, as my new mom had three children of her own and one more on the way. There wasn't time to focus on me or to help me heal due to all the demands a young mother experiences. What resulted was a very difficult relationship between Mom and me.

Over the years, there were many arguments and much tension between us. I felt unloved, unheard, unappreciated, undeserving, and unimportant. I also felt inarticulate, afraid, anxious, falsely accused, and carried regret that my biological parents had died. I did not feel like a part of the family; I felt like an outsider. I have no childhood memories of my mom telling me she loved me or hugging me. There was very little personal interaction between us and most often when we did interact, she found ways to belittle me, to find fault, and to make it clear I was a thorn in her side. Since I didn't know any differently, I came to accept this as the norm. But it took its toll. Like so many in dysfunctional family situations I came away from my childhood feeling like a victim and hopeless.

My awareness grew as the years passed. I realized that I was unhappy and afraid but that others didn't feel the same way. Shyness was rampant; I was anxious all the time, petrified to walk into a room, a store, or a gathering of any sort alone and afraid to talk to anyone I didn't know (or hardly knew). I developed my own avoidance technique to deal with my fear early in childhood. I would move my eyes into a partial cross-eyed place. It was subtle enough that no one could notice, but it was completely effective in blurring my vision so I could hide from others. If I couldn't see them, they couldn't see me. I did this into my teen years when I brought the habit into full consciousness and made the decision to stop. It took determination because it was so ingrained. Along with the eye blurring, I became good at presenting a façade of "I'm okay." I believed if I pretended hard enough, it would be so. It got me through those painful years in a way that I didn't have to expose or express myself.

I tried to reach out to my mom as a teenager but my attempts mostly fell on deaf ears.

She said, "I don't like all this frank talk."

Fortunately, I had close friends who nurtured me and gave me a clearer idea of what family could mean. What developed was my determination to not give up on myself but to find answers. Instead of thinking Mom had to be the one to change, I looked for answers in other ways. I became deeply motivated to "fix myself."

First, I began moving—literally. I went to college in the South, then I moved to Arizona, Vermont, New York City, and finally, Los Angeles. Some people suggested that I disconnect from the family completely. I never chose that option. Instead, I moved away to avoid recurrences of hurts and wounds and to find out who I really was. Second, I went into therapy as a junior in college. I didn't know what else to do. The constant anxiety ate at me, and it was hard to go through each day with so much fear, even though I rarely knew what I was afraid of. I did not want to live that way anymore.

Therapy was great. It helped me gain perspective. I saw the good things I had in life, which added balance to my viewpoints. I appreciated all the resources my family had provided, the good education and the opportunities made possible as a result. And I also came to understand my patterns and belief systems. For example, a self-identity I had locked into despite excellent grades was that I was "inarticulate." I believed I couldn't properly express myself because of my many experiences growing up when no one listened. I had assumed (unconsciously) that no one would ever be able to understand me because I spoke so poorly. Therapy helped me realize I was articulate, and I had misinterpreted others not listening to me as being my fault. Wow! What a great breakthrough! There were many other A-ha! moments. For 15 years, I went to three different therapists totaling six years of therapy. Of course, I also grew up in those same years and learned a lot from experiences I went through. I matured, became a responsible adult, got an undergraduate degree in anthropology, did field work with Native Americans, got a masters in business (MBA), had two children, and struggled to figure out what to do in life.

I also came to understand more about my mother from a psychological perspective. I realized she was insecure and lacked self-esteem and self-love. One summer I was back East visiting my parents while my sisters and their kids were there. One of the children, Lisa, who was about two or three, played outside with older cousins for an hour or two. When she toddled back into the house and into the crowd of people who were around, she saw her mom and ran toward her with a big hug. My mom was visibly upset.

She said to Lisa, "Don't you love me anymore?"

Lisa had no idea what she meant but squealed with delight as she hugged her grandmother.

My mom was upset that Lisa ran to her own mom first before her and thought that meant Lisa didn't love her!

Mom didn't have the many opportunities we have available to us today because she was born before many women joined the workplace. She was extremely intelligent and could possibly have been a CEO of a Fortune 500 company. Instead, she volunteered, often moving to the top one in charge. For example, she became the president of the alumni associations at both her boarding school and her college. She never received a paycheck, the reinforcement of worth we mostly take for granted now. She caught up with meeting societal expectations for her socio-economic level and background. She became a gourmet cook, a big entertainer, and often did things because it was expected of her rather than because it meant something to her. I don't think she was even self-aware enough to know how stressed she felt with the pressures of entertaining.

What follows are the theories I developed as to why she and I had so many problems. First, Mom did not get along very well with her sister, my birth-mom. I thought perhaps the animosity between them was transferred to me. Second, I could see that Mom made choices based on how they would appear to others rather than what was really important to her. I felt she must have taken me into the family because of how it looked, not because she wanted five children or because she loved me. Once done, she had to live with the burden of two new girls, now five in all, with the balancing act being a difficult one. Therapy enabled me to see my mother as a real person with her own issues and problems. I saw her as wounded herself, struggling to do the best she could. It still hurt that she didn't love me, that I was unimportant to her, and that she would find fault with me every chance she got. Yet, I always wanted to find a way to improve our relationship.

Three important things did *not* happen for me as a result of therapy. One: therapy did not resolve my issues with mom. Understanding helped but was not enough. Two: I never got over the chronic anxiety. It was present whether things were going well or not, and I could not find a way to get rid of it. Taking medication never was an option, as it never occurred to me at the time. Three: even though I could recognize my patterns and understood their origins (at least based on the therapeutic model of this life), I could not seem to change the patterns. I got to the point that whenever a "mother" figure came into my life, someone who found ways to judge me as inadequate, I could see right away that my problematic "mother" pattern was repeating itself. Even though I had moved away from my mom, I was having similar issues with others whether it was a boss or a coworker, a mate, or even someone I thought of as a friend. I realized I brought the pattern with me and could not escape it. I didn't want the pattern so I kept searching for answers.

How did this pattern with my mother affect my life? I'm sure most of you will understand that feeling unloved and as if I was the problem affected all my basic viewpoints about myself. I felt undeserving, unworthy, a failure, a loser, helpless, and hopeless. And these beliefs permeated my life on every level. I had no self-confidence, chronic anxiety, complete self-doubt, and whatever good was in my life, I often didn't see it or couldn't accept it. Basically, I saw myself as an emotional basket case.

Joan Culpepper and the Higher Self Information

HIGHER SELF QUOTE

Practice makes perfect. In any instance, when one is training to reach into higher levels, it is necessary to utilize those exercises as often as is possible. There are many things that go on in the everyday mundane world to distract your attention, but it is the responsibility of each individual to make the time and take the effort to instigate these practices in order to continue to grow and expand beyond each level. Too many people view Joan as having effortlessly sat down one day and Eureka! the skies opened and information poured in. This, of course, is untrue and it was in the consistent practice of working as often as possible with every individual that she was able to move one step at a time into the point she currently resides. Consistent practice is needed and necessary on the part of individual.

Hello Fortune! Meeting Joan Culpepper was the luckiest moment of my life. This was the next step I brought in for myself, though I didn't realize at first that I had co-created the meeting. I was a complete newbie to alternative ways of thinking and perceiving. But from the first day, I knew it was something incredible. The Higher Selves in that first reading in 1983 gave me a technique to deal with my anxiety and within a few days, it was gone! From that moment on, I was sold and took all of Joan's classes and workshops and never missed an opportunity to learn more.

The Higher Selves told me in a reading with Joan that before I was born, I knew my biological parents would die young. I had agreed to be their child, as they needed some type of energy from me in order to progress in their evolutionary process. We had all co-created this before birth and I had forgotten (as is normal). So after they died, I blamed myself (as children often do) and had not gotten over it. The person I planned to be with long-term in this life was Mom. She and I had issues to deal with and had agreed (again ahead of time) that she would bring me into the family. The Higher Selves had not yet explained the term Soul Scramble, but later I came to understand that her patterns and my patterns fit together perfectly. Her behavior toward me would activate my preexisting patterns so severely that I would do exactly what I did. My severe pain was the great motivator to drive me into a seeking and searching pattern to heal myself. My part of the bargain, though, was to then help Mom heal her pattern; but this came much later.

First, I learned about neutralizing. And I worked on all my issues, including my relationship with my mother. (By work I mean doing the neutralizing and empowering.) The information about neutralizing was as new to Joan as it was to all of us. We learned together from the Higher Selves during Joan's Wednesday classes. Despite confusions with the new information, I worked on my patterns/belief systems (both regarding Mom and many other things) slowly but surely. I was unable to get information from the Higher Selves for myself as yet, so at this point, I just worked on the issues and problems I was aware of.

Three years later, Joan reflected Charlie. Pieces of the puzzle about how the soul works and how it relates to us in this life began to make sense. I started to see my relationship with Mom from that larger perspective (the helicopter) that I've talked about and our difficulties became opportunities for me rather than problems. I also realized that my patterns were in place before I was born into this life and that it wasn't Mom's fault. That was huge. I saw Mom in the role of motivator who triggered all that I carried. This shift in my thinking spurred me to dig deeper and deeper into the well of Altered Realities I carried and to neutralize them. And I did.

The next jump in improvement came when I learned about the Astral and the self-identities we had all built there. Immediately, I started including all my Astral Altered Realities in my neutralizing exercises. At first, I neutralized the Altered Realities I had built during this life. Then I called in all the Astral realities from every life that I had on this planet. And lastly, I called in my entire conglomerate Astral identities from the entire Human Kingdom Universe! I didn't want to leave anything to chance. I wanted to move out of the victim mode and did not want to continue to empower whatever residue or dregs I had left within my own etheric bodies. Neutralizing these Astral energies had the physical effect of actually making me feel lighter. It was as if a huge load of pressure was taken off my back. It was this noticeable lessening of the "weight" on my physical body that told me in my gut just how powerful that negative Astral energy was and how important it was to neutralize it.

During this time, though I consistently worked on myself, I did not consistently work on my relationship issues with Mom. Being 3,000 miles away from her, I tended to do more work just before a trip East, while there, and then maybe for a couple weeks after returning. I also neutralized a situation when I would see a "mother figure" show up in my life. I was rewarded by the reduction of the stresses and strains when I was with Mom. Problems were still there—she was who she was—but I was not nearly as hurt or upset by her. I was still cautious when around her, as I still didn't want to give her cause to say negative things to me. But there was perceptible improvement.

One indicator of the positive shift occurred when my father became ill. He had indolent lymphoma and from diagnosis to death he lived about six years. He did not suffer much and for a while he was even convinced they had misdiagnosed him. Toward the end, however, he was quite ill though he still took nothing but Tylenol for the pain. At this point, his five daughters (including me) would take turns going to Florida where my parents lived so that Mom always had some support and help. When it was my turn to go, the decision was made that another sister would have to be there at the same time, so that Mom would not have to be alone with me. This may not seem like good news but it meant I was able to go! In this difficult time for Mom, if she had not wanted me there at all, I wouldn't have had a choice. Surely that would have been the case had I not been neutralizing those magnetic energy identities related to our situation. This was progress, and I felt included for the first time.

CHAPTER 26
Healing Sessions on Mom

Dad's Request

Dad died in 1999. And about a year and a half later while I was out running, Dad came to talk to me. I was neutralizing (as I often did while running) when I realized that I was being pulled up into the Astral. I was already amalgamated so I wasn't afraid, just confused. I was taken to the positive Astral and I saw maybe a dozen people there who were Astral workers. When I got my bearings, someone walked toward me with Christmas tree-type lights hanging around him!

I said, "Dad, what are you doing with all those Christmas tree lights around you?" He said, "I didn't want you to miss me."

I burst out laughing because he knew well that my ability to pick up psychically could be sporadic. Once I had him in my sights, however, the light images he projected disappeared, and we conversed for a while.

Dad was not alive; he was in Heaven—between lives. We have the techniques from the Higher Selves enabling us to work with those both out of body in Heaven and those in body but are not in our presence. Over time I have developed an ability to see or sense someone whether out of body or in body but "at a distance" (meaning at that time I am not with that person). But Dad had it right. I'm not perfect at it and cannot guarantee when I'll "get it" and when not.

There are two issues that I would like to clarify. The first is when I work or talk with someone in body but at a distance; I usually talk with him/her at the mind level because the person is in body. We all operate out of the mind level while alive. There have been situations where the mind level is not able to fully understand what I am asking, so I then ask the soul of the person to come forward. For example, in Chapter 17, I discussed getting information about a friend's brother, Joe, who had died 50 years earlier. As you recall, Joe had already reincarnated and was an eight- or nine-year-old boy living here in the United States. So when I called him in, it was the boy who presented himself. Because the mind of the boy did not remember his prior lives, I then asked that the soul of that individual come forward. That was how I was able to learn of his prior life.

The second significant issue involves Free Will. If you work with others at a distance or out of body, you often won't have their conscious consent. This could bring the possibility of trespass into play. However, when working with the Divine Energies, we can do no harm and we always work at the highest level. Free Will is a soul level decision and not made at the conscious or unconscious mind level. Remember my earlier example when the passengers on a plane about to crash are willing at the mind level that they not die and yet each of them does die. If there is one or some that do not die, it is because those souls were not yet ready to make the decision to die. When doing healing work with someone, there is no trespass if we are properly amalgamated. If the person does not want the healing energy, it will not penetrate. The Divine Energies do not force or control the humanities. If the soul does want the healing energy, it can accept it and hold it in his/her soul banks until such time, it is ready to use it. It may use it slowly over time or may take in all in the next day, month, year, or lifetime.

My dad's purpose for reaching out to me was that he wanted me to do healing work on Mom. He explained that she had had many lives wrapped up in a Soul Scramble so entrenched that it had been impossible for her to break free. He said that between each life, she understood what she needed to do in the next life but since she forgot her purpose while in body each time, she just kept repeating the scrambled cycle again and again. (This sounds a lot like Charlie, doesn't it?) Dad explained that since he had his own repeating cycle, he knew it was important for her to forgive herself while in body. This was key. If she could take that step, he said, she would be able to heal the whole Soul Scramble. He didn't explain the scramble in detail but gave me a general outline.

He said that Mom had a deep sense of guilt and shame that came from her belief that she made serious mistakes in her lives and was at fault. When the shame about herself and her faults would be triggered for some reason while in body, her coping mechanism was to blame and denigrate someone else. This had the short-term effect of making her feel better about herself since others would focus on the scapegoat and not her. "At least (she would feel) I'm worth more than that terrible person." The reality eventually hit her that she had made an innocent person out to be the villain and then the shame hit her again. Much of this was not conscious for her but would happen out of knee-jerk reactions time and again based on the entrenched Altered Realities that she had created for herself. It was a vicious cycle built on a bed of self-loathing and shame. She was a good person but could not see or accept it because of her misunderstandings and false self-beliefs.

In response to Dad, I said I would work on Mom. The plan was not to work on her in person but to do the healings at a distance. I foresaw a big obstacle. Since it was Mom's choice to take in the healing or not, I was worried that her deep negative feelings toward me would make her more prone to reject the energies. Dad and I decided that I should use a surrogate healer—a family member (I will call him Josh), who was well loved by my mom and was also my good friend. Josh was still incarnate on the planet, so I telephoned him to ask if he would be part of the healing. He agreed.

The Setup for the Distant Healings

You have no need to worry that there might be a trespass of some sort. Each soul receives at the level what it desires to receive. So in some instances you will note healings that take place very quickly because those souls have the desire to take the healing energy. In other instances, you will see no results at all, as far as healing is concerned. So while in many instances miracles can happen, if that soul does not desire it (for whatever reason) then that soul will take in the energy and use it at some point in the future now. Thus, nothing is ever wasted.

Using Higher Self techniques, I would amalgamate and simultaneously bring both Josh and my mom (both at the mind level as they were both alive) into my presence, visualizing them in front of me as if we were in the same room. Because I didn't want Mom to see me, I stood behind a symbolic two-way energetic mirror that the Higher Selves helped me create where I could see and hear Mom and Josh while they could not see or hear me. While they talked, I would do the healing work, both neutralizing and sending in the empowering Divine Energies.

The first three sessions worked really well. I no longer remember what went on in those sessions except that I phoned Josh after each one and told him what had transpired. I'm sure he was humoring me on some level, but Mom did feel the energy (though not consciously) and thought Josh had sent it to her. I was fine with that.

The problem came with the fourth session. It started out as usual, with both Josh and Mom in front of the two-way energetic mirror while I did the healing work. A few minutes into it, at a point where Mom was complaining about how difficult living with Dad had been, the energy mirror dropped! It disappeared!

Mom and Josh turned toward me immediately and Mom said to Josh, "What's she doing here?"

I quickly said I was stopping by and then I took myself to a safe distance where I could set up another "blind." From there, I started sending Mom every Divine Energy I could think of to calm and soothe her, as she was visibly anxious and confused. Then, right at that tense moment, Dad arrived beside me! And I said emphatically and anxiously, "Dad, this isn't a good time," as I was madly doing all I could to help improve the situation. "Mom isn't a big fan of yours at this moment." I didn't want Mom to see Dad and to become even more upset!

Dad said to me calmly with great sadness in his voice, "Don't worry. She can't see me, and I already know how conflicted her feelings are about me."

At this same time, Josh opened up. Because he was an honest person, he told her the truth that I was doing the healing work, not he. He wanted to be beside her to be sure she was okay and to give her comfort. Slowly Mom calmed down, accepted the situation, and the session ended.

I know even those few sessions helped Mom, but I didn't do any more on Mom because I was so shaken although I continued to work hard on myself. A year or two later, I visited her in Florida with no one else there to buffer my visit (!), when we decided to go shopping. I drove. At some point, Mom turned to me and said something nasty (I don't remember what) and I was not hurt by it! I didn't have to force myself not to be hurt or to pretend not to be hurt because the hurt was just not there. Instead, I giggled and poked Mom in the side and said, "Did you just hear what you said? It was so silly!"

And with that she laughed, too. She was able to bypass completely what could have been a start to a series of nasty comments and instead, the incident was funny. The "dance" of our Altered Realities as they went through their knee-jerk action and reaction sequences was over. My Altered Realities were no longer there. Thus, without my normal reactions, hers were not being triggered. This situation was a huge change. What could have been a very painful moment turned into the solid beginning of our new foundation.

CHAPTER 27

Mom's 90th Birthday

As long as you are willing within your heart of hearts to fulfill, you cannot fail. When you move to heal another and use the instruments that are 5th Dimensional energy symbols, if you sincerely desire to fulfill that function, if your purpose is pure, you can do no wrong. Your Higher Selves will guide and direct you and will enact on behalf of the patient whatever is required. You can do no wrong when you are sincere in your motives and pure in your purpose.

We have a tradition in our family, when there is a significant event such as a big birthday or major anniversary, various family members do skits, give some special toast, or sing songs whose words are rearranged to fit the occasion. So at Mom's 90th in 2006, I decided to say something important to her to honor her life. Mom had planned a week of fun and celebration in Florida, and the entire extended family and many dear friends were attending. My relationship with Mom had improved every year, and I could only relate to feeling unconditional love for her. I was free and clear from my old baggage of bitterness, anger, confusion, pain, and misunderstandings.

My change toward my mother may seem miraculous or part of the impossible realm, but that is the nature of neutralizing. You release old patterns, viewpoints, and belief systems and either slowly or suddenly (from your conscious, waking perspective) the things that bothered you before are no longer there. There is no need to force yourself to think positive (a technique that often doesn't work), as the thought forms, the habit imprints, and emotional blueprints are gone. They are no longer drawing in Astral energy or activating the energetic replay buttons. So from that deep, rich feeling of love, I wanted to say something important and supportive of her.

A few months prior to her birthday celebration, while working on myself (neutralizing), the Higher Selves showed me a big piece of the puzzle related to my mom, bringing even more expansion to my understanding. It was related to those very early months after my birth parents died (a time period outside of my conscious memory). This information they provided was the deeper psychological reason behind the great disconnection between Mom and me in this life—the trigger for my current life's fears and anxieties. Clarity struck me, and I saw how the problems Mom and I had were neither her "fault" nor mine. They were based on situations and conditions unforeseen and misunderstood.

I knew from the moment I thought about giving a toast to Mom at her birthday celebration that I would talk about this *a-ha* moment including all my love and understanding with it. I wanted her to clearly know in consciousness that despite our differences in the past, there was no blame. I would not talk about Soul Scrambles or pre-life choices. That was not relevant for her. What was relevant was that our problems were born from a situation that was not foreseen or understood. It was also important that she knew that all our problems were behind us now.

Bringing this out into the open was a big step for me. So once I wrote the toast, I decided to send it to Josh. I thought he might suggest ways for me to tighten it up. Instead of being supportive, he was against my saying any of it and continually tried to talk me out of it. I was completely surprised and with his continued insistence that I not give the toast at all, I started having self-doubts. Finally, I went into frequency to ask the Higher Selves. "Am I so wrong to want to do this?"

They said, "There is someone here who wants to talk to you." It was Dad. Instead of paraphrasing what he said to me based on my memory, I have replicated here much of the e-mail I wrote to Josh right after Dad talked with me. (FYI: Dad had had the benefit of being educated by the Higher Selves.)

Written to Josh (Edited for Brevity)

Dad told me that it was important that I don't take your advice. He understood my reasons for sharing my talk with you, and it was fine that I did. He explained, however, that you are coming from the point of view of the consummate diplomat, having beautifully developed your diplomatic skills as the way to manage complicated or potentially hurtful situations.

He said this was not what is needed for Mom at this time. A diplomat is successful because he can get a point across when everyone at the table communicates in the same language and knows the underlying meaning of the words, spoken and unspoken. The diplomatic language often talks around the truth instead of saying the truth head-on. There is an important place in the world on a daily basis where diplomacy is needed and is often the best way to go. This is not the case here.

Dad said Mom doesn't have enough time left for diplomacy to work. She needs the whole truth (though not truth bashing) all at once even though she will not fully understand what I say or what others will say that night, as she will have had too much to drink. Plus, she will forget most of what was said in a week or two. I was to send her a copy of the toast for her to read and reread. What wouldn't happen is an immediate win for Mom. Dad said we are going for the longer-term win that can come from hearing what she needs to hear—my truth.

Dad explained that I am in a unique place. A number of things had to happen for me to be ready to do what I'm planning. One, the insight and understanding had to be there. That in itself is difficult and can take great effort to get to. However, because of the neutralizing work I've done on myself (and my life issues), I have had the benefit of true insight. Two, true forgiveness has to have occurred. Given my experience with Mom, that would have been difficult. Yet the forgiveness I feel is real and deep. Three, there also has to be purity of purpose and sincerity of motive. Luckily, those are not so difficult for me as apparently I have long carried those motivators. (In other words, I would not manipulate a situation for my gain but only because I thought it was important for Mom.) Four, it takes great courage to stand up and say the words. Many may want to say them but would find reasons to legitimize not doing so. And five, there has to be real love (or Higher Heart Consciousness) there as well, which there was and had been there for a long time despite the circumstances.

Because all of five conditions were present and satisfied within me, my words would be a powerful healing event. Not only would they help heal Mom, but they also would bring healing energy to all present. The words would penetrate into the subconscious bringing the powerful light of truth and love to Mom and even to everyone else. Mom may have a negative reaction at first, but the light will activate the start of real healing. Now and then she would think of the words, as she rereads the sent copy of my toast. When she dies, she will have understood them and taken in the healing energy. For her, it will be the start of her true self-forgiveness, the first step she needs to take in order to move toward proper self-love and out of her Soul Scramble.

Dad then verified that I had chosen to be with her in this life because the situation would provide me the motivation to do the self-healing I was determined to do. Many of my issues (and Mom's) were from many lifetimes and personally, I wanted to deal with and heal as many of mine as I could in this life. In return, I was determined to give Mom the chance she needed to heal herself whether she consciously asked for it or not. Dad also explained that my resolve to speak out came from my knowing unconsciously that my toast was to be of utmost importance for her.

Dad wanted me to understand the benefit of beginning the self-forgiveness and self-love while in body. When out of body, Mom had understood her pattern and was determined to change in the next life. It just didn't happen because of her powerful Altered Realities. I knew that Dad, too, had recurring Soul Scrambles. So, at the end of this conversation, I said, "But Dad, you didn't have the benefit of healing your patterns in your lifetime. So what is going to happen to you?"

He said, "*I will plan in my next lifetime to have someone just like you to be there for me with the truth when I need it.*"

Of course with that, I burst out crying. And needless to say, I did the toast.

The "truth" Dad speaks of is the misunderstandings and resulting hurts that were the foundation of our problems. It was not that Mom was a bad person. She was a good person who had been suffering through lifetimes of deep shame and guilt. In this life, I was the one who should have held the most bitterness toward her. By speaking to her with love, understanding, and respect, it truly got her attention. I had healed to the point where she could feel my unconditional love, which opened the door for her to heal as well.

The Toast and the Results

HIGHER SELF QUOTE

All that Originating Source is, was, and will be you are also. There is nothing wrong in this reality, in your life that you do not have the power to correct.

I began by addressing everyone in the room:

Some of you may not have expected that I would stand up tonight to pay tribute to my mother as many of you know, for most of our years together there has been discord and disconnection between us. It is for this reason that I am exactly the person that needs to speak as I hope my words will carry the depth of meaning and love that, at 90, Mom deserves.

For most of my adult years I have been working to understand and to heal the hurts and misunderstandings between Mom and me. Although I have been successful with many issues over time, it was just this summer that I came to that "a-ha" moment which resolved the remaining confusion for me. This is what I would like to share.

What many of you know is that when Janet and Eddie (my birth parents) were killed, I was 18 months old. Mom and Dad did the right thing and opened up their home to me in truly less-than-perfect circumstances—there were three little kids underfoot and Mom was pregnant with her fourth. Now, me, a pre-verbal toddler in diapers arrives. Understandably, this was an overwhelming time for

Mom. The short-term solution was clear, and my moms' parents and siblings jumped in to help. I was sent to my grandparents' summer home in Maine where each aunt-and-uncle pair would come for a two- or three-week visit to help care for me. I don't know all the details, but I've been told each family spent two or three weeks with me before returning to their home. At the end of the summer, I returned to Mom and Dad either soon after or just before my sister arrived, a newborn with all the normal demands of time and attention.

Here is what occurred during this time that became locked in my unconscious. First, from my child's perspective, I lost my parents when they didn't come home. Then, the series of aunt and uncle visits, each of whom loved me and encouraged healing and connection, would end when their "turn" was up. I would begin to bond with them as new "parental" figures, then they would just "go away." Without anyone realizing the significance, every adult I became attached to I "lost," effectively traumatizing me again and again. The unforeseen result was a pre-verbal child, with very little understanding, found it unsafe to connect with a parental figure. I became afraid of everything and came to distrust connection and intimacy as it meant to me the loss of a loved one. When I returned home, I was closed to any effort on Mom's part to love me due to my unconscious fear of losing someone else. My a-ha moment was that no matter what effort Mom put into making a connection with me, I was almost impossible to reach. My responses would easily have been misinterpreted as rejection. Thus Mom and I never really had an opportunity to bond as parent and child, though the importance of bonding wasn't even "out there." By the time I had my kids, however, much of what I read and learned about dealt with the importance of bonding.

Once I grasped the significance of this, I was then hit over the head with the insight of how difficult it could have been for Mom! It could be likened to a time when a friend of your child comes over for the night. You might enjoy having the friend for the sleepover, but when the parent comes to pick the friend up, as much as you and your child enjoyed it, you are glad that he or she is going home. Just having another child around requires more of your time and attention. There may be additional disruptions/arguments/upsets or you just want the house to go back to "normal." Remember, this isn't your child. There is no parental bond here. This is similar to what I believe happened for Mom at least in the early stages. And it was due to circumstances and was nothing intentional. She had made the choice to give me a home, but in effect, with me too afraid to connect and trust, it was like I was that friend who never got picked up. Of course, I can't be sure that Mom had any such feelings. Also, we were related so there was more between us than this simple scenario.

As I thought about this, I came to understand the struggle it could have been for Mom, although perhaps very little of it was completely conscious. I'm sure she did what she had to do and perhaps thought little about it. In those days, therapy was less of an option for help than it is today. Mom would have few, if anyone, to turn to for understanding and solutions. The sympathy would most likely have gone to the recently orphaned child.

Though the difficulties between Mom and I were pervasive and unresolved, in many ways I had a good childhood with family, friends, and fabulous opportunities provided for me. Yet, there was much pain underneath for both of us. I've now come to see that this pain carried a beautiful silver lining. Because of it, the motivation to understand was constant and powerful in my life. Being in a different generation than Mom meant doors and concepts were available to me that were not available for her. In some ways, I realized I was the lucky one. Mom had to cope the best she could. I can't possibly know all that was problematic for her, but I can empathize with the possible issues that she could have faced.

Now I addressed Mom directly:

So tonight, Mom, I am here to say that having you as my mother was the source of so much good in my life and without you, I would not be half the person I am today. Indeed, you chose a difficult road, and I deeply appreciate the significance of your choice. You more than followed through on your commitment to me even though there were tough times. My hope is that by talking to you tonight, I've brought you even a little of the light you so deserve and that this will help you resolve some of the remaining issues for you. I want you to hear me when I tell you all the issues are completely resolved for me, and you have my deepest love and support. This is my true gift for you—one that I am so glad to have the opportunity to present. So yes, I am the one who needs to acknowledge you at this very deep level, to tell you I love you with all my heart, and to thank you for being the wonderful person you are. And, of course, Happy Birthday.

When I finished, I gave Mom a huge hug and repeated how much I loved her. I could tell she was unsure really of what just happened. She hugged me back even in her confusion. She'd had a lot to drink, and I believe she was limited in her ability to process what I said. When I left her to go back to my seat, eight or ten people came up to me right away to tell me how moved they were. Many were crying and even Josh came up to me to apologize (though I had already understood). I was a bit upset about the attention coming to me instead of going to Mom, so I felt quite awkward. At the same time, I was also amazed at the results.

The next morning something extraordinary happened. I was in the dining room having breakfast when one of my niece's husbands came up to me. He knelt down on the floor to talk to me eye-to-eye and said, "I can't thank you enough. After I heard what you said in your toast, I went up to our room and said goodnight to my kids in a way I never had before. You have changed my relationship with them forever."

No one at this family reunion had any idea how incredible a moment that was for me. This was beyond my wildest expectations. It completely validated what Dad had said about the toast helping others and as a result, it bolstered my confidence that it would also help Mom truly heal. All I can say is, "Dad, thank you for supporting me!"

The Next Six Years

We have told many of you often that you are the power, that you are the miracle. This means you can make an effect in your life and the lives of others once you have reached the point of accepting within yourself the idea you do have the power.

Mom lived until four days before her 96th birthday—four years short of a century. During those six years, I would come to visit once or twice a year. I would spend long hours with her even though it was hard to get a conversation going. Slowly, she was losing her short-term memory, growing hard of hearing, and moving slower and slower. I played simple card games with her using the open-hand method you would use with a child. She was always a game person and she loved it. I also would bring my computer over and show her some of the funny or interesting e-mails that I knew she would enjoy. Lastly, together we did grade-school-age crossword puzzles. She was a long way from doing *The New York Times* puzzle she had been good at in the past, but she loved it anyway and each time she got a word, she was so proud of herself. Of course, we would walk around either when she was using a walker or when she had to use a wheelchair. Sometimes, she didn't remember I was there or had been there the day before. But the many moments together were warm, loving, and so very special. There was no more squabbling. We found time to play, to enjoy a meal together, and pass the hours connecting in small ways. I didn't do any more healing work on her because Dad came in to tell me that she had forgiven herself (at the soul level) when she was about 93 or 94.

At the time of my last visit with Mom, when we walked down the hall, a friend stopped to talk with us. Mom introduced me as her daughter from California. Then she said, "Janet and I didn't get along before but I have completely forgotten why!" Then Mom turned to me with a questioning look and said, "What was the problem?"

I said, "Who cares, Mom? We are getting along now, and this is the happiest time ever for me!" And Mom just laughed with joy in her eyes and love in her heart. My Soul Scramble was gone as was hers, and we had healed all we needed to heal.

The love we came to share is a treasure that lives way beyond her death in more than one way. First, it lives on as inspiration for the people who can find hope that they, too, can resolve their difficult relationships. Also, the whole process with my mom was and continues to be a large part of the motivation behind this book. It propelled me to understand and learn about how each of us chooses our parents and the general circumstances of our lives before we are born.

Mom didn't know much about my journey but it didn't matter, for when it was time she welcomed me with open arms. She was open to a loving connection between us and to moving out of the old stuck places that she and I had been in for so long. She could have held on to the past and shut me out. But she didn't. This is the measure of the woman I call my mom. For this takes great courage; this takes being able to forgive; this takes great understanding. Because of Mom, I have become more balanced, healthy, and happy than I could have ever been without her.

Forgiveness

HIGHER SELF QUOTE

*There is **no** Divine Forgiveness needed to come from outside yourself. The only Divine Forgiveness that is important exists within you.*

By the end of her life, Mom had brought in true forgiveness of the self. This is the process of truly, in the heart of hearts, forgiving ourselves at the soul level for whatever our soul believes it has done wrong or believes it is lacking. If each individual on the planet unraveled the mysteries of its soul, each individual would find the originating lifetimes of the false beliefs where their various misconceptions took place. Once we understood them, it might be easy to forgive ourselves. However, few of us will ever have that luxury. Not only are Soul Scrambles complex, but they also contain lifetimes of misconceptions. Luckily, understanding them is not required! Once we recognize that we are "trapped" in a scramble or even just a difficult situation, we can then see that we are exactly where we need to be. We can begin to neutralize starting with that exact pattern.

If you were asked to forgive a person who was responsible for the deaths of hundreds of thousands of people, could you do it? Most of us couldn't. But what if you were then shown the absolutely horrific lifetimes that person had endured prior to being the person you knew? Would it be easier to forgive them then, knowing why and how they got here? When those of us who were in Joan's Wednesday class first heard Charlie's story, we felt such overwhelming compassion and love for him. We had the benefit of hearing most of Charlie's story from a big picture point of view and with that understanding, forgiveness was easy.

Neutralizing is the key to the big picture point of view. As you work with neutralizing, you will peel back layers and layers of all the energy identities that are a part of the pattern. You will clear the blueprints of guilt and fear and doubt and everything else active within it. You will also neutralize the "Astral yous" that reflect the same identities. And you will empower your continued unfoldment by activating and directing Divine Forgiveness into your energy fields. The whole process will lead to self-forgiveness no matter how intensely you blame yourself (or someone else). It is not a process of forcing yourself. It is a process where you find your way to your true worth by neutralizing the blinders, the false beliefs, the pain, the shame, and all that holds you attached to what you wrongly perceive as flaws, either your own or someone else's.

CHAPTER 28
After Mom's Death

HIGHER SELF QUOTE

A soul once released from the body in the form of death carries with it into its own hereafter whatever conditions existed within its Soul/Mind at the point in time the death takes place. This means it also carries with it imprints insofar as physical impairments are concerned, causing that soul (even in disembodied form) to still continue in physical handicaps.

I spent a week with Mom in the spring of 2012 and three more days with her in the early summer. I knew that it would be the last time I would see her. We had such a beautiful time together and when I left, I experienced both grief and a sense of peace. By late summer and early fall of 2012, Mom began to fail. Her body was giving out from old age. In mid-October, we got about a two-week warning that her death was imminent. I worked on her right away, hoping to clear away anything that might make her suffer more or to dissolve any fears of dying. I also called in Jane & Company to help with her crossing over. Mom died four days later. The sisters decided on a date for the memorial service—Mom was cremated— and I planned my trip back East. We had the memorial service in early November 2012 and celebrated Mom's life!

Two weeks after she died, I wanted to contact her. I called her in (at the soul level now that her mind had joined with the soul—the minds of the past) and she "came in" with Dad. The sense I got was that she was leaning heavily on his arm and was not really aware of what was going on. Dad did the talking and explained that Mom was still very connected to the belief that she was weak and confused and could not get around without leaning on him. He explained this is common when people die; often they still believe they have to deal with the body or the illness left behind. He told me he was there for her as her support system and for me to check in a month or two to give her time to adjust.

After the memorial service, there was to be one other event the following summer of 2013. We were going to bury Mom's ashes next to Dad's in his family cemetery in Vermont. I knew this service would be another opportunity to speak. I had spoken from my heart at Mom's memorial service in November, telling all those attending a little about my journey with Mom and how much it had helped me. For me, that service was a time of closure. Now, with this new opportunity, I thought I would go in and ask Mom if she wanted me to say anything for her.

Mom's Message

HIGHER SELF QUOTE

Whether a soul is out body or in body it is of no consequence; each soul must learn to forgive the self.

Mom was excited about the possibility to "talk" to others from Heaven. But the first thing she told me was that she had her Heaven legs on now! She said she no longer felt like she had to lean on Dad and was able to go where she wanted when she wanted. She also said to tell everyone she loved them, and she would be there at the ceremony. The significant message she wanted me to convey was that even though it may have seemed like she lived too long, it wasn't until the last three or four years of her life that she took a very important step. While we could have been thinking she had little quality of life and that it would be gentler to let life go, she productively used that time to make shifts toward accepting and forgiving herself. She was adamant that I let everyone know how important self-forgiveness was in life. We often misunderstand who we truly are and react out of those confused and painful places doing things we aren't happy with. And Mom wanted me to convey it is never too late. Finding self-forgiveness was the treasure that made all those years worth it to her.

This opportunity to speak for Mom created nerves and questions. My friends, clients, and readers knew and accepted what I did for a living, yet there were family members who would be at the ceremony who either didn't know or did know and judged it negatively. So speaking up meant I would walk through the final door of proper self-acceptance. I wanted to pass on Mom's words, but I had some old doubts thinking maybe I would open myself up to criticism and attack. However, I saw this concern as an opportunity. I began neutralizing the fears and misgivings that could have prevented my speaking altogether. .Instead of backing out, the neutralizing dissolved my self-doubts and fears and I walked out of that "closet," stood tall, and delivered the message.

Afterward, many people didn't say anything to me, but many did. Those that spoke to me were supportive, interested, and caring. Some shared some very private moments with me such as when they, too, were in contact with a loved one or had gone through a near-death experience. They appreciated having someone to talk to, and I appreciated their support!

In addition to the connection with Mom relating to the burial service, I also heard from Mom recently during some healing sessions. She came in to help me heal the hurt from experiences with her while I was a child. Even though we had healed our relationship and there was unconditional love between us, there had been events and experiences in our past that had left me feeling "less than." She took full responsibility for how she had treated me and added her Light to mine to neutralize the residual trauma and pain. By helping me, she in turn accelerated her own continued evolutionary soul growth. Also, she told me she had healed her scramble and moved up in frequency and would be taking on a new life, which would be completely different than it would have been had she not learned to forgive herself.

Mom shared that in prior lives, not only had she been an alcoholic and a rage-a-holic but also had put the priority on external acceptance by society. She would take on their rules of right and wrong, presenting to the public what she thought would make her acceptable. However, what was lost to her was real meaning and depth in relationships and true happiness. She also felt she had mistreated people, with the result of taking on tremendous guilt and shame. She had found it hard to live with herself. She coped by engaging in anger or alcohol or meaningless activities to help her avoid looking at herself. Yet now, she was excited about planning her next life where she wanted to be of service and to help others.

How This Applies to Other Situations, Conditions, and People

Our lives are complicated. We rarely know why (in a deeper sense) we were involved with various people, had the families we had, how we landed a great career, why we got stuck with chronic illnesses, etc. It is "normal" to fall into the blame game at least at first. In the case of a difficult relationship, it holds us to the belief that the other person is "bad," undeserving, and worthless. This couldn't be further from the truth. The other person is caught up in his/her own messy scramble and the two of you fit together perfectly. You have chosen to be together to become aware, just as Mom and I were. Blame slows our progress by closing the door to self-exploration and healing. It doesn't mean that you stay in the line of fire while you work on your patterns, issues, fears, and doubts. No one has to be mistreated or harmed in order to learn and evolve. It is, however, to our benefit to ask, "What energetic part do I carry that is being triggered off and/or is calling in this mistreatment, difficult relationship, or hurtful situation? What part of *me* needs to be healed?"

In approaching difficult situations in this way, you put the focus where it can be the most helpful—on yourself. If you wait and wish for others, someone, something to change, the result most often will be nothing will change for you. Even if someone, something else does change, you will just recreate (manifest into your outer reality) the same problems with different people or scenarios, much like I did with my "mother" pattern. *The work that needs to be done is on healing yourself.*

What healing the self does is to disrupt the "dance." When we fall into a repetitive pattern with another person or people, it becomes a series of steps that are action, reaction, reaction to the reaction, etc., and symbolically the two people (or more) proceed moving around the "dance floor" like a couple who follow all the steps of a dance by rote. When one person heals him or herself, they take themselves off the dance floor and the other person flops around not knowing where to go or how to act. There is nothing for that person to react to. The one that left the dance floor and the person left alone both can look up and see that there is more to life than that dance and that they don't have to follow those steps by rote. New ideas, concepts, feelings, and thoughts now have the space to come in and be noticed. Healing ourselves is a powerful tool and affects everything else and everyone else, directly or indirectly.

CHAPTER 29

Personal Soul Scramble 2: The Spiritual Teacher

We do not wish to belabor the point but want to emphasize the importance of the responsibility that every receiver of information has. It is the responsibility to listen to it with ears that hear and to evaluate (based on your own consciousness) that information regarding its value to you and its application in your everyday life.

I'm including yet another personal scramble for two reasons. First, because I want you to know that I understand the material in this book at the personal level, and I'm not free of issues/patterns/worries/etc., just because I'm sharing it. Like all of us, I have many misunderstandings and deeply entrenched belief systems I have carried from prior lifetimes into this one. Second, and even more importantly, I want to show you that what we carry is complex. We have and have had many Soul Scrambles. And they tend to overlap and affect all of us on a daily basis.

Spiritual Teacher Soul Scramble

I have had many lives in which I was a priest or a priestess or a spiritual leader on different planets during different time periods. I was in positions of spiritual leadership and authority where part of my responsibility was to teach or instruct students or initiates in various different spiritual paths, depending on the lifetime, location, and culture.

What happened was that I often laid aside the body devastated about my behavior because I ended up in many of these lives doing something taboo. I would have an affair with another priest or an initiate, which was completely forbidden. I was inevitably discovered and thrown out, excommunicated, and judged unfit. Over time, I built up a substantial belief that I was a great failure. I had not kept my oaths or allegiance to my faith. I kept sabotaging myself and brought forth into lifetime after lifetime those feelings of failure, tremendous shame, and a deep fear that it would happen again. Upon hearing this from the Higher Selves I thought, "Okay, I've screwed up big time. Why are they telling me this?"

The Higher Selves explained it wasn't that simple, and my feelings of failure were based on a major misunderstanding. While I was in the position of teacher or leader in most of these lifetimes, I had very deep feelings of doubt about what I was teaching. I kept questioning my faith and the information I imparted to the students. I felt strongly that it was limited and illogical and/or erroneous. But I didn't share my doubts with anyone else. That would be a great sacrilege and would likely have meant death or imprisonment by the higher authorities. These extreme sanctions kept me from questioning the religion and also meant I suffered greatly with self-blame. So the doubts in these lifetimes multiplied and took over my waking moments. I felt disloyal to my faith, my colleagues, my oath, and my students. I was overwhelmed as I could neither accept the idea of letting the students down nor could I handle the deep spiritual conflict within me.

It was because of this conflict (according to the Higher Selves) and because of hating the idea of being disloyal to my oaths that I would choose in those many lifetimes (sometimes consciously and many times unconsciously) an out—to go and do something taboo. I couldn't live with the belief that I was betraying everything and everyone I knew, including my students and myself. So I would have the forbidden affair. At some logical place, it felt less devastating to be kicked out of the leadership position because of having a forbidden relationship than to be unveiled and exposed as a spiritual fraud and to disappoint those who had believed in me. Besides, expressing doubts in most of these particular lifetimes meant I would be executed for heresy. Keeping my mouth closed also meant staying alive.

No matter what the reasons for the behavior, my choices meant that I suffered tremendous guilt and shame. Lifetime after lifetime, I wanted a chance to do it over and get it right. I would choose to return to some other spiritual mission and tried in the new life to rectify my wrongs, to be the proper leader and advisor. Easier said than done. For just like Charlie (as is true for all of us), when we take on a body, we don't remember the purpose for that life or even if there was a purpose. And therefore, I would repeat the pattern again and again. The Altered Realities carried within my etheric bodies led me around by the nose. The guilt and shame continued to be empowered and further entrenched.

Before I incarnated into this current life, I was determined again to get it right—to expand my thinking and to understand what went wrong and why. I had wanted to find ways to resolve and dissolve my feelings of failure and shame about my previous behavior and to forgive myself. Fortunately, being killed off for heresy is not an issue here in the United States. Prior to taking on the body, I had also set up the circumstances of my life that led me to Joan Culpepper, although I hadn't remembered any of this. We had been together in many prior lifetimes. It was a good choice as her Higher Self information resonated deeply, and I took to it like a thirsty woman would take to water.

To clarify, I have been fortunate to learn of many of my past lives, sometimes in detail but mostly as general descriptions around a pattern that I was focused on clearing. There are many avenues to discovering past lives, whether from a past life reader, the Higher Selves, guides, or a hypnotherapist who regresses you. However, it is not necessary that you learn of any lives. A close friend and neutralizing buddy of mine does not believe in past lives at all. She uses her upbringing and current emotional issues to understand and clarify her patterns. It is extremely effective as to what issues to neutralize, and she has changed much in her life already. Again, belief is not required with this work.

In this life, I had another the chance to become a Spiritual Teacher. As you know, when Joan laid aside the body, her family gave me the copyright to her information. Wanting to share the knowledge with the world, I proceeded to do the best that I could. I wrote my first book, started giving workshops, web-radio shows, and private sessions. The process of moving out into the more public eye triggered for me concerns in many areas. I questioned how I should teach the information, what parts of it I should teach, and in what order. I would compare how each class I taught went to how I wanted each class to go. I felt doubt and thought I should have done better. I also had this deep sense I was responsible for every person who heard me, and struggled to be clear so as to avoid misunderstandings. Fortunately, the one thing I did not have any doubts about this time was the information itself. I have not and still do not doubt what I am giving out. I am thankful for that!

When I started the path of teacher in this life, I didn't know the Soul Scramble I operated under. But I still had no problem neutralizing those feelings that made going out to the public difficult for me. Slowly, with the neutralizing I did, my fears gave way to confidence in my teaching, as I brought in deeper levels of self-acceptance and self-forgiveness. I also found much conscious expansion and improved my own connection with the Higher Selves.

I came to understand that not only does the teacher have a responsibility for the information, but that the listener has an equal responsibility for what he/she takes in. As listeners, we all have the responsibility to be discerning. We do not have to accept what we hear hook, line, and sinker. Take in the words and ideas and try them on. See what fits and what feels right to you and leave the rest behind. Each soul needs to decide for itself what works for him/her. So if some part of the information is incorrect as explained, then I do not need to beat myself up about it, nor does anyone else. My intentions are good, and I explain the viewpoint as best I understand it. It is okay later (when discovered) to explain the same information in a more expanded way. There is no requirement that we be perfect out of the gate because we can add, correct, or supplement as we go. This may seem obvious, but it took me time to see it.

The Higher Selves explained—from the standpoint of my students in those prior lives—that I did not need to feel as if I had failed them. First, the students were there for reasons of their own. Many who I taught were in those spiritual environments to learn the exact spiritual information I taught. Even though to me it seemed limited and erroneous, to them it was an expansion of the concepts they had held previously. As one evolves, as you now understand, we do it in steps in the same way we would teach a child about the birds and the bees. You don't start out telling a 5-year-old the information on reproduction in the same way you would explain it to a 15-year-old. As their ability to understand grows with age, you expand the discussion by going into more details and complexities. Most of the novitiates in those lifetimes got the exact level of information that was correct for them in this part of their soul's journey. And it was also their responsibility to accept or to question. It was theirs to either resonate with or to reject. Each soul moves upward, expanding its consciousness bit by bit over its many eons of lifetimes, looking for the next higher step on the truth ladder. And I had chosen to help these souls discover a new consciousness that for them was important. I had not failed those students.

Also, there were some initiates/students who thought the truths I taught were too limited (like I did). And that was okay as well. They came to learn discernment and to think for themselves. These students left the order because they were ready for the next level of expansion of information. I had not failed them. By leaving, it meant they were successful in their step forward. Because I taught them a limited truth that they were ready to move beyond, these students were propelled to look further for a more expanded viewpoint. This meant they stood on a solid foundation at that frequency level and would not backslide. This part of the Higher Self information fascinated me because it meant that even though I felt great shame about those lives, I had not betrayed my students. I helped all those that I taught, just not in the ways I had believed I should have. I had completely misunderstood the situations over and over again.

In addition, the Higher Selves explained I also had honored my internal compass. I listened to my doubts and found a way to leave the spiritual practices I couldn't make peace with. This was a testament to my going within and not just accepting the viewpoints of the external authorities. For me, the spiritual teachings were off the mark. I handled it the way I did, as there were few options. But again, what seemed like a deep weakness on my part was instead a strength. This is a clear case of a Soul Scramble loaded with misunderstandings. We all have them, and they are based on misinterpretations and limited viewpoints from the societies and situations we have lived in. Happily, I am now in a situation where what I teach is not dogma, and there is no need to convince anyone that what I share is right *or that they must believe it.*

Conclusion

HIGHER SELF QUOTE

The Higher Selves remind us to love ourselves where we are, accept ourselves where we are (knowing that we are not defined by our outward circumstances) and practice proper love of self and the celebration of the self.

The great news is that once you heal your scramble, it is done. We can't go in reverse. Once we move up to a new higher frequency level of truth, there is no backsliding. The evolutionary process is very clear on this. When situations and conditions come into our lives that trigger us, these can become good opportunities to become aware there is still work to be done. And as we continue to do the neutralizing, the situations will come up less often and less intensely because we don't have to get to the very end to have improvement. At some point (like with my mom in the car when what she said did not hurt me at all and left us giggling), we will discover that the healing is complete and we are on the firm foundation of our new level of understanding.

Our beliefs become limitations and prevent long-term expansion and movement forward. If there is a conflict/confusion/problem, we can neutralize the misunderstandings and all the underlying causes—known and unknown. We will bring in great clarity of vision and expanded perception, and we can be in the helicopter directing our lives from the much wider perspective. Sometimes the shifts come in quickly and sometimes they take a while. It is all part of the process. Every individual is that snowflake, and yet there is hope and help for all.

PART VI

The Neutralizing Process
and Its Practical
Applications

CHAPTER 30
Essential Evolutionary Concepts

All life (on all levels) is connected to the Originating Source by the Pure Soul Essence, which is the perfection and the reflection of what ultimately gave birth to it.

All life from the smallest grain of sand to the highest level of Originating Source is exactly the same within that Pure Soul Essence level; it just processes in different forms of energy and at different rates of speed.

Pure Soul Essence

The Pure Soul Essence is the vehicle that allows the interchange of all experiences, energy, knowledge, etc., to move between the Originating Source and its aspects (souls) and back again. Without it evolution would not exist. Without it there would be no learning, no growth in vibratory frequency, and no existence. Evolution is not its only purpose. The Pure Soul Essence also gives us the ability to neutralize. It is the powerhouse we all carry.

In Chapter 1, I described the Pure Soul Essence as the part of the

Originating Source held within every soul from the lowliest grain of sand to the highest most evolved being. It is everything that the Origination Source was, is, and is becoming! I use the analogy that the Pure Soul Essence is likened to our DNA. Just as every cell in our body has full double helix of DNA—whether in the skin, the kidney, or the lungs—every soul in the universe, known and unknown, has the Pure Soul Essence. All souls are expressions of the Originating Source, just as our cells are expressions of our DNA.

Let's take this analogy a step further. Because every soul is part of the Originating Source, we are all manifestations of that energy, although we operate at different frequency levels. Let's use our own body as a microcosm of the much larger and infinite whole. Within our own physical body we have parts that are extremely dense—our teeth and bones—and we have parts of our body that are less dense, such as the various tissues and organs. We have fluids such as lymph and blood and saliva, which are even much less dense. There is no question in our minds that all these parts belong to our body even though they look different, behave differently, and respond differently to various stimuli.

The same is true of all the physical manifestations in the known (and unknown) universe. We all are part of the Totality of the Originating Source. And we carry all that Originating Source experience, its purity, power, knowledge, perfection, and balance at that Pure Soul Essence level. This idea is so huge that even if we can accept this concept on an intellectual level, we would have a hard time grasping the enormity of it. In our minds, the Divinity (the Originating Source) seems like it must be something more powerful and something disconnected from ourselves. And we might wonder, if we are equal to all that, why aren't we manifesting it? Good question.

We don't manifest all of what we are at that level because no one told us much about it before, if ever. Because we carry so many blinders of misunderstandings, misinterpretations, and false beliefs from eons of lifetimes, we carry layers and layers of thoughts, habits, and emotional blueprints that make it difficult to connect with this concept. All of us arrived into this life with limited viewpoints and entrenched Soul Scrambles that make becoming aware a long process.

Imagine yourself in this analogy. You are like a lonely fish that lives and swims deep within the ocean near the bottom, where there is no light of knowledge and understanding. This fish feeds and reproduces. It feels small and insignificant, unimportant in the scheme of things as the narrow limits to its existence have blocked out and blinded it to the significance of itself and its universe. But what if this fish decides to swim out of its comfort zone? In the beginning, it might not experience much of a difference, but it keeps moving. It takes a long, long time because the weight of the vast ocean is holding it to a very tedious and slow process. Yet, it keeps swimming up and up and up. After many harrowing experiences with the unknown, the fish is rewarded. It sees light for the first time! With that light, its vision becomes more acute and the fish sees more life and beauty than ever before. A plethora of animals and plants thrive there. It spends every day soaking in all that this new world offers. This motivates the fish to continue to swim upward. When it arrives at the top of the ocean, it finds a world with infinite surprises—atmosphere, land, plants, and animals. Of course, it also encounters many unknown dangers and problems. It has had to learn to avoid boats, other bigger fish, and stormy waters. Its learning curve goes way up.

The fish realizes it is being noticed and looked at by the other life around it. With its new awareness, it looks carefully at itself for the first time. Instead of a little, dull, insignificant fish, it discovers it is beautiful. Its body and fins are gorgeous, reflecting the light in a myriad of colors. It is part of a grand and special world. It comes to understand that it is as important a part as anything else it sees.

We are like this imaginary fish. We begin our journey in the Human Kingdom, barely aware of the world or who we are in it. We have no context to understand the universe and all it has to offer. But we are on our journey of discovery where we learn and grow and slowly move up the frequency levels of awareness. As we do so, we both create and move through our blinders and the energetic layers littered with the false beliefs we had taken on and still carry. They are heavy and make it difficult for us to "see." Slowly the "light" penetrates, and as we move through each layer, the dark shifts from black to gray. It is these layers that have held us prisoner, keeping us from knowing who we are in all our glory.

For eons, we were unaware of the existence of the Light of our Pure Soul Essence, let alone its power. Yet the Light has always been there for all of us all the time, just as it had always been there for the fish, even though it didn't know of it for so long. It just takes time for the fish and for us to reach that level of understanding. When we do reach those higher levels of awareness and learn to use the power of the Light, we can use that energy to accelerate our journey and expand our viewpoint. The end goal is to know that we are beautiful, pure, perfect, unlimited and equal with every other soul.

This is the journey we are all on, and we make this journey on our own timing, in our own way. All roads lead to Rome (awareness), and no one way is the best way. There is no judgment, no better than or worse than. And this journey will take us to the purity and perfection of who we truly are, to knowing that we are our Pure Soul Essence and to live out of that place. Until then, we have the Pure Soul Essence to use to help us on our journey.

Now that we know about it, how do we use it?

Focused Thought and the Amalgamation

HIGHER SELF QUOTE

Within this Pure Soul Essence you carry the absolute Totality of Originating Source that gave birth to you, and you are not separate from it. You carry within you, at the Pure Soul Essence level, the ability to create within your own right, to access all knowledge, wisdom, and power from the highest Totality of All That Exists. The Pure Soul Essence Energy is there, waiting, until each individual decides to use the energy.

Until we know about our Light—the Pure Soul Essence—it is only potential power, untapped and unused. The Pure Soul Essence carries the Divine Will frequencies and as such, is unable to trespass our Free Will nature. It won't come in and fix our lives. Instead we have to invite it in and give it permission to help us, like when I discussed the super-duper computer with only potential power until we turn it on and ask it a question. We know how to turn on a computer, but how do we turn on our Pure Soul Essence? We have a simple "turn-on" switch. It is our *focused thought*, the holding of a thought in our minds for a few moments.

Using this focused thought, we activate our Pure Soul Essence by becoming *one* with it. This is amalgamation. You can think it, sense it, imagine it, or say the words, "I am my Pure Soul Essence." Perhaps you can picture your inner Light as a flame of a candle (or a spark of light) that grows and intensifies until you stand in that Light, glowing, beautiful, larger than life. I like to use the symbol of the sun, something so powerful in life that it immediately gives me the mental and emotional connection to the incredible power of the Pure Soul essence. As you focus, the Light expands past your physical and etheric bodies as large as you wish until you are the huge beacon of Light extending into the atmosphere and beyond. This focus is how we activate the powerhouse we carry. This is the amalgamation or the merging with and becoming one with our Divine Light. This is how we give it permission to move into our Free Will arena.

We also amalgamate with the Originating Source and the Higher Selves. When we amalgamate with the Originating Source, it is our guarantee that we are utilizing the Divine Energies at the *highest level* we can at any moment in time. When we open ourselves to this infinite resource of Divine Energy, it cannot come to us in its full strength. If it did, it would kill us. So the energy de-intensifies down to the highest frequency levels that we can use. Tomorrow or next week, we would be able to use even higher levels. So why would we ever want to work with lesser frequencies? It wouldn't make sense.

The Higher Selves, too, are very important as they help direct the energy. They are us. (See Appendix II.) If it is the knee that needs healing but we mistakenly send it to the elbow, the Higher Selves would direct it to the knee. Whether it is energy from the Originating Source, the Pure Soul Essence, or the Higher Selves, all sources work at the Divine Will level and can do us no harm. The amalgamation of all three puts us firmly in place as the directing identity with infinite power, infinite wisdom, and as if we are carrying the "Hammer of Thor." The 4th Dimensional, human thought, habit imprints, and emotional response blueprints are so weak and powerless in comparison, they are like matchsticks to this hammer.

When we amalgamate, we are asking for the Divine Energies to move in to help us. These energies carry the power to improve all aspects of our lives. Without it, when we think, speak, and act in our lives, we create the matchsticks that are our energy identities. These are the words, habit imprints, and emotional blueprints we try to render harmless. By using the amalgamation, we bring all the Divine power into the mix.

For example, we all know the power of love. When we say affirmations about love without being amalgamated (I am love, I am loved, I am lovable), we build our positive matchstick piles, one small matchstick at a time, hoping the pile will get big enough to change our lives for the good. However, if we amalgamate and activate Divine Love using our focused thought, we bring the divine power of love that carries all the purity and perfection and empowers us at levels we can only imagine.

Also, the amalgamation brings us into a state of the Highest Ideal. The Highest Ideal from the Higher Self viewpoint means that while we are in a state of amalgamation we are not only protected from possible negative energies, but the actions we take could not harm ourselves or another. If we mistakenly think we need to heal the digestive system and the real cause of the problem is the nervous or hormonal system, that is what will be healed whether we are aware of our mistake or not. I recently did a healing at a distance by request by the mother of someone with severe heart problems and a collapsed lung. I was told that it was the left lung that had collapsed but while I was directing the energy to the left lung, I kept seeing the energy going to the right lung. I wasn't sure why but thought maybe it was getting strengthened to do the work for both lungs. Three weeks later I heard from the mother that she had been mistaken and it was the right lung that had collapsed.

We will also receive the information and energy at the highest level. The Highest Ideal means we are always moving on the highest road, the highest frequency, the deepest healing, and the greatest understanding that we can reach in that moment in time. With the next amalgamation, we will be working again at the next highest level in that moment, etc. Even when we are not completely conscious and aware of where we need to go or what we need to do, we have given permission (by amalgamating) at the Free Will level for the Divine Energies to be the power behind our movement forward.

Therefore, why not be more proactive and amalgamate first so that the only energy that we call on is the Divine Energy that can do no harm? I suggest that we do so.

Last, visualization techniques often are used as a calming exercise, to put you in a positive frame of mind, or to help you create what you want in life. Although these are valid and useful techniques with great benefits, the use of symbolism as described by the Higher Selves is not the same. Instead, we use the symbol because we are part of the Human Kingdom, and it is difficult to sense or imagine pure energy. We are visual beings and the use of a picture, sound, words or color (any symbol) for something to focus on facilitates the process. The symbol is used as a focal point **but** it is *what is behind that symbol that is important.* Even the words, "I am my Pure Soul Essence" are symbols for the Divine Energy we all carry.

In all of the work I do and all I share about the Higher Self information, symbols always represent powerful energies that we normally can't see, hear, or feel. By focusing on the symbol, we open up a portal that unleashes and/or releases the potent energy behind it. Because the technique activates the energy that the symbol represents, there is flexibility as to what symbol you use. If you wish to use a river, a strobe light, a musical note, or a drumbeat to be your symbol for the Pure Soul Essence, there is no problem. Ten different people can have ten different symbols, and if they use their conscious focused thought to activate that Pure Soul Essence Energy, any symbol will be as effective as any other.

CHAPTER 31
Neutralizing and Empowering

Step 1: Awareness

HIGHER SELF QUOTE

Too often consciousness is mistaken for having the eyes open. Instead, consciousness of your life situation—true consciousness of your life situation—is the power to alter it, to change it.

Now that we understand so much more about our human journey, we recognize at the soul level we have many imprints and Altered Realities that create the situations and conditions we experience in our outward reality. Even if we don't know any details, we are aware we have Soul Scrambles and we have (most likely) come to this life with the desire to heal them.

We understand our Soul Scrambles are unique and made up of misconceptions, false beliefs, judgments, and limited truths. We understand that while we were in the Human Kingdom Heavens before our birth we made the decisions as to the circumstances of our current life in hopes that those situations would bring us to the point where we seek and search for answers. This planet is now a prime spot to heal because of the high frequency of energy present and growing. I now encourage everyone to take this awareness (which has already given you a huge jumpstart on changing your life for the better) to the next level. I suggest using life's experiences that are out of balance, unhappy, uncomfortable, scary, etc., as the starting point for neutralizing!

Step 2: Neutralizing

HIGHER SELF QUOTE

When you have located the Energy Identity that pertains to the condition you wish to heal, surround it and isolate it in a symbolic circle. If you will look to the right of it, you will see an invisible force field with a circular outline exactly like this Energy Identity you have isolated. But this form is invisible because it is unfilled. Use your right hand and fill that form with light. Now using your left hand, move that Energy Identity very slowly into the lighted form. They become neutral. This appears as gray, the combination of black and white. Draw in that neutralized Energy Identity and dissolve it into the light of your own beingness.

Once we become aware of our patterns (and this is easy as we begin where we are unhappy) and of the Pure Soul Essence Light we carry, we can address the Altered Realities and energy identities we carry at the etheric levels.

The minute you think a thought (habit or blueprint), energy is created that moves into both your etheric bodies and into the Astral. Once created, the energy cannot be destroyed. What we can do is to change the nature of the energy. We can remove the magnetic power that it has and then we can amalgamate (merge) this new neutral energy with our Pure Soul Essence Light. Neutralizing is the name the Higher Selves gave the process over three decades ago.

I mentioned earlier that we use our Light to bring the magnetic power of the thought form into a neutral state thereby rendering this energy harmless. Imagine you have two beakers of liquid. The liquid in each are exactly the same in amount yet one beaker has liquid with the most basic pH and the other liquid has the most acidic pH to an equal but opposite degree. When you pour the liquid from one beaker into the other, you then have a liquid that has no pH at all. It is completely neutral. Yet, you still have all of the liquid; none was lost. This is what happens when we neutralize thought energy (as described above in the Higher Self quote). The Light moves in and matches all the thought forms in the exact size and shape. When the process is over, we still have the energy (though now neutral), but the magnetic signature is no longer present, no longer drawing to it other energies that would empower it.

Neutralizing the Habit Imprints is different, as you may remember. The imprints are deeply ingrained ruts in an energy field that propels us to action. And the deeper the ruts or imprints, the stronger the habits are. What the Light does when we direct it to neutralize is to fill in the deep crevasses, thereby deactivating the propelling force. It is as if we have taken out the firing pin of an automatic weapon. It is no longer able to be part of the action. Neutralizing disarms our habits.

What happens when we neutralize the Emotional Blueprints? We do *not* neutralize the emotions. Instead, we neutralize the energy that holds the emotions attached to an event. The energy is like a Velcro or energy field that holds the blueprint together. When the energy is neutralized, a blueprint no longer exists. The emotions are freed from the event—they are no longer attached—and when the event recurs, we no longer have the replay button. Instead, we have a real choice as to how we feel about an event.

My analogy for this is one of a vendor holding helium balloons of three different colors. If we want to buy a balloon, we have to choose from the limited colors he offers. If he lets go of the balloon strings and the balloons float away, the limitation is gone. Now we can choose from the much bigger variety of balloons that aren't blown up yet (back at the store). Emotionally, neutralizing blueprints is freeing and opens up our emotional world. Since we often work on negative emotional blueprints, this means there is now room for more objectivity, positivity, and understanding in our emotional state around events and experiences in our lives.

When we neutralize, the Pure Soul Essence Light is working simultaneously on the total package. We can work on one element at a time (the thought form, the habit imprint, or the emotional blueprint) or all of them at once. I also recommend with every pattern, issue, or belief you want to change, that you neutralize any and all energies and Altered Realities that are either *directly or indirectly related* to it in any way. This covers more bases.

Lastly, we can simultaneously neutralize our Astral Identities, which is a good thing. We direct the Light to the Astral, asking it to neutralize the same energies we work on in our etheric bodies. Or, we can just sit down and do a neutralization solely on our conglomerate Astral Identities. I've used both techniques at different times and both are effective. Because we continue to build new "Astral yous," I recommend we neutralize them over again from time to time.

Step 3: Empowering

By consciously thinking and creating any positive image of yourself in your etheric bodies, and then energizing it by becoming consciously aware, from time to time, of this Energy Identity, you will have created a willing servant. It would be wise to infuse each of these created Energy Identities with the concept of amalgamation with the Higher Selves. This then allows the Higher Selves and their higher knowledge to be in charge of these particular creations.

Empowerment is also important. Most of us have learned that thought energy is one of the most important energies in existence. Thinking positively has taken the world by storm, and we cannot avoid being conscious of it. The magnetic nature of each thought, though important, does not match in comparison to the Divine Light Energy we carry in the Pure Soul Essence. We could think "I am rich" or "I am healthy" a hundred times a day for years and still not create enough positive Altered Realities to ever match or overpower the negative ones of financial lack and illness that we have created over eons of lifetimes. And of course, we know that positive thinking does nothing to reduce the negative in any way. Instead, the energies are attracted to and empower like positive energies. The negative ones are left untouched and continue to magnetically draw in those situations and conditions that will further empower them.

In addition, the process of repeating positive affirmations is slow. To *accelerate* it, after we neutralize a pattern, we can *empower* the opposite belief/pattern. Using the financial lack pattern as an example, after we have neutralized it, we then activate and bring in the Divine Material Abundance Energy to empower our own small "I am rich" Altered Reality. The immediate results are huge in comparison. Always amalgamate the Higher Selves with any Altered Reality you are empowering. This is your guarantee that the positive energy won't in any way combine with negative Altered Realities (as is certainly possible), as this can result in the manifestation of some pattern that is not in your Highest Ideal. We all have a push/pull type of feeling about things and the emotional blueprints can be complicated. So as a precaution, I make sure that whatever I am empowering is amalgamated with my Higher Selves (or my Highest Ideal).

The Exercise

I give my students, clients, and anyone who is interested a one-page sheet or laminated card with a simple neutralizing exercise because I want everyone to have the simple tools to amalgamate, neutralize, and empower. And I provide it here as well. There is no requirement that anyone need be extra special to do this work. Anyone can do it, and it doesn't require long periods of schooling or lots of money. It needs the awareness, the focused thought, and the amalgamation process. When saying (out loud or to yourself) the bolded phrases below, spend a few moments on each one. They are not to be said by rote like reciting the alphabet. This activates the focus of attention that is the all important turn on switch.

The first version comes with an explanation. The shortened version is a cheat sheet that you can copy and take with you anywhere.

Neutralizing on Your Own:
Version with Explanation and Short Version Cheat Sheet

- **I am My Pure Soul Essence Light.**

  This is your Divine Light that every soul has from Originating Source. You can see it, sense it, or imagine it using a symbol such as a spark of light, a flame of the candle, or the sun. When we amalgamate with (or become one with) the Light, the Pure Soul Essence encompasses the totality of our beingness (our physical and etheric bodies). Our focus of attention gives permission for the Divine Energies that you carry to move in and to help you at the Free Will level.

- **I Amalgamate with the Originating Source.**

  Because our Pure Soul Essence is always connected to the Originating Source, by consciously focusing on amalgamating with it, we expand the connection and invite in the infinite resources of All There Is. It is also our guarantee that we will work at the highest frequency level that we can.

- **I Amalgamate with the Totality of My Higher Selves.**

  This brings the connection with the higher, more evolved aspects of ourselves into the process. They facilitate the de-intensification of the Divine Energies to the level we can handle them. They also keep unwanted masqueraders and negative energies out of our energy field.

- I Release the Patterns, Issues, Fears, Doubts, Worries, Hurts, Fatigue, Problems (or anything else) into this Light to be Neutralized.

  The dark negative energy identities and altered realities from the conglomerate of your etheric bodies will move out of your etheric bodies into your Light. As they hit the Light, the energies will be neutralized. Spend as much time releasing as you have time for. You might take 3, 10, or 30 minutes. Every bit helps because once neutralized, it is permanent.

- I Absorb the Neutral Energy into My Light.

  Now this neutral energy will be absorbed into your Light, thereby empowering your Light. We don't want to leave the neutral energy out there. Being neutral, it becomes whatever it touches. So it could empower some negative energy identity that you or someone else carries or that the Astral carries. Therefore, this is an essential step but occurs quickly. You can also connect this step with the neutralizing one by simply stating/seeing/intending that as the negative energies release into your Light, they are neutralized *and* absorbed in one step.

- I Send My Light into the Astral to Neutralize My Astral Identities Related to This Pattern.

  You can visualize or sense a beam of your Light moving into the Astral like a laser that seeks out the "Astral yous," neutralizing them on contact.

  When done with the neutralizing steps, we begin the empowering process. You can do both at the same time or even go back and forth between the two.

- I Activate and Bathe in the Divine Energies and Ask the Higher Selves to Amalgamate with My Empowered Energy Identities.

  This empowers your positive energies. There are an infinite number of Divine Energies. Just as when light moves through a prism you can see that it is comprised of colors, in the same way Divine Light carries different elements, each as powerful as the other. Some examples are Divine Love, Forgiveness, Clarity, Hope, and Understanding to name but a few. You can change which Divine Energies you activate any time. Amalgamation with the Higher Selves guarantees that a positive energy will not add strength to a negative manifestation.

SHORTENED VERSION: Cheat Sheet

- I am My Pure Soul Essence Light.

- I Amalgamate with the Originating Source.

- I Amalgamate with the Totality of My Higher Selves.

- I Release the Patterns/Issues/Fears/Doubts/Worries/Hurts/Fatigue/Problems into this Light to be Neutralized.

- I Absorb the Neutral Energy into My Light.

- I Send My Light into the Astral to Neutralize My Astral Identities Related to This Pattern.

- I Activate and Bathe in the Divine Energies and Ask the Higher Selves to Amalgamate with My Empowered Energies.

More on the Exercise

The wording I provide in this exercise is a starting place. These words unleash a powerful process—the release of the negative energies from our etheric bodies and the activation and use of the Divine Energies. Again, focus on each phrase for a moment. The order of the phrases can be changed, and soon you will find yourself moving into your own wording, sensing, and processing. It is about the focus. If you have experienced the conscious healing meditations that I do in class or on web-radio, you will know that I change it up every time. You, too, will find yourselves becoming freer and freer to express your inner senses.

Even though the wording can vary and the order of the steps can change, a couple of the actual *words* you use are important. You have read about the Astral and understand that whether we intend to or not, we can call on Astral energies we may not want. It was with long explanations that the Higher Selves let us know what happens with the unwanted Astral energies when we pray to God and thus, recommended that we use the term Originating Source instead. The term carries a neutrality in the sense there are not centuries and millennia of Astral energies built up around it.

Another example would be the *higher power.* It automatically sets up the possible connotations that there is some higher being who runs the show and we are its puppets, inferior in some way. We now know that we are all equal. We are all expressions of Originating Source. And in the Human Kingdom, we are the directing identity.

Another possible substitution you would now be aware of is *guides.* If you wish to have your guides come forth, please use the term. But if you want to have clear access to the frequency of information from the Higher Selves, they cannot trespass your Free Will decision or push aside a guide you have called or have allowed in.

In addition, if while you are working your mind wanders or you get interrupted, you would need to amalgamate again. The amalgamation is part of a conscious process that is maintained as long as we hold our focus of attention. I often do my neutralizing and healing work while I walk. And I have my focus pulled away for many reasons such as someone talks to me or something interesting or worrisome is happening with the traffic pattern. Once I am ready to continue the work, I re-amalgamate. It takes but a few moments.

The Divine Energies have more to each of them than what you might think. For example, when we call on Divine Power, it would not carry the negative perceptions of power that we may have here, such as control, manipulation, or something self-serving. When we connect with and use Divine Power, we are connecting with our Pure Soul Essence power—the Light we carry that is all the Originating Source was, is, and is becoming. We are not receiving power from an external source nor would we necessarily experience the mundane manifestations of power. Instead, we enhance our connection to the Pure Soul Essence, our purest, most perfect and potent point of power.

Also, from time to time a new aspect of this infinite Divine Energy presents itself. For example, a few weeks ago I worked on someone who was completely disconnected from herself, her passions, her gifts, and her worth. She always put herself last in any situation. After I explored much of this pattern and its causes to help the client neutralize, the Higher Selves suggested that I activate the "Divine Yes." This was to help her bring the "Yes" to herself, her value, her opening, her expression, her self-connection and to empower the self-commitment to stand up and be counted. It was awesome, and I now use it often.

By using conscious and focused thought, we accelerate our evolutionary movement up the frequency levels of understanding. This powerful Pure Soul Essence Light will make the rest of our journey more joyful with fewer blocks and less fear, trauma, and drama. Problems that appear will be less intense, will occur less often, and in time, they will become minor blips and disappear completely. Our lives will manifest opportunities and possibilities never dreamed of. It would be as if the fish, instead of slowly and doggedly swimming to the surface, was able to hitch a ride on a deep-sea submarine as it came up from a deep dive. The ride would speed up its journey to the new world.

The use of our Light will do the same.

Example: How I Worked on My Mom Issues

Now that you have the technique, how do you start and where do you start? At first, you are in a place of pain, confusion, and insecurity. So you begin with the first thing/aspect that comes up for you. That's what I did. Reading about my process can help get you started on your own. Please keep in mind that even if we are confused, doubtful, and afraid, it works anyway. All will make progress, despite what we may think. Just begin with what you know. You don't have to know the second step before you do the first one. It will unfold.

The Victim Mentality

Neutralizing: I began with the obvious. I felt so much like a victim, and it seemed like I was powerless to change anything. I had tried hard to move out of this belief system, and I placed my hopes on this new technique. I released into my Light the whole victim pattern, feeling like a victim, acceptance of being the victim, feeling I deserved being a victim, anger at being a victim, lack of control over my life, powerlessness, misunderstandings, and misinterpretations about being a victim. I also neutralized being a victimizer in case I had been one as well and wanted at the soul level to experience being a victim in order to atone for something. Who knew what I had or had not done in other lives, so it didn't hurt to do both sides of the coin. Moreover, when we blame someone for something happening in our lives, we become a victim and the other person becomes a victimizer. And vice versa. The worst is when we blame ourselves for something because we are both the victim and the victimizer. And blame was rampant at me, to me, and from me. I wanted it all gone.

Empowering: Divine Power and Love, Divine Clarity and Understanding, Divine Balance and Harmony, Divine Self-Acceptance and Self-Forgiveness, Divine Connection, Resolution, and Self-Realization

False Accusations

Neutralizing: An element of the victim pattern that stuck out for me was the feeling of being falsely accused. Mom (due to her Soul Scramble) often lied about how a situation unfolded between us or about what I did or did not do. She was clever when she did it, as there were rarely any other witnesses to the events or no one else willing to stand up for me. And she would tell many others her version of the situation. It was often months or even years later that I would find out about the distorted and hurtful lies, now so long past the event that the damage was done and the opportunity to set the record straight was long gone. And the false accusation pattern reappeared in my life from other quarters. So this was a big one in my mind, and I neutralized around it often at first. I didn't want those energy identities that accepted being the scapegoat or the "bad guy."

Empowering: Divine Clarity and Insight, Divine Forgiveness, Love and Understanding, Divine Justice, Truth and Self-Connection

Anger and Bitterness

Neutralizing: I worked on bitterness, anger, and frustration. I often felt when I was young that life was unfair, and I was angry at my mother and at the universe. I worked many angles of this including the neutralizing of all anger in all situations and the whole belief system that fairness was actually something real and to be expected. I released all the energies I had created while being angry and expressing that anger to others. I worked on shame and guilt because after an episode with Mom, I would often turn the anger on myself. Self-blame was rampant as I often believed I was at fault.

Empowering: Divine Balance and Harmony, Divine Clarity of Vision and Expanded Perception, Divine Self-Acceptance and Self-Connection, Divine Forgiveness and Understanding

Lack of Self-Love

Neutralizing: This led me to neutralizing self-attack, self-loathing, lack of self-love, lack of self-respect, and self-value. Then I turned it around and worked on the patterns where others attacked me, not loving me, not respecting me, or valuing me. I asked myself, "Did I deserve love?" And just in case I believed somewhere that I didn't deserve to be loved and respected, I neutralized that, too, along with feeling that I was unlovable.

Empowering: Divine Love and Self-Forgiveness, Divine Worth, Respect and Value

Invisibility
Neutralizing: Part of this was the feeling that I wasn't seen or heard or noticed. The Altered Reality example (see Chapter 21) of the unnoticed child on a busy street was one I carried in my own etheric bodies. It fit my feelings perfectly, and I dissolved that one as fast as I could, calling in all those directly and indirectly related. I also neutralized the part of me that didn't notice others. Not only did I feel invisible but also many times didn't see others. Being invisible was a pattern I worked hard to dissolve along with the opposite, others being invisible to me. As you will recall, I had the habit of blurring my eyes for my early years in order not to be seen clearly by others. When you do that, you don't see others clearly, either. So invisibility was a two-sided issue and both sides were ripe for neutralizing.

Empowering: Divine Vision and Hearing, Divine Presence and Wisdom, Divine Courage and Confidence, Divine Expanded Perception

Poor Relationships
Neutralizing: Relationship issues of all kinds were also fodder for my focused thought. I neutralized all communication difficulties,

misunderstanding, patterns of being subservient, trying to please, self-sacrifice, and accepting less than equality and kindness. Also, self-sabotage came up as I thought of ways I aggravated the situation (mostly at the unconscious level) with Mom and any relationship. I included, too, my relationship with myself on as many levels as came up for me. I worked hard and often to neutralize all them.

Empowering: Divine Communication and Message, Divine Understanding and Self-Acceptance, Divine Plan, Resolve, and Resolution, Divine Relationships, Family and Connections, Divine Forgiveness and Equality

Pain and Suffering

Neutralizing: One of the biggest parts of the pattern I worked on was the vast amount of hurt, pain, suffering, and grief on psychological and emotional levels that dogged me throughout my childhood and beyond. Usually, I worked the conglomerate energies—the thought forms, habit imprints, and emotional blueprints—all at once, but sometimes I projected into my Emotional Response Body to work directly on the blueprints. They were deep, dark, and entrenched. I would see them symbolically as huge haystacks standing in a field. When I cleared the energy holding them in place, I watched the stacks become smaller and smaller as the attached emotional responses were freed. Then I would find that, like an iceberg, the haystack was just the tip of the blueprint. The rest of it was below ground level. Many times over the years I would send a stream of Light down into the well of suffering to reduce it more and more. I came to understand through my own process just how much suffering and pain we have all experienced over the eons of lifetimes. It took a big effort on my part to dry up those wells of agony. However, each time I went in, I could sense the well was less and less deep. It was as if the rest of the iceberg was melting.

Empowering: Divine Joy and Happiness, Divine Healing and Harmony, Divine Choice and Freedom, Divine Resolution and Solutions, Divine Courage and Confidence

Fear of Expressing Myself

Neutralizing: Being afraid to speak up and express myself was also a big issue. My mom intimidated me. She had a strong personality and was not afraid to let me know when she thought I was wrong. I usually clammed up. It was such a seasoned reaction that I did it without thinking. Coming into consciousness about this one was a long haul, and it had its origins somewhere back in my many reincarnations. I have neutralized this one often and discovered that the fear of consequences ran very deep. In many lives I was killed off, imprisoned, tortured, excommunicated, exiled, etc., for speaking from my heart. This fear was also a part of the second Soul Scramble of the Spiritual Teacher that I shared above. I still neutralize this one from time to time because now that I am sharing this spiritual work, I want to make sure my heart and voice are open, clear, and without fear.

Empowering: Divine Expression and Communication, Divine Nurture and Acceptance, Divine Unfoldment and Destiny

Fear of Authority

Neutralizing: There was a pattern that many of you may think is insignificant. I did at first. I had a deep fear of anyone older than me. Even if that person was only one year older, I immediately felt inferior, incompetent, and wanted to hide. Of course, I understand now this was attached to my deep fear of authority. It usually was not operational around my family or close friends but was deeply imbedded in my psyche. It took time for me to actually see this as important to neutralize. Once I got to my 30s, I often was around older people (not old but just older than me), and I noticed that I projected onto them some of my mother's traits.

I remember an incident in the early days when I was taking all of Joan's classes. I had a few friends that wanted me to start a little group with them so they could learn all that I learned. I wanted to but was afraid to ask Joan for her permission. Joan lived and breathed the Higher Self work she brought forward. She didn't judge others and was supportive of everyone's efforts to learn and to share. Anyone looking at the situation would not see any reason for me to be afraid of asking her. But I was. When I finally asked her, taking many weeks to get the courage, she was thrilled with the idea and said of course! I then realized it was time to deal with my fear of older people/authorities. I began to neutralize them. I recognized it was holding me prisoner to inequality and to the belief that those external voices were more important than my own. This was one that gave up many of its layers fast. This was tied to my mom because she had been one of the first authorities in my life, and I had absorbed her viewpoints about me as my own.

Again, our scrambles are complex and interwoven and most likely we will not understand them totally. Luckily, it doesn't matter.

Empowering: Divine Equality, Divine Clarity, Divine Courage, Divine Vision, Divine Understanding

Neutralizing My Astral Self-Identities

When the information came in on the Astral, I worked hard on all the Altered Realities that were my "Astral yous." Every pattern I uncovered related to Mom was carried in the Astral, too, so I was not shy about neutralizing as much as I could. I made sure to do all of them more than once because I knew I still created them with every thought. I was motivated! Sometimes, I would work on one or two identities and other times, I would work on neutralizing the totality of my conglomerate Astral energies.

You know I was successful in dissolving this scramble, and it enabled me to help Mom dissolve hers. All of you can do this work. You begin with any problem or pattern or emotional issue you may have. Take one or two elements of it and begin there. Or if you want, start with the whole scramble. You can do this.

The Evolutionary Thrust

Every single soul is Divinely Willed along the path of higher evolution. In the Human Kingdom (at the Free Will level), the idea of Free Will is valid in that it allows the individual the expression to do what it wants to do, to make decisions that it wants to make, to choose or not to choose whatever it wishes. And yet in the underlying Pure Soul Essence level, the human soul is Divinely Willed.

As humans, we are in a Free Will Kingdom and we make those Free Will decisions from the soul level. Yet, paradoxically, despite our Free Will, we are also Divinely Willed. But how can we operate with both Free Will and Divine Will at the same time?

Divine Will River

Think of Divine Will (an infinite flow of Originating Source Energy) as an inconceivably huge river running through the entire universe—both known and unknown—constantly moving from the lowest and densest frequency of energy to the highest, lightest, and most expanded frequency level. Every soul in the universe is in this river or this flow of Divine Will Energy. It only flows in one direction, as the direction of the river is never reversed. As souls move along the river, they move along in evolutionary frequency always moving upward. The river is gentle, never forcing a human soul to go faster than it is ready to go. The three lower kingdoms (Mineral, Plant, and Animal) move slowly but efficiently down the river because, being on Instinctive Will, the souls move with no resistance. However, at the Human Free Will level, the souls make their own decisions and their own choices. They have an infinite number of choices within this river of energy as to what to believe, how to live, and where and when to play out their journey. But no matter what they choose, we are all still on the river, still moving in the same direction as every other being. As humans, we all get confused, lost, afraid, doubtful, misdirected and often blame, surrender, fight, resist, defend, dare, and so much more. Yet, no matter what we do or where we go, we are always part of the evolutionary movement up the energetic river flow of Divine Will.

It is our Pure Soul Essence that connects us to this Divine Energy. All souls at every level in the universe are forever connected and carry all that the Originating Source was, is, and is becoming. Even though Charlie thought he was a soul lost, no soul is ever lost. This is why: the Pure Soul Essence connection is there forever. We are aspects or expressions of the Originating Source, and there is nowhere to go but with the flow. There is no place where there is no flow, no place to escape. There is no going backward.

Any move forward in evolution is permanent. Once a soul has made a step forward and is firmly in place, the soul cannot regress or move backward. In the 4ᵗʰ Dimensional reality, it may appear many times that souls step back. But what you view as a soul regressing is really personality and psychological distortions an individual soul must work out. These distortions are unrelated to the soul evolutionary standing that is permanently in place. And when ready, the soul will move forward once more.

It is in this way that we have Free Will while still operating within Divine Will. The river is symbolic of the Divine Will current, which we are all on, regardless of our level. Free Will is part of the complex flow of this evolutionary energy, operating within its specific parameters, just as Instinctive Will and Spiritual Will do.

In general, there are three ways that the humanities move through the flow depending on where they are in their journey. And none of the ways is wrong, bad, lucky, or unlucky. We are where we are when we are there.

1. Sometimes we are like a *passive leaf* in our journey, and we go where the flow takes us. This can mean our movement can be slow sometimes. When barriers appear, the leaf can be held up behind the block for hundreds or thousands of years. We may act in a passive manner because we carry a deep belief system that tells us we need to let the universe guide us. Sometimes we are the leaf because we have had several difficult lifetimes leading up to a lifetime where we decide to take a sabbatical on movement forward in order to heal from those traumas.

Sometimes we don't understand that we have a choice to travel any other way, either because we have just begun the journey or we have not been introduced to the concept as yet.

2. Other times, souls will *actively resist* the movement of the flow and will purposely take shelter at some place behind some barrier and build a home there for hundreds or thousands of years. The reasons we decide to move out of the flow on purpose may be because of fear—thinking that around the bend is a giant waterfall, or we get stuck on one pattern, a Soul Scramble, that we can't seem to find our way out of. We could also be waiting (at the unconscious level) for a situation, condition, or person to appear that we believe will fix us or make our lives better. And waiting for those external saviors can take a very long time.

3. The third situation is when we become *active partners* with the flow and anticipate barriers by working to avoid them and actively working to escape the barriers if they couldn't be avoided. The choice to actively stay in the flow and to move down the river of energy (or up the frequency level) could be because we are ready to become all we can be. Maybe we understand at some level that we are the directing identity of our lives and our journey. Or perhaps we are just fed up with the pain and suffering we are going through and decide we don't deserve it any more.

Of course there are infinite reasons for any soul to move in any one of these three general patterns. And we have all processed at different times each way. But while we are held within this gentle energetic flow of Divine Will, we continually make our Free Will decisions. The Divine Energy, though, carries us all in the general direction and guarantees us all to continue on our evolutionary process. There is *no* fate or destiny in the human level where the Divine Energy is calling the shots. We are still the directing identity, choosing to float along, choosing to move into a waiting pattern or choosing to use our Free Will to cooperate with the movement. Since I have benefited so greatly when I took the reins, I cannot help but encourage people to choose the third option, especially because now we are getting more help than ever before because of the *Evolutionary Thrust.*

Evolutionary Thrust

JOAN CULPEPPER QUOTE

It is time, in the evolutionary movement right now, where everything is getting ready to make a giant move forward. Things are different now than they were even 2,000 years ago at the evolutionary frequency level. In the last 2,000 years we have advanced the equivalent of 10,000 years of evolutionary frequency. And in the next 2,000 years, the evolutionary movement, in its totality, will increase by about 100,000 years.

The Originating Source is fed by all of our experiences—good, bad, or indifferent—across the Pure Soul Essence connection. Every experience of every soul at every level continually feeds into that connection. Not only are there an infinite number of souls across the universe within the four lower dimensions, but we must also consider there are many, many more dimensions (which I briefly introduce below) where the number of souls could be viewed as infinite to the infinite power. Therefore, Originating Source is in a constant state of evolving and growing and experiencing based on all that is fed to it by all souls on all levels. And every soul benefits from that because we also get the feedback. We are all that Originating Source was, is, and is becoming. We don't consciously know we're getting the feedback. But this Pure Soul Essence is our connecting link to the totality of all life and all levels.

The evolutionary movement is in the process of making a major thrust forward, and this is what the Higher Selves term the Evolutionary Thrust. The Evolutionary Thrust is the speedup of evolutionary frequency of the Originating Source as it prepares to take a giant leap forward. To go back to my analogy of the Divine Will energy flow, the Evolutionary Thrust speeds up that flow. The river of Divinely Willed Energy in which we are all connected has begun to move more quickly. And because we are part of it, connected by the Pure Soul Essence, we are being carried along at a quicker pace. Every single soul at every single level will, as a result, make this giant step forward simultaneously with the Originating Source. This is Originating Source pulling all souls forward in what would be viewed as an evolutionary leap. In addition, as previously mentioned, the flow of the evolutionary frequency is increasing at a exponential rate, meaning it is having a huge effect on all of humanity and all souls!

HIGHER SELF QUOTE

The Pure Soul Essence of each individual could be viewed symbolically as connected to the Evolutionary Thrust like a lighted rope. As the Evolutionary Thrust continues to process and build momentum, that beam of light pulls the individual along at the Pure Soul Essence level. As the pulling along takes place, individuals will undergo a proportionate acceleration of cleansing and purifying of the Altered Realities.

We are pulled along by the speedup of the divine river, moving into higher and higher frequencies; we will also be moving through the clarifying process of all that we carry at the Altered Reality level. We do not get the luxury of bypassing any of the patterns we need to become aware of, to release, and to neutralize. We cannot miss any of the steps of evolutionary movement up the frequency ladder by just waiting for the Divine Will Energy to do it for us. What it does mean, however, is that we will be stepping up the timing. Our emotionally imprinted experiences and Soul Scrambles that have collected through so many lifetimes will become part of the *pull-through process*, enabling us to clear out these unwanted patterns more quickly in order to stand in a state of purity.

Before the Evolutionary Thrust began, using the flow (river) of energy analogy, you could view the gentle flow as having little effect on our journey as humans. If we got stuck behind symbolic "boulders" (our Soul Scrambles) for example, the slow flow did little to move us along. It was gentle. As a result, we could be stuck there for 50,000 years before that slow flow would have any effect on us. An eon of time might be needed for us to become aware there was a way out (a different perspective to our problem which would result in movement forward again). However, with the increase in the flow due to the surge of thrusting energy, imagine the flow now pushing our awareness of the boulders so that we find our way out more quickly. Do we still have to deal with the boulders? Yes, we have to meet every block, every issue, every scramble, and cannot avoid even one. But it is as if the increased flow telescopes the action. If a problem or scramble may take 10 years to resolve, now it could take but one year. The question when we come face-to-face with the problems is, "Do we dig in our heels and resist dealing with them? Or do we do everything we can to help clear the blocks?"

What approach we use will determine how difficult or how smooth our journey is. Will there be a respite after some problem is resolved? Perhaps. However, it is also possible that there will be no respite or only a very short one. The flow takes us to each issue faster than before and will continue to do so at an ever-increasing rate.

The Consequences of the Evolutionary Speed-up

HIGHER SELVES QUOTE

This thrusting movement forward brings each individual to higher and higher levels of awakening, whether it be at the unconscious level or at the conscious level.

The Evolutionary Thrust moves us through an awakening process. And though normally we think of awakening as a positive thing, sometimes it may seem to have a negative bent. The awakening can happen at the unconscious level and often we are being pulled along this evolutionary momentum faster than we can easily assimilate. This can cause fatigue, a sense of apathy, or feeling as if our brain is on stun. It can create a loss of memory. Think of the movement going as fast as the speed of light. We have a thought. But we move so fast with the thrust, in an instant we have moved beyond the thought. Yet we're still standing in this reality with the knowledge that the thought was there but we cannot find it, we cannot remember it. Processing the awakening, therefore, presents the need for adjustments and assimilation that we are not even aware we need since much of it is occurring at the unconscious level.

On this planet (and all planets housing human souls), as the energy of evolutionary frequency continues to process the thrust, many humans have and will continue to hold on to the only reality that they are accustomed to—the reality of what they believe in. They cling hard to what they know, for it's the only thing that gives them any kind of security. Over time, the "stand fast" determination can continue to become more emphatic, more overt, and far more intense. As a result, we have and will continue to see fanaticism pertaining to the belief systems carried by those individuals. However, as the Higher Selves have said:

We wish to assure each of you that every soul at every level (regardless of any act or intention on the part of the soul) will ultimately, through the Evolutionary Thrust itself, go through what could be viewed as major pull-throughs that assures the soul's return to the Originating Source.

Because of the Evolutionary Thrust, there is a pulling process from the Originating Source that reaches, touches, and pulls all souls at all levels through the places they may be stuck, including those who have moved into the fanatical place or any type of "digging in the heels" action. This is the giant pull-through and happens because of the Pure Soul Essence connection. A pull-through often manifests as some sort of crisis in the life pattern—an illness, some type of serious loss, an unexpected major change, an accident, or natural disaster that has major consequences. We still have to address anything and everything standing in our way. Instead of taking each evolutionary move one slow step at a time, the pull-through causes us, in an energetic way, to run as fast as we can. The process can be intense and upsetting, especially if there is limited understanding as to why we brought the event or situation into our lives. When we come out on the other side and have moved up the ladder of understanding, we often appreciate the instruction and are better off. But it can be hard to see that while we are experiencing it.

Even though it may seem things happen to us that we don't choose and fate is involved, this is not the case. At the soul level we are the ones that choose the issues and conditions of the pull-through. We are never victims.

Being the passive leaf or the active resister to the Evolutionary Thrust flow would intensify the pressure, stress, fatigue, drama, and the pain in our lives when we could have been more proactive about it. Fortunately, we have the neutralizing process from the Higher Selves to allow us to be the pilot that steers effectively past the barriers and gives us the ability to dissolve those blocks we do get stuck behind. And it also allows us to get through a pull-through we hadn't been able to avoid more easily as we now have the techniques to neutralize all the emotionalizing.

HIGHER SELF QUOTE

The Evolutionary Thrust could bring to mind the idea of chaos, which would appear to many as if it has and will continue to become worse. However, chaos is only a centering point between the old order and the new order. For a new order to exist, the old order must first be torn down. This then appears (through the eyes of the individual viewing it) to be a state of chaos.

I encourage all to shift their viewpoint to the positive idea that the evolutionary momentum is taking us into higher levels of consciousness. It does so as it brings to the surface within all souls upon this planet (and on other planets) whatever each soul believes it must experience in order for it to move through that tunnel of soul darkness to the other side. This is how we will process so that we can stand in a cleaner and purer state. This can seem like chaos, in our own lives and for so many around the planet. But again, we cannot bypass anything that needs to be addressed. Thus, the pull-through compresses all experiences each of us determine at the soul level that we need to go through, resulting in the dialing up of the intensity. And this can create painful situations and individuals can feel as if they have been turned inside out.

In summary, there are three options we generally have as we move through life or through the Divinely Willed evolutionary flow. We can be the passive leaf, the active resister, or the invested participant who works with the energy to be discerning, pro-active and intending to help the self. Being aware and actively working to facilitate and ease one's process can greatly reduce the difficulties as well as the number of barriers we need to get pulled through.

Evolution

HIGHER SELF QUOTE

It is important to remember evolution is eternal and never-ending. You might view the Originating Source symbolically as being compulsively obsessive about bringing back to it all of the souls it has "aspected out" and about continuing its evolvement and expansion. Each time a soul or a planet returns to that Originating Source, it is expulsed outward again into Outer Dimensions.

Clearly, not evolving is not an option. We have a long way to go before returning to the Originating Source. After the Human

Kingdom (the 4th Dimension), there are three more dimensions, the 5th, 6th and 7th. The 8th and 9th Dimensions are the incubatory and preparatory dimensions that prepare all souls for the return to the Originating Source. At that point, the souls are "aspected out" again to the next higher series of kingdoms or to what the Higher Selves call the *Outer Dimensions.* You can view this symbolically like the scales on a piano. The very lowest key on the piano is the dense world of our Mineral Kingdom/Dimension that we live with. So the 2nd note would be the Plant Kingdom, the 3rd the Animal Kingdom, the 4th would be the Human Kingdom, etc. The next 3 notes would be the 5th, 6th and 7th Dimensions. Therefore, the 1st complete 7 notes, 1 scale, would symbolically be the reality we live in, each note indicating a new dimension as they move up in evolutionary frequency. There are no 8th and 9th keys on a piano scale so for the sake of the analogy we'll ignore those for the moment.

On the piano, after the first 7 notes (the 1st scale), a 2nd scale begins at a higher frequency. Then there is a 3rd scale and a 4th, etc. Therefore, as you go up the keyboard, the notes "A" through "G" repeat in scale order again and again at a higher pitch as you move up. Similarly, this is what happens with evolutionary movement. It is like the process of moving up the keyboard, one scale at a time with each dimension moving into higher and higher in frequency levels. Just as the notes "A" through "G" repeat at higher frequencies going up the keyboard, so do the dimensions in the evolutionary scale. Therefore, the 1st level of the first Outer Reality is likened to the Mineral Kingdom of our scale but it is running at a much higher frequency (a higher pitch). The frequency level of the Mineral Kingdom in that Outer Reality is higher than the 7th Dimension of the Reality that we live in.

It is almost impossible to imagine what it is like in the Outer Dimensions. The Higher Selves have told us that evolution has produced 4 Outer Realities all with 7 dimensions (plus the 8th and 9th that are the "birth canal" to the Originating Source each time) and each one operating on higher and higher frequency levels.

Our reality scale—the one that starts at the very bottom of the piano—is the most recent reality birthed by the Originating Source. That is why I said in the beginning of the book that Originating Source is infinite eons older than the Milky Way Galaxy. As long as the known universe has been around, it is but a drop in the ocean of time compared to what has come before and what is still unknown.

Final Perspectives

We now understand how the soul and the mind are part of the totality of who we are. We know how the soul communicates with us. We are aware of what to pay attention to in our lives and how to see the negative events and situations are opportunities the soul uses to propel us to awareness and healing. We know we are the directors of our own destiny. We can decide whether we want to be a leaf, a resister, or one that cooperates (by neutralizing our negative energies) with the speedup of the river of Divine Energy as it telescopes our issues to come up sooner and closer together. Lastly, we have the healing techniques, the focus of attention, and the motivators to use them.

Our increased awareness has moved us away from the old system where the soul and the mind operated separately. The conflict, confusion, and ignorance meant that both parts of us worked with one symbolic arm tied behind its back. The mind tried to power through the life as if it was in control, but was instead being led around by false beliefs, solidified truths, self-identities, and misunderstandings carried at the soul level. The soul, in attempts to bring awareness, clarity, and healing screamed at us by manifesting problem after problem only to be ignored.

SOUL PSYCHOLOGY has woven the picture of how our journey within the Human Kingdom is set up to bring all of us to full consciousness. It brings us to the place where the soul and the mind work as a team—the soul leads us to where and what we need to heal and the mind then uses the techniques to accomplish all that our soul desires. Together, they can be our powerhouse enabling us to accomplish more in a year than what we had accomplished in many previous lifetimes put together.

With our self-awareness, we can look around the globe. What we often see are the wars, climate changes, upheavals, conflicts, natural disasters, torture, imprisonments, murders, and much suffering from many quarters. What more can we see about our world from our new, more expanded viewpoint?

First, every situation involves individuals that have chosen to be part of the problems. There are no victims, only the perception that there are victims. We can ask ourselves some new questions now like what could the individuals be learning in that situation? Why would they choose to suffer like that? What kind of journey could those souls have had up to now that would lead them to live the way they do? We would not have answers for these questions but *we now have the questions!* Instead of blaming/judging/criticizing/attacking, we can have more levelheaded approaches, different types of resolutions, and viable solutions. The focus would be on the underlying causes of the problems rather than using Band-Aids that temporarily stop the bleeding but don't heal the wound.

Second, our knowledge of the Evolutionary Thrust will add more to our new perceptions. We realize if our individual problems are being telescoped, intensified and sped up, it is happening globally. And each situation, event, and upheaval involves many individuals, all of whom have an opportunity to process and learn what they have chosen. Not all of those involved will be moving through the event in the same way. Some will be leafs, passive and unaware that they can be more proactive and self-aware. Others will cooperate with the speed-up of the evolutionary movement and will actively participate in finding answers and ways to resolve the situation. Still others will be active resisters to change, digging in their heels, inside feeling fearful, threatened, or confused. All three types will be involved in any event resulting in the appearance of chaos in the world. Because the Thrust is increasing on a moment-to-moment basis, there will be an increase of what *looks like* global chaos as the many hotspots unfold in confusion, turmoil, and disorder. The chaos signifies the old order is being dissolved to make way for the new. For some, the transition will be easy or easier. For others, it could mean great suffering, fear and/or even rage.

Every soul is going through the Soul/Mind detox, the confrontation with their own inner "demons of the mind" (the false beliefs, limiting truths, and misunderstandings) in order to neutralize and clear them to move into a state of balance and harmony within. Some are going through it at the conscious level but many more are going through it at the unconscious level, leading to a constant struggle to understand what is going on. The many conflicts around the world are the result of the billions of people going through this process at the same time. As more individuals become aware that the battle between dark and light does not mean person against person but is going on within themselves, there will be a shift worldwide.

Third, because the Earth's soul is evolving in a manner that moves parallel with the souls housed upon it, we can also understand that it, too, is going through its own detoxification. It is cleansing and purifying just as the humanities are doing. As we care and respect our fellow man, we care and respect our planet. The natural disasters are the mechanism through which the planet's body cleanses itself. Few particles on the planet are still pure. Having housed life for millions of years, the particles have been housed in more bodies (whether plant, animal, or human) than we could count. In this way, the particles have taken on their own pollutants and toxins which are experiencing the speed-up of the Evolutionary Thrust as well. We may see more natural upheavals and planetary changes. With the determination and focus by so many worldwide to learn about and prevent ecological disasters, we are doing and will continue to do what we can as planetary cohabitants.

I mention the increases in worldwide individual and societal upheavals as well as the natural disasters because often doomsday prophets surface that feed on the fear we all carry. I offer another perspective here. Just as Charlie is not a soul lost, nor is anyone or anything else—no mineral, plant, animal, human or the planet Earth—a lost being. We will move through the cleansing process to the other side of balance and harmony. The tide will turn, as more and more people cooperate with the energy, taking on an increasing awareness and using it to help themselves and others. We don't know the timing. In a Free Will arena, probabilities change daily, but we will reach a tipping point without needing everyone to be aware. At that point, there will be a powerful tide moving the humanities toward the respect, caring, understanding, and acceptance of themselves, each other and all souls. And the tide is already building steadily.

I wish everyone success on their journey, and hope you now understand the path all souls take. Clarity allows us to be more accepting and loving to ourselves and all others. This practical, non-judgmental approach sees all individuals as equals and asserts there are *no* patterns too negative or outrageous or unreachable with the Higher Self techniques. Everyone can use these tools and succeed in changing their life patterns.

I am always available for questions and help. (See Appendix IV.) I encourage everyone to get started or to continue using this information to turn your lives around just as it did mine!

APPENDICES

APPENDIX I
GLOSSARY

1st Dimension—The first level of evolutionary soul consciousness/awareness. It consists of the Mineral Kingdom and is governed by Instinctive Will.

2nd Dimension—The second level of evolutionary soul consciousness/awareness. It consists of the Plant Kingdom (the flora) and is governed by Instinctive Will.

3rd Dimension—The third level of evolutionary soul consciousness/awareness. It consists of the Animal Kingdom (the fauna) and is governed by Instinctive Will.

4th Dimension—The fourth level of evolutionary soul consciousness/awareness. It consists of the Human Kingdom (incarnate and disincarnate) and is governed by Free Will.

5ᵗʰ Dimension—The fifth level of evolutionary soul consciousness/ awareness. It consists of the Inner-Planetary Kingdom (Inner-Planetaries) and is governed by Spiritual Will. All humans eventually "graduate" into this dimension.

5ᵗʰ Dimensionals—The overall term that refers to the souls that have graduated to the 5ᵗʰ Dimension. They are also called Inner-Planetaries.

6ᵗʰ Dimension—The sixth level of evolutionary soul consciousness/ awareness. It consists of the Spiritual Hierarchy Kingdom and is governed by Spiritual Will.

7ᵗʰ Dimension—The seventh level of evolutionary soul consciousness/awareness. It is governed by Spiritual Will. There is not much information about this dimension—yet.

Altered Realities—Altered Realities are complex energy identities that exist within our etheric bodies. They consist of thought forms, emotional blueprints, and habit imprints generated by each soul as he or she lives each life. The Altered Realities exist at the etheric level and are in a genuine *state of being*—though soulless and mindless—that a Soul/Mind has created for itself. They each have their own energetic dwelling place (that we have created through thought), social grouping, and philosophical beliefs. If you are able to sense at the energetic level, you can talk with them to find out when they were created and what they think, feel, and believe. Altered Realities exist in each person's private etheric field as well as in the Earth's Astral band.

Amalgamation—The joining or blending of your own energy field with the energy field of the Higher Selves, the Pure Soul Essence, and/or the Originating Source. Amalgamation is done by imagining, sensing, or verbally stating the following: *"I am one with my Pure Soul Essence Light and I ask that it fully encompass the Totality of my physical body and my etheric Bodies. I become one with the Originating Source of All There Is. I am amalgamated with the Totality of my Higher Selves."*

Amalgamate—To move into the state of amalgamation. A person amalgamates to become one with or merge with Divine Energies. This gives them permission to become part of and active in your Free Will pattern.

Animal Kingdom—*(See definition for 3rd Dimension)*

Astral—A term for energy fields that surround the Earth and contain the projected thoughts of all the humanities past and present. It could be viewed as the planet's Thought Form Body. The energies in the Astral are soulless and mindless and are heavily weighted by the negative as compared to the positive. The Astral is not Heaven, though it coexists with Heaven and all souls move through the Astral Chakra System upon laying aside the body in order to get to Heaven.

Attachee—A human being, incarnate on this planet, who has a disincarnate human emotionally attached to him or her. A disincarnate cannot attach to another human unless that human carries something at the Soul/Mind level that gives the disincarnate permission to be attached. This is usually not a conscious choice by the attachee and is not the same as possession.

Chakras/Chakra System—Energy exchange points that are part of the etheric energy body system around the physical body.

Channelling—The merging of the mind of a human being (who is incarnate on the planet) with the soul of a disincarnate human (who resides in Heaven) in order to communicate and pull in information.

Conscious or Consciousness—There are three elements to the concept of Consciousness.

1. The state of being actively aware of your thoughts, your physical body, your current state of mind, and all that is going on around you.

2. An attempt to keep your focus on specific thoughts or a specific state of mind without transient thoughts.

3. The continuum of levels of soul awareness within the Soul/Mind.

Creative Body—An envelope of energy surrounding each human being that contains all of the soul's potential creations as they exist at this point in time. The Creative Body uses your thought forms, habit imprints and emotional blueprints to slowly weave the pattern that filters through and manifests into your physical reality. It is here your outward physical life is *manufactured*. This manufacturing process takes place over a period of time prior to its manifestation into the physical. The Creative Body can be "read" to determine what you are creating for your future.

Creative Life Force Energy—The compelling force within all souls at every level. It is an impersonal Divine Energy that creates based on the nature and quality of the fuel it has to work with. In the Human Kingdom, this includes the thought forms, habit imprints, and emotional blueprints.

De-intensify—The process of moving an energy's frequency to lower levels thereby permitting it to be used safely within a lower dimension.

Dimensions—Evolutionary frequency levels that represent the evolutionary stages of a soul.

Disincarnate—A human out of body living at the soul level in the Human Kingdom Heavens.

Divine Energies—Energy (in its purest form and highest frequency) that comes directly from Originating Source. While Divine Energy exists in a state of totality, it also is made up of infinite elements (such as Divine Love, Divine Forgiveness, Divine Mind) that can be utilized individually. All Divine Energies are de-intensified down to the level accessible by the soul wishing to use it.

Divine Light—The Divine Energies of the Originating Source.

Divine Material Balance—A Divine Aspect of Originating Source that has been infused into the soul essence of the planet Earth. It carries the "I have" concept in perfect balance. The energy helps us materialize the abstract into the concrete. All human souls on this planet chose, in part, to reincarnate here for help from the planet. Materializing into the concrete is not only about money; it is about the manifestation of anything into a material form. This includes financial security, the health of the physical body, our gifts and talents, and our relationships.

Divine Will—Divine Will is one of the powerful aspects that makes up the conglomerate of the Originating Source of All There Is. The Divine Will aspect is the energy that moves us along our soul's evolutionary path. It is not imposed upon us in the Human Kingdom but offered if we are *willing* to take it in.

Emotional Blueprints—Patterns held in the Emotional Response Body that govern how we will respond emotionally to any given situation. A blueprint is a response pattern built up from previous lifetimes. In this life, when an event occurs, the response pattern is triggered, releasing an emotional reaction from the past that greatly colors (discolors) how we experience the event in the present. Note: When you do work within the Emotional Response Body, you are neutralizing the blueprint, not the emotions themselves.

Emotional Response Body—An envelope of energy surrounding each human being in which emotional blueprints are held.

Emotionalizing—The act of processing an emotional reaction and losing the rational self to that reaction. By being aware that you are emotionalizing, you can stand within the center of the emotion— not *be* the emotion. You allow the emotion to be whatever it is and properly process it by releasing it into the Light.

Entity—This often refers to a disincarnate human, a human soul that has laid aside its body and resides in the Human Kingdom

Heavens. An entity is still a member of the Humanities and is part of the Free Will Kingdom. Just like the term "human," there is nothing innately negative or positive about the term "entity."

Energy Identities—The term used to signify all the thought forms, habit imprints, and emotional blueprints that each soul creates and accumulates over the span of its entire journey through the Human Kingdom Universe. They are soulless and mindless energy forms, energy without Soul/Mind reasoning and consciousness.

Etheric—A general term that refers to the non-physical plane and is most often used by the Higher Selves when referring to the energetic space around the physical body.

Etheric Bodies—The Thought Form Body, the Emotional Body, the Habit Body and the Creative Body (as well as other bodies) that occupy the etheric space around the physical body.

Evolutionary Thrust—The process where Originating Source makes a leap forward in its own evolution, pulling *all* souls with it through Pure Soul Essence connection from a lower energy vibration into a higher energy vibration.

External Authorities—Those individuals in any part of one's life that are presented or seen as having more expertise, experience, knowledge or wisdom than someone else.

Façade Soul—The 4ᵗʰ Dimensional soul that is taken on by the 5ᵗʰ Dimensionals who volunteered to return to the Human Kingdom. Even though the term "façade" is being used, it is no less real than the true Human Soul. They must abide by the same rules and regulations of the Human Kingdom and are subject to the same processes.

Female Nature—Every soul carries within its totality both elements of the female and of the male. As each human soul moves through its evolutionary journey, it reincarnates as both males and females in many lives. The full scope of the soul process—both the male characteristics and the female characteristics—is experienced, discovered developed, and eventually balanced. (See Male Nature)

Free Will—The energy level of the 4th Dimension relating to the fact that souls on this level possess total and complete power and responsibility for all circumstances surrounding their lives. No trespass of any human soul is possible; what happens to someone must be agreed to at the soul level. (It is important to note that Free Will is held at the unconscious or soul etheric level.)

Habit Body—An envelope of energy surrounding each human being in which our habit imprints reside. It carries the energy that propels us to action.

Habit Imprints—The energetic forms created in the Habit Body every time we think a thought and/or we do an action. Every thought and action creates an impression in the Habit Body energy field. Habit Imprints carry no conscious thought, though they can be deeply ingrained, and they carry the propelling energy behind our oft-repeated actions. The deepest imprints are responsible for our most ingrained habits.

Heaven—The energetic space where human souls move upon the laying aside of the body at the end of each life. The soul carries with it whatever conditions exist within its Soul/Mind at the point in time the death takes place. Souls stay there until they incarnate into the next body. And the humanities in place in Heaven are from all the planets within the Human Kingdom Universe, not just Earth. It is no requirement that you be a good person to get in. Heaven is a part of the Human Kingdom Universe, and it is still in the Free Will arena.

Higher Selves—5th Dimensional Soul Aspects that carry and project de-intensified energy and informational frequencies into the Human Kingdom in order to assist in the evolutionary process of the four lower kingdoms. Being from the Divine Will frequency level, they do not trespass the Free Will of the Humanities.

Highest Ideal—While in a state of amalgamation, we are processing from the Highest Ideal. This means we are moving on the highest road, the highest frequency, the deepest healing, and the greatest understanding that we can reach in that moment in time. With the next amalgamation, we will work again at the next highest level in that moment and so on. Even when we are not completely conscious and aware of where we need to go or what we need to do, we give permission (by amalgamating) at the Free Will level for the Divine Energies to be the power behind our process and our movement forward.

The Highest Ideal protects us from possible negative energies; the actions we take cannot harm ourselves or another person; when asking for information, we will receive it at the highest frequency level we can reach; and when we ask for energy for any purpose, we also will receive it at the highest level that we can process.

Human Kingdom—*(See definition for 4th Dimension)*

Human Kingdom Heavens—The etheric space that houses disincarnate human souls.

Human Kingdom Universe—This is where all the humanities exist. It includes Earth and countless other planets that house the four lower kingdoms. It also includes the Human Kingdom Heavens where the humanities go when out of body between lives.

Impress—This is the unconscious guidance or communication that our Higher Selves would use to encourage us to some action or to an expanded understanding. They cannot trespass and would only influence us in the Highest Ideal. We always have the option to follow or not to follow the impress.

Incarnate—A human in body living at the mind level on a planet that houses human souls.

In Frequency—The process a human uses in order to enter into and communicate with the Higher Selves at the 5th Dimensional frequency level.

Instinctive Will—The energy level of the 1st, 2nd, and 3rd Dimension where souls on these levels go through their evolutionary process based on instincts.

Inner-Planetaries—*(See definition for 5th Dimensionals)*

Inner-Planetary Kingdom—*(See definition for 5th Dimension)*

Jane & Company—A term coined by Joan Culpepper to refer to a specific group of disincarnate human souls that she and other healers met in the early 1980s. These souls were at a very low level of evolutionary understanding and were often misguided, unaware, and at times, destructive. Eventually, Joan Culpepper (with the help of the Higher Selves) led this group of disincarnates through an educational process that allowed them to not only choose to move out of their stuck belief systems but also to form a grassroots organization that would help others in the Heavens who were in similar situations. Jane & Company is still there helping other disincarnate or about-to-be disincarnate humans.

Light—The symbol that is most often used to represent and activate the Divine Energies. This symbol also represents the Pure Soul Essence, the Divine Energy contained within each soul.

Male Nature—Every soul carries within its totality both elements of the female and of the male. As each human soul moves through its evolutionary journey, it reincarnates as both males and females in many lives. Thus, the full scope of the soul process—both the male characteristics and the female characteristics—is experienced, developed, and eventually balanced. (See Female Nature)

Masqueraders—Disincarnate human souls who pretend to have higher knowledge. These souls seek out those who they can teach, guide, and direct (whether incarnate or disincarnate) for their own manipulative or devious reasons. Although many may not come from a place of purity, some masqueraders sincerely believe that they know best. Like all souls who reside in the Human Kingdom, masqueraders can be educated and assisted in moving into higher levels of evolutionary consciousness.

Master Teachers—Disincarnate human souls who are trained by 5th Dimensionals to be of service to the humanities. Laying aside the body does not automatically create a Master Teacher. The Master Teachers are high-level 4th Dimensionals who decide to take on the thousands of years of training necessary to become Masters. They offer help by guiding humans through their evolutionary process.

Mind—The mental and emotional process within the current life—how you think, feel, react, and process your experiences. Every time we incarnate, our soul takes on a newborn body and a mind to go with it. It is new for every lifetime. The mind then becomes the mechanism that allows the soul to experience and learn while we are in body. At the time of physical death, the mind of each life then rejoins the soul to become a part of that conglomerate.

Mineral Kingdom—*(See definition for 1st Dimension)*

Neutrality—The Higher Selves use the term in two different ways.

1. The state of mind between belief and disbelief and between truth and untruth.

2. The harmless energetic state where the thought forms, the habit imprints, and emotional responses move after being processed by the Divine Energy.

Neutralizing—The act of rendering the energy identities carried within our three etheric bodies harmless. It brings our thought forms into a non-magnetic state, fills in the habit imprints to disarm the power of their propellant energy and dissolves the energetic bond within an emotional blueprint that holds emotions attached to an event. This process brings all three simultaneously into a state of neutrality, using the Divine Light that we each carry within our Pure Soul Essence.

Originating Source—The neutral, balanced and impersonal energy that is the originating source of all life and includes all life. This is another term for God/Allah/Universal Source, etc. yet it carries an expanded meaning. It is used instead of the more common words, as it is free of personal connotations and personal bias and does not trigger the Astral energies.

Outer Dimensions—Where souls go to continue their evolutionary movement after they have completed the 7 dimensions in our reality—mineral, plant, animal, human, 5th, 6th, and 7th dimensions. The 8th and 9th incubatory levels prepare them to return to the Originating Source. At that point, Originating Source gives birth to them into the first dimension (likened to our mineral kingdom but at a higher frequency level than our 7th dimension) of the first Outer Reality. There are at least 4 outer realities.

Plant Kingdom—*(See definition for 2nd Dimension)*

Proper Self Love—The cultivation of a strong, positive, and conscious relationship with the self, based on our true perfect identity and not on our outward expression. It is the internal complete awareness and acceptance of the perfection and beauty of one's soul; it contains no self-judgment.

Pull-Through—Pull-throughs occur during upward frequency shifts when individual souls *choose* to be pulled through to the next level of "conscious awareness" in a short period of time and at an accelerated speed. These souls experience what they would normally have gone through without an evolutionary frequency upsurge but during the speedup (the Evolutionary Thrust), it is done in a compressed manner and often experienced and perceived as chaotic.

Pure Soul Essence—The divine part of every soul that is a part of, and directly connected to, the Originating Source. It is the highest, purest, most perfect part of each soul. Focusing on your Pure Soul Essence activates the eternal connection with the Originating Source and allows us access to all its knowledge, wisdom, and power in our free will arena.

Reflecting—The process that a human (in body) uses in order to mirror or act out what an entity (disincarnate) wishes to express or communicate. The incarnate human remains in complete conscious control of all his/her bodily functions and mental abilities throughout the entire process. This process differs from channeling in that the disincarnate does not merge its soul with the mind of the human reflecting it.

Solidified Truth—An Altered Reality so heavily intensified over time by the thoughts of the humanities that it is perceived as a fact. The belief in this truth is so powerful that it becomes *absolute and unquestionable* in the mind of the believer.

Soul—The conglomerate energy of awareness built up over eons of time. Knowledge and higher levels of understanding are gained as the soul experiences lifetime after lifetime. It is a conglomeration of all the minds of the past. After death, the mind of the current life joins the conglomerate soul energy. As the soul evolves, it moves up the frequency ladder into higher and higher states of awareness and understanding.

Soul Aspect—A part of a soul that has "broken off" or "aspected out" to experience and express its own individual existences. Each part is separate but equal in the same way an amoeba that divides creates two amoebae that fully function. It can be an aspect of a human soul or a 5th Dimensional Soul. Aspecting happens at every level of evolution including the Originating Source. All beings are aspects of the Originating Source. Each and every aspect contains the Pure Soul Essence.

Soul Fracture—This is a Soul Scramble gone so dark and deep that it has resulted in the soul's choosing an insanity pattern.

Soul Psychology—The study of how our prior lifetimes of experiences (both incarnate and disincarnate) have led to the creation of the belief systems, the unconscious conditioning, the soul scrambles, and the self-identities that have permeated and defined us in each successive life as we have journeyed through the Human Kingdom Universe.

Soul Scramble—This is a term used to indicate a dysfunctional, limiting, and often painful pattern in our lives that holds us firmly stuck in a rat wheel of repetition of unwanted situations. It is often born from personal events and/or cultural conditions when a mind makes (and locks into) one or more erroneous conclusions and misinterpretations during its life experiences and/or during the death experience. The scramble further develops during the long and problematic path of many lifetimes because a soul continues to accumulate and entrench more misconceptions (as it adds the experiences from each new life) becoming imprisoned in its false beliefs. A Soul Scramble will affect a soul's choices in most of its subsequent reincarnations, thus propelling a soul on a difficult journey. In time, the soul will unscramble its false beliefs and misunderstandings that are at its foundation. This process will lead the soul to deeper understandings and will enhance its sense of self-awareness and its evolutionary growth.

Soul Set—A Soul Set is when with the laying aside of the body, the mind of the prior life remains fixed upon the experiences of that past life. This can happen when death occurs if the mind is overwrought with distress, discomfort, jealousy, anger, or any intensely powerful emotion. These types of powerful emotions can lock (set) a soul's focus of attention to the life it just left instead of toward its conglomerate soul. In other words, it locks into experiences of that prior life with such an intense focus that the soul holds onto that mind aspect while in Heaven.

Spiritual Practices—Within every human culture, there are religious and metaphysical customs unrelated to the secular world of everyday life. The practices (such as how to behave and what to believe) are dictated, directed, or encouraged by those with the spiritual authority and are usually followed by many within the society.

Spirit Guide—A disincarnate human who has reached a high frequency in its evolution and made a decision to move into service for the humanities. There is formal training in place for the guides to learn and develop the necessary skills.

366

Spiritual Will—The energy level of the 5th, 6th, and 7th dimensions where the souls on these levels consciously agree to operate on Divine Will.

Surrogate—Someone who, during the process of distant healing, stands in to represent the person being healed. While acting in that temporary role, the surrogate becomes the instrument through which the healing energy can be projected. The healing energies that are received by the surrogate are then infused into the one being healed. Surrogates can be used for healing either an incarnate or disincarnate human.

Thought Form Body—An envelope of energy surrounding each human being in which every thought from every lifetime resides.

Thought Forms—Collections of thought energy that are held within the Thought Form Body. With every thought, an energy is created that has its own magnetic signature. All thoughts are attracted to like thoughts. These groupings of like thoughts (the thought forms) continue to magnetically attract more like thoughts. Because we have had thoughts from the first moment we arrived in the Human Kingdom, we carry with us an infinite number of thought forms, ranging in size from minute to huge. Thought forms exist in each person's private etheric field as well as in the Earth's Astral Band.

APPENDIX II
More on the Higher Selves

As explained, the evolution of a soul begins at the mineral level and then proceeds over eons of time to the Plant, the Animal, and then to the Human Kingdom. When human souls have progressed through all the levels of human, they then are ready to graduate into the 5th Dimension. Upon graduation (which takes place solar system wide—not one individual at a time—and involves moving *both* body and soul into the higher frequencies), these souls move into the Spiritual Will Kingdom. They take on Divine Will as a conscious choice (while the first three kingdoms are Divine Will at the unconscious level). The choice means that those in the 5th Dimension take on a service commitment to help the four lower kingdoms evolve.

How does this relate to all of us? How do we access and connect with those expanded 5th energies and expanded information? There are *three* ways.

First, every human soul (no matter what human frequency level it is on) has a 5th Dimensional that oversees its progress in its evolutionary movement. This means that there are 5th Dimensionals behind the scenes helping all of humanity and would aid any one of them should they be asked. (Although 5th Dimensionals perform many tasks, most of those tasks will not be discussed until a future book on Soul Evolution.) *Anyone and everyone*, then, has access to 5th Dimensional energy by using the power of focused thought to amalgamate, which then gives the permission for that Divine Energy to become active in our Free Will Kingdom.

Second, there are human souls who have moved into the highest levels of human evolution and often have parts of their soul—soul aspects—that have actually reached that 5th Dimensional frequency level. They carry elements of the soul process (aspects) that vibrate to the level of that higher-level energy stream. This happens even though the human has not yet graduated into the 5th Dimension. These souls then have direct access to the knowledge and wisdom from that 5th Dimensional evolutionary stream of energy. There are many millions of souls such as these on this planet today due to the evolutionary movement of the planet itself.

This aspecting process happens at every level of soul evolution. For example, there are animal souls who have parts or aspects of their soul process that have reached into the frequency level of human. We all know animals (don't we?) that seem almost human. It is because they, too, have soul aspects that have reached the human frequency levels.

Third, there are 5th Dimensionals that have volunteered to return to the Human Kingdom to give more hands-on help to the evolutionary process of the four lower dimensions. These 5th Dimensionals are present here in body housing a human soul as a façade or an overlay "on top of" its *True Soul Essence*—its 5th Dimensional Soul Aspect. It doesn't mean that these people—5th Dimensionals with a façade human soul—are aliens. They carry a dual soul nature in the same way some carry a dual citizenship for two countries.

Upon the return to the Human Kingdom, an aspect of the 5th Dimensional soul (its True Soul Essence) has de-intensified down to a lower frequency of energy that will not harm the humanities. It then takes on a human soul which overlays its own 5th Dimensional soul essence. The human soul is necessary because they must obey the rules and regulations of the Human Kingdom Universe. And these rules include the requirement (one of several) of operating within the Free Will pattern as opposed to the Spiritual Will that exists within the 5th Dimension.

When this third group of souls de-intensified their 5th Dimensional Soul Aspect to move into the Human Kingdom, they left soul imprints of themselves at each frequency level. This created a chain or a ladder made up of these Higher Self Soul Aspects. These aspects connect the lowest frequency of the True Soul Essence (which is anchored within the façade human soul) to its 5th Dimensional self that still has its beingness within the 5th Dimension. This powerful ladder-like connection facilitates the ability of the human façade soul to access the higher frequency levels of information and energy.

There are many millions of these dual souls present on this planet (while many trillions have been operational in the Human Kingdom Universe for eons of time). They are currently here on Earth in the millions in order to help with the evolutionary concepts that are in process. For the most part, these people are unaware of their dual soul nature, though at some inner level they likely could sense it and would resonate with the idea. Because they are in the Human Kingdom, and have been for eons of time, they go through and experience the human condition just like all of the humanities. Thus, everything in this book relates to them as well.

No matter which group any soul is in on the planet, all have access to the higher frequencies of 5th Dimensional information and energy. And in every case, the energy streams come from the Divine Will level and must be invited in. Both the second and third group of souls have the seat of the 5th Dimensional energy within, meaning that the Higher Selves are held within and are a significant part of the soul process. The common concept that the Higher Selves are the higher evolved parts of ourselves is thus valid. The first category of souls—those who have not yet developed soul aspects reaching the 5th dimensional level—do not have the higher energy streams anchored within. But this does not hamper them in any way should they want to access the energy. And it is not necessary to know which of the three groups you are in.

Connecting to the Higher Selves

When connecting to the Higher Selves, dismiss the idea that it is similar to how a medium or a channel brings in information from a human soul who has laid aside the body and is residing in Heaven. Your Higher Selves do not reside in Heaven (though the souls that carry the human façade or overlay do return to Heaven between each life, as again they must obey the rules and regulations of the Human Kingdom). Channeling is used to bring in information from other souls within the Human Kingdom. It is a person-to-person, long distance call so to speak. Bringing in information from the Higher Selves is a different technique. The Higher Selves suggest that if you want a symbol for what you would be doing when bringing in your HS information, you could view yourself as a receiving station—as satellites that pick up pictures (symbols) and words from electronic broadcasts. We could view tuning in to the 5th Dimensional energy streams in a similar manner.

Thought is an energy. We tend to think it is horizontal in nature because we think one thought and then another and then another. It can seem as if thought unfolds in front of you in a horizontal linear path. But the true nature of thought as described by the Higher Selves is vertical, running from lower frequencies of energy to higher and higher ones. Every concept (idea) is carried at every frequency level. The higher the frequency, the more expanded the thought (concept). For example, the thought about what our relationship is to the universe many centuries ago was that the Earth was the center of the universe with the sun revolving around us. This concept evolved in time to where we came to understand that, instead, the Sun was the center of the universe with Earth revolving around it. And with more expansion, we came to understand that the sun is not the center of the universe either but rather the sun is just a part of the Milky Way, one of thousands of galaxies (known and unknown) that are made up of infinite numbers of suns.

It is important to understand the vertical nature of thought because the way to connect to the Higher Self energy streams is to move into the higher frequency levels of thought. The phrase used to describe the connection process with the HS is *going into frequency.* It is a conscious movement up the levels of thought until we reach into the frequency levels that are 5th Dimensional in nature. And because the frequency is so high there, the information and knowledge is beyond the frequency level of thought that we have here in the Human Kingdom.

Joan Culpepper's Process

The focus that led Joan to be able to pull in the Higher Self information started early on. She (who carried the dual soul nature) responded to her Higher Self *impress* (the unconscious guidance that she could choose to follow or not) to work from the highest level downward as opposed to the lowest level upward. She chose to follow the impress (not even understanding what it was at the time) and would not call forth Spirit Guides and Master Teachers and instead always asked for information from the Originating Source. This focus was significant because it allowed Joan to tap into the highest level of evolutionary information attainable in any moment, with her abilities constantly improving. Over time, she was able to reach into higher and higher levels of thought until she reached the 5th Dimensional frequency levels.

With the top-down intention, Joan activated the flow of the information from the Originating Source information down the frequency levels, de-intensifying as it goes, through the 7th Dimension, into the 6th Dimension, and then down into the 5th Dimension. When the energy gets to the 5th Dimensional level, the 5th Dimensional souls there act as intermediary transmitters, continuing the de-intensification until it reaches the level a Joan could handle. (If we got Originating Source information without the de-intensification, it would kill us.) Even though de-intensified, it carried with it all the purity and perfection of the Originating Source. In this way, Joan was able to go into higher and higher frequency levels reaching into the 6th Dimension level before she ended her career.

The Higher Selves are part of the Divine Will Kingdom and act as facilitators for the de-intensification process. Because they are a part of most of us, it is easier to reach into and to understand the higher frequencies. We are familiar with them because they are us, part of our conglomerate soul. Talking to the Higher Selves in some ways can be like having a conversation with yourself. Don't we do that already?

Going into Frequency

Everyone moves into frequency in a slightly different manner, and each individual processes it differently. My process often works where I download an entire concept, understand it instantly, and then have to find words to explain and unfold the information. Joan got the information directly in words as if reading out of a book and then would get symbolic pictures when relevant to further flesh out an idea. No one way is better than another.

One simple technique for those who wish to try going into frequency is the following: amalgamate. Imagine yourself centered in your expanded Pure Soul Essence light with the 5th Dimensional energy stream also being within you, symbolically anchored there. Then, imagine this light of expanding thought moving upward, symbolically higher and higher until you cannot see the top, as it is going into infinite expansion, like an escalator moving into the sky. Then consciously see or sense yourself riding up the escalator, moving upward into higher and higher levels of thought. The escalator symbol carries you upward effortlessly. Go as high as you can and then when you slow down and stop, begin to ask questions of your Higher Selves or work on healing and neutralizing. You will find that answers and solutions will come, often ideas you never thought of before. You will find the healing process to be more profound. And in time, whether right away or many times later, you will know at the inner levels that you are connecting to that Higher Self frequency. You may see symbols or light. You may pick up concepts, pictures, sounds, colors, or even nothing. Ideas and visuals may come to you in the moment or through dreams or will show up in your mind as you do the dishes a week later. You will always get help, answers, information, and energy from that level, whether you get something consciously or not. Sometimes it just takes time for us to be sure that we are hearing and/or experiencing it.

Learning to go into frequency is like developing any skill or technique. We have to practice, practice, and practice. Some will tap in easily and some may take longer to develop the skill, which is the way with any ability. We all can do it. I wish you the best with it!

APPENDIX III
Preview of Book Three: Jane & Company

Jane and her cohorts are disincarnate humans that will fill the pages of my next book. They reside in the Human Kingdom Heavens and the work Joan did with them provided the forum for a significant part of the Higher Self information on the Human Kingdom Heavens.

About 30 years ago, a friend of a friend of Joan Culpepper's asked for help to heal her brother, Michael—not his real name for privacy sake. Michael had severe mental problems and the psychiatric community found it difficult to treat him effectively. Joan agreed to do a healing session and set it up with herself acting as the surrogate for Michael (who was not present) with a healer named Joe who was trained by the Higher Selves, and a mutual friend who would take notes. These three had come together before to do healings for others. Although the foundation of the work used neutralizing techniques, the Higher Selves used the opportunity of the smaller healing sessions to provide even more techniques, including how to do healings at a distance, how to heal someone in Heaven, and how to heal an aura, just to name a few.

On that first day when they worked on Michael, they learned from the Higher Selves that Michael had an *attachment* with a disincarnate human, Jane, who followed him around working to bend him to her will. He was in body and she was in Heaven. Jane had a Soul Set where she had locked into an unrequited love relationship from the last time she was in body over 300 years ago. Michael was the object of her desire in that life, and she wanted to hold onto him forever. Fortunately, at the start of the healing session, the Higher Selves came in and explained the concept of attachment, how a disincarnate soul attaches itself to someone living in body. This attachment process is not the same as possession. Instead, it is a situation where the disincarnate follows the person around and manipulates him or her through the power of thought or other techniques. The human in body then is the *attachee* who is being influenced by a disincarnate human. Michael was the attachee.

The Higher Selves gave Joan and Joe the basic history of when and where the attachment began and how it was relevant to Michael in this life. Then Jane stepped forward and Joan reflected her for the first time. Jane was not processing out of a high frequency of human awareness and did not understand she held both herself and Michael stuck in their evolutionary journey. Her focus was solely on being in love with him. Because it had been a situation of unrequited love, Jane would manipulate Michael in ways that made him look crazy to others so that he would not develop a closeness to anyone else. Whenever Michael would begin to make a new friend or get a new job or move to a new place, Jane would (through the power of thought) get him to do something mean or bizarre so that the person (or boss or apartment manager) would no longer want him around. His scary and offensive behavior made it impossible for Michael to make and keep connections. He was evicted at times and even arrested. These tactics made sure he was "hers." Because Michael's behavior looked like mental illness, there were continual attempts over the years to get proper medications and treatments for what was wrong. (Caution: this does not mean that all mental illness is caused by an attachment situation. Schizophrenia is a legitimate diagnosis and can be very treatable. In this particular case, though, Michael was not mentally ill.)

Disincarnate human souls in Heaven are still part of the Human Kingdom. As a result, Jane was in the Free Will Kingdom and she could not be forced to leave Michael alone. She had to want to stop voluntarily. The first healing became a series of sessions, one every couple of weeks. At first there was time spent getting to know each other—Jane and Joe and Joan. During these sessions, the Higher Selves not only educated Joan and Joe with many new concepts about the soul and the Heavens, they also helped educate Jane.

Jane's increased awareness blossomed when Jane was introduced the first time to another disincarnate, Charles. (Not Charlie, by the way.) Charles was also attached to someone in body—someone he had loved during his last life in body. However, the attachment played out very differently than Jane's. Per the advice of the Higher Selves, Joe and Joan encouraged Jane to act as a messenger. They suggested that Jane get to know Charles, share with him what she was learning, and to then return to fill in Joan and Joe with all she had learned. It was Jane's interactions with Charles that brought her to the understanding that both she and Charles (and the other disincarnates she came to know who were also attached) were hurting themselves and the people they loved.

After the first few sessions with Jane, the Higher Selves encouraged Joan to open up the process to others of us who attended her weekly group. That's when I joined and was present for the next two plus years. This new group (made up of growing numbers of disincarnates as well as those in body) pursued the mission to educate and increase awareness of those souls in Heaven that were stuck for whatever reason. Jane (as she became more and more aware) joined forces with Joan, Joe, and all the rest of the expanded group to find other attached disincarnates, to educate them, to assist in healing their incarnate attachees, and to encourage them to detach. The term Jane & Company came to refer not only to the original group of disincarnates but also to all of those others in the disincarnate realm who were educated and joined them in their service mission. Jane & Company continues to work under the tutelage and supervision of the Higher Selves. Jerome, the Master Teacher, also works with them.

The idea of attachment may seem scary, especially because sometimes the human in body is not aware of what is happening. Michael had no awareness at all except that he kept thinking he heard voices. Jane (and other disincarnates) often did the manipulation by sending her thoughts toward Michael in a steady stream that the attachee "heard" either consciously or unconsciously. (Again, not all people who hear voices have an attachment. They may have some sort of schizophrenic psychosis. In reverse, not everyone who has an attachment hears voices.) An attachee does not have to obey what the voice says, but because the voice can be insistent, often the attachee gives in. It was in this way that Jane manipulated Michael. If the attachee simply said no to the voice (and meant it), there would be nothing Jane (or any other disincarnate) could do to force him (or anyone in body).

Whether or not one is aware of an attachment, there are two avenues of help for anyone who is involved with this type of situation. One, neutralizing is the key to eliminating toxic relationships in your incarnate world *as well as* your disincarnate world. Two, Jane & Company continue to educate those in heaven who are stuck in their evolutionary movement.

The process of attachment between a disincarnate and a human in body is no different than a problematic relationship between two people in body. We are all aware that some individuals are codependent or partners in a relationship where one person is dominating and controlling and the other does his or her bidding. Whether between two living people or one living and one dead, the relationship is rooted in the belief systems carried by both. One person wants the power and the other believes it is powerless and cooperates perfectly by allowing the dominance. This is why neutralizing is the basis for healing the attachment situation. It dissolves the belief systems that hold us all prisoner whether we are in body or not.

The full story of Jane & Company, in heaven and the physical world, will be the next book I write. You will meet many disincarnates including TJ, Thor (not the god), Aggie, Preacher Boyden, and more who will become your friends. You will learn much more about the soul, evolution, and the Heavens. New ideas will be introduced and illustrated with Jane's story, continuing the expansion of your perspectives about life, death, and the soul. It is a true story of a unique partnership between those in body and those out of body that has developed over time. Not only is the story fascinating, but also this interaction has left an indelible and powerful service footprint that continues on both sides of the veil within the Human Kingdom Universe.

Additional Resources

Website: HigherSelfVoice.com (or janetrichmond.com)

My website is a one-stop resource for all things related to the Higher Selves and the neutralizing work. In it you'll be able to view my Calendar of Events for future workshops, Meetups, radio shows, and more. You can read two free chapters from my book *CHOICES* and listen to archived radio shows. Join the Higher Self Voice mailing list to keep on top of the latest information. And you can also purchase my books, CDs, and catalytic art as well as schedule sessions and sign up for various events.

Testimonials on the Overall Self-Help Information:

"For decades, I experienced continuing rounds of anger, blame, shame spirals, and hurt aimed at my parents. By utilizing these techniques daily/weekly, I have experienced a steady healing in those behaviors as well as in other patterns. Thankfully, I was able to heal my relationship with my parents, most especially with my

father. The changes I made within me were so successful that by the time he passed away, I loved him totally and found that I had no unfinished business with him. I could let him go in peace."
—Lynne K., Winnetka, CA

"Finally, I know how to get rid of my negative thoughts! I used to feel like the dunce at the back of the class because no affirmation, positive thought, or silver lining was ever able to penetrate the abyss of my depression. Where I once saw only despair, I now see a future full of fun and laughter."
—Kathy P., Reseda, CA

Book 1
CHOICES: Neutralizing Your Negative Thoughts and Emotional Blueprints

My first book is a detailed look into the unconscious mechanisms that run our lives. Did you know that no amount of positive thinking will overcome the magnetic energy of your negative thoughts? Did you know that once you think a thought it lives forever? Did you know that to have foundational change (rather than a Band Aid) your energetic baggage must first be neutralized? Positive thoughts connect with positive thoughts with no effect on the negative thoughts already in existence. *CHOICES* not only explains this crucial misunderstood element but also offers the simple tools that *anyone* can use to begin getting real change in their lives. It clarifies the idea that our beingness doesn't end at the skin, as it describes the world of our etheric bodies and how all that we store there affects us. It specifically explains how thoughts interact with emotions and habits and how they all are woven together to create what we manifest in our lives. Last, it shows how we can neutralize the baggage so that we are free of its magnetic influence. *CHOICES* uncovers the amazing unseen world we carry with us at all times.

Testimonials on *CHOICES*

"My theory on spirituality is that universal laws should be easy, not complex. Advancing spiritually should be fun and not considered work. Janet Richmond and her Higher Self information follow this pattern. The meditation in her book is simple. After a few times, I already had it pretty much memorized. If we can separate our emotions from whatever occurs in our lives, we can break these patterns and deter the thought process that makes us continue to recreate these events. And neutralizing the emotional blueprints does just that!"
—Elliot M., TX

"I've been reading and re-reading your book since I got it. It's incredible—so helpful—so clear—so absolutely positive. Thank you!"
—Nancy B., Thousand Oaks, CA

"I received your book several months ago and it's now my 'middle of the night can't sleep' favorite! I really like it and wanted to find a source to purchase it at wholesale for my store, The Crystal Voyage. I dropped a note to New Leaf Distributing to let them know it's a really great book. Thank you!"
—Crystal, Crystal Voyage Bookstore, Tacoma, WA

"Janet has written a fabulous book introducing everyone to the wisdom of the Higher Self information along with a practical guide to put these exercises into practice. It is flavored with her own personal wisdom, grace, and understanding. This book is so powerful! You CAN make more enlightened choices!
—Lynne, Winnetka, CA

Monthly Healings: Higher Self Voice Meetup Group

Within this monthly group, you can expect a very relaxed atmosphere and a chance to connect with like-minded people who are eager to use the Higher Self techniques toward a more self-empowered life. It is an opportunity to get a jumpstart for self-healing as I do short individual sessions for several people in each group or a general healing for all present. All present are active participants in every healing and benefit from the intense group energy and the focused neutralizations.

Testimonials from Meetup Groups

"Janet's Meetup was so powerful for me. Janet is very gentle but effective in her delivery of knowledge and guidance. The tools that she has provided are just what I needed. Thank you to Janet and all of the guests. It was a night to remember."
—Marinda, LA, CA

"I've been going from meetup to meetup looking for answers. Here, I have finally found the answers I have been looking for."
—Zeke M., Reseda, CA

"What a fantastic evening! The work is so helpful and clear. I got the best night sleep I've had in months! Now I'm reading your book and loving it! Thank you for all your insight!"
—Nancy B., Calabasas, CA

"I can't wait for the rest of the classes. Janet is a beautiful soul that has that a wonderful intent. If you want to explore 'Light Energy,' this is the class."
—Noelle, Sherman Oaks, CA

Visit my Meetup page at: www.Meetup.com/HigherSelfVoice
for more information.

Web-Radio Shows

On my weekly web-radio show in 2011 and 2012, I discussed the many expanded aspects of the Higher Self information that changed my life and can change yours as well. They are packed with personal insights, healing meditations, fascinating interviews and co-hosts, as well as up-to-the-moment information directly from the Higher Selves. In 2014, the shows became process-oriented with individual healing opportunities for people who either call in or e-mailed me with a healing request. All healings are set up to benefit all listeners as well. They are powerful experiences and ongoing. All past shows have been archived and indexed on my website, janetrichmond.com. The direct links are below.

http://tinyurl.com/hsvradioarchive
http://tinyurl.com/hsvradio

Testimonials on Web-Radio Shows

"I first heard Janet on Contact Talk Radio (CTR) in January 2012 and began to listen to her live and archived shows. I also am able to attend her monthly meetups. The guided healings and the Higher Self information that Janet has taught me has been life-altering. I have learned to heal myself and to change the negative patterns that had me emotionally drained for years. Also, Janet has also helped my mom through her guided meditations. Although my mom does not understand English very well, by solely listening, she felt the energy and the neutralizing helped her tremendously with the serious depression that she had been struggling with for years. My mom still says her mantra, 'I am my Pure Soul Essence Light' daily with a big smile on her face."
—Tina A., Pasadena, CA

"I just wanted to let you know that never before have I experienced from an archived radio show anything close to healing energy. But something happened when I listened a few minutes to you. I have to say, you're onto something in your soul level connection and your *voice* is apparently doing instant karmic healings. I am grateful and will continue to work with these downloads."
—Name Withheld

"I've been listening to your shows. I listened to the worthlessness one (my big issue) last night and slept like a baby afterward. You must understand what an insomniac I am. I can't remember the last time I didn't need to take something to put me to sleep. But I didn't need to last night. Thank you so much!"
—Nancy P., Glendale, CA

"I loved the healing you did in today's show. I felt such a sense of love, peace, and connectedness. I've been replaying the show you did with me that focused on releasing fatigue and self-criticism of wanting to be perfect and am now shifting to easily allowing in self-love. A few days afterward, I met with a friend and received a message from her saying I looked fantastic, flawless, and gorgeous and she was proud to have me as a friend. Talk about a huge shift. Much gratitude to you for your amazing work!"
—Denyse B., Lakewood, CO

"Thank you so much for the show you did on blog talk radio on July 21. I have listened and re-listened to it, making many notes. I was crying and my eyes would pop open in shock at some of the things you said.-Whether it was me you sensed directly or not, it helped me immensely. I hope you felt the energy of appreciation and gratefulness that I sent back to you, but I wanted to make a

point to let you know how thankful I am. Your message and the healing have had a huge impact on my life."
—Andrea

"I listened to the show . . . and was blown away! Janet, you are fantastic. I listened to it all, and it is just wonderful. I am looking forward to learning more."
—Margaret N., Melbourne, Australia

"I listened to the healing twice today. Just hearing these words made me cry from the deepest of my being. Even though I had no conscious memory/association with the events you described, inside I knew/remembered and the floodgates just opened. It connected many dots about feelings of isolation, disconnection, and feeling ugly that I had experienced. A huge burden has lifted its weight from me. I realize that it is special to be on Earth today. Also, it has increased self-compassion and self-acceptance enormously. I now understand that these blocks weren't because I wasn't willing, smart, or 'whatever enough,' but that it stems from eons of lifetimes!"
—Eline V., Netherlands

Private Sessions: Healing

Private sessions allow you to tackle the issues or problems that are personal to you alone and tailor the healing to the specific goals you want to accomplish. It is an effective and intense way of using the 5th Dimensional information and is perfect for anyone wrestling with resistant patterns. The Higher Selves of the person worked on leads me to uncover the issues at the soul level (related to what the individual wants to heal) that are tied up in soul scrambles and misunderstandings. It reaches into and dissolves deep levels of the underlying causes of the pain and difficulties one is going through. Each session lasts approximately 60-75 minutes and can be conducted in person (at my home in Los Angeles), on Skype, or over the phone. There is no difference in the quality of the session either way. Private sessions are not restricted to one person and can be given to several people as a group. If you and a friend or family member (or any type of group) wish to have a private session (for personal issues you wish to work through), then this is a great opportunity to learn and heal together.

Testimonials on Private Sessions

"I can't even describe to you how I felt leaving your house after my session that day. The meditation was the first time I was able to really feel the light inside of myself. It was an extremely powerful experience which opened up something new and beautiful in the bigger picture of Me."
—Kayla, West LA, CA

"I called Janet for some help with deep issues and she responded by giving me a healing—she calls them private sessions. I call them milestones. My friends have noticed my transformation as much as I have. A private session is like singing a beautiful and inspiring melody with someone, in this case, Janet."
—Kim T., Toronto, Canada

"Because of your work, I feel like I can handle *anything* that comes along. Nothing, not even cancer, can throw me, if I just do the meditations. I know they'll bring about changes that will help in any situation. Now I know I can deal with anything that comes along. I don't feel powerless anymore! Thanks for that!"
—Nancy P., Pasadena, CA

"There are many practioners but few healers; you are an amazing healer. I appreciate your ability, wisdom, and kindness."
—Cynthia Q., Sacramento, CA

Catalytic Art

I use a unique technique given to me by the Higher Selves to incorporate the Divine Energies into art in order to create or help manifest a desired change within one's life pattern. The picture becomes a conscious focal point, energies on paper, which catalyzes the individual's life pattern wherever needed, whether for healing, resolution, release, empowerment, and/or manifestation of specific situations or conditions. The energy continues working slowly and consistently for one's lifetime, bringing change to higher and higher levels.

Testimonials on Catalytic Art

"This is an awesome pic! And the painting is even more amazing in person! Yeah for Janet Richmond and her talents! "
—Diana, LA, CA

"My catalytic art picture has been working perfectly for me for many years. I got one to help me find a perfect place to live back when I could only afford a very small studio apartment. Not only did I find a special one-room place, but every time I have moved, it is like magic and something perfect is available. I now own my home and have the artwork hung as a prized possession. I have been blessed!"
—Maureen, LA, CA

Original Recordings of Joan Culpepper

Joan Culpepper's ability to go into frequency and pull in the Higher Self information was nothing short of phenomenal. Although there are hundreds of documents that contain the transcribed material of Joan's many sessions, nothing compares to the experience of hearing her voice as she went into a conscious meditation with the Higher Selves. Of the over 800 recordings, I have chosen 10 to have digitally mastered so that you can hear firsthand as Joan brings in the Higher Selves to impart high frequency information.

Contact Information

For questions, comments, requests of any type, my e-mail address is janet@janetrichmond.com.

To do more exploring, my website is janetrichmond.com or higherselfvoice.com

ACKNOWLEDGMENTS

I am ever grateful to Joan Culpepper for her intention and determination to share the Higher Self information with others and to her daughter, Trish, for giving me permission to share it with the world. I am continually amazed at how far I have come from the scared little girl—alone, emotionally crippled, and hopeless— to where I am now. I don't have to pretend anymore, to present a façade to others based on what I think they want me to be. I am myself—genuine, real, and joyful. I become more of my unlimited nature every day and find myself looking through the expanded lenses of understanding toward all of humanity. The world makes more sense than it ever had. I want the same for all people, and this book is my way to pay it forward.

I also want to thank my editor Lorraine Fico-White of magnificomanuscripts.com. I found her by a recommendation from someone I didn't know and never looked back. I am a writer not because I love the act of writing but because I have something to share. Thus, my writing style was *not* carefully crafted by education but developed with the birth and incessant use of e-mail. It was this way of communicating with others that I developed my chatty, informal, relaxed, and truly rumpled writing style. Lorraine's brilliant eye transformed this book into something more readable and accessible. For that I feel endless gratitude and appreciation. (Readers will thank her, too!)

Last, but no less important, I give my heartfelt thanks to those who have supported me in my journey—my friends, clients, listeners, children. In many ways they have played a significant role in keeping me focused and on track with a gentle, helpful and consistent wind at my back. They also have inspired me often with ideas and insights for my own personal growth that facilitated and accelerated the unfolding of my career.

ABOUT THE AUTHOR

Janet Richmond grew up in a small town in Connecticut, often described as a bedroom community of New York City because most households had a commuter who either drove or rode the train to and from there for work. Her schooling included The Masters School in Dobbs Ferry, New York, the University of North Carolina at Chapel Hill, and the University of California, Los Angeles where she received her Masters in Business Administration. She started her own business management company and supported her family for 20 years, raising two children as a single parent.

Janet "discovered" Joan Culpepper in 1983 with her first psychic reading. The Higher Self information had such a powerful impact that Janet dove into learning all that Joan offered. When Joan moved out of state four years later, Janet committed to working with the life-changing material. She not only used the neutralizing techniques consistently on herself, but also in her work with many others. She developed her catalytic art, displayed it at shows, and taught others how to do it.

Janet wrote her first book, *CHOICES: Neutralizing Your Negative Thoughts and Emotional Blueprints* upon receiving the copyright to the information in 2006. Janet wanted to share Joan's legacy with the world. Once Janet sold her business management company in 2009, she moved into other metaphysical arenas. She currently facilitates monthly meetup groups, hosts a web-radio show, and conducts private sessions utilizing a soul scan technique given to her by the Higher Selves where she scans the soul process for causes of patterns behind the problems in this life. She also continues to create her catalytic art, conduct various workshops, will soon present interactive live tele-classes, and as requested, will be offering workshops to make certification available.

Janet currently resides in the Los Angeles area.

Made in the USA
San Bernardino, CA
20 November 2016